The Disclosures from Germany

The Disclosures from Germany

I

THE LICHNOWSKY MEMORANDUM

THE REPLY OF HERR VON JAGOW

Translation, Introduction and Notes
By MUNROE SMITH

II

MEMORANDA AND LETTERS OF DR. MUEHLON

Translation, Introduction and Notes
By MUNROE SMITH

III

THE DAWN IN GERMANY?

The Lichnowsky and Other Disclosures
By JAMES BROWN SCOTT

NEW YORK
AMERICAN ASSOCIATION FOR INTERNATIONAL CONCILIATION
1918

9504

It is the aim of the Association for International Conciliation to awaken interest and to seek coöperation in the movement to promote international good will. This movement depends for its ultimate success upon increased international understanding, appreciation, and sympathy. To this end, documents are printed and widely circulated, giving information as to the progress of the movement and as to matters connected therewith, in order that individual citizens, the newspaper press, and organizations of various kinds may have accurate information on these subjects readily available.

The Association endeavors to avoid, as far as possible, contentious questions, and in particular questions relating to the domestic policy of any given nation. Attention is to be fixed rather upon those underlying principles of international law, international conduct, and international organization, which must be agreed upon and enforced by all nations if peaceful civilization is to continue and to be advanced. A list of publications will be found on pages 255 to 264.

TABLE OF CONTENTS

I

The Lichnowsky Memorandum
The Reply of Herr von Jagow

Reprint of INTERNATIONAL CONCILIATION No. 127, June, 1918

INTRODUCTION

The Lichnowskys are a family of Upper Burgundian origin, a branch of the house of Granson. They have held estates both in Austrian and in Prussian Silesia since the 17th century. In the *Almanach de Gotha* for 1849 they were described as "possessing" one town and forty-five villages with 21,620 inhabitants. The title of prince was first conferred by the King of Prussia toward the close of the 18th century. Early in the 19th century the Lichnowskys became princes in Austria also.

I

Karl Maximilian, sixth Prince Lichnowsky, was born in 1860. He served for a time in the Prussian army, in which he holds the rank of major, and then entered the diplomatic service. In 1885 he was attached to the German embassy in London; later he held diplomatic positions in Constantinople, in Bucharest, and in Vienna. During the latter part of his residence at Vienna he was first secretary of the embassy. Transferred in 1899 to the Berlin Foreign Office, he served there, as he tells us in his memorandum, for several years (1899–1904). After eight years of retirement from the diplomatic service, he was sent to London in 1912 as German ambassador.

As his memorandum shows, Prince Lichnowsky is in many respects a diplomat of the older school. He is not of that oldest school, described as men sent abroad to lie for their country's good, for he is obvi-

ously a truthful man; nor is he of the Frederician school, cynically described by the Great Frederick himself as spies, for he is clearly an honorable gentleman. He tells us, in fact, that he had no espionage fund. That fund was expended in England by other agents, with whom he had no relations. The Prince is old-school in his belief that the relations between states, and even the great issues of peace and of war, are mainly determined by the relations established between their diplomatic representatives and the persons who play leading rôles, in society as well as in politics, in the countries to which the representatives are accredited. He is, on the other hand, a modern diplomat in his recognition of the importance of keeping in touch with the leading men in commerce, industry, and finance, and of influencing general opinion, at least so far as this can be done by public speeches reported in the daily press.

In his general view of German foreign policy, Lichnowsky is distinctly of the Bismarckian school. He declares indeed that Bismarck made a mistake in allying Germany with Austria and with Italy; but, given the situation created by those alliances, the policy which Lichnowsky steadily advocated and still defends is that which Bismarck consistently followed in the later years of his chancellorship and insistently recommended, after his retirement from office, in public speeches, in the press and in his posthumous memoirs. Germany's duty to Austria-Hungary, according to Bismarck, was limited to defending the integrity of the Dual Empire. Germany had not undertaken and should not undertake to support Austrian schemes of expansion in the Near East, for Germany had no interests in the Balkans.

In all collisions of interests and of ambitions between Austria and Italy, Germany's rôle was that of the disinterested friend, and therefore of a possible umpire. Similarly, in all collisions of interests and ambitions between either of its allies and Russia, Germany was impartial. So only could Germany maintain its traditional friendship with Russia, which seemed to Bismarck, as to Lichnowsky, of the highest importance.

Bismarckian again is Lichnowsky's conviction, clearly implied although not definitely stated, that the German Empire should have been satisfied with the position it held in Europe before the present war. He also believed, with Bismarck, that Germany's colonial expansion should be limited to such gains as could be secured without war, particularly without conflict with Great Britain. His chief efforts, during his two years in London, were directed to this end, and were attended by a degree of success which he does not overstate.

In his acceptance of these Bismarckian traditions, Lichnowsky was, at least from the point of view of Berlin, distinctly old-school. Ever since the retirement of Prince Bismarck there had been a growing conviction at Berlin that Germany had interests not only in the Balkans but also in Asia, and that these interests were to be realized by putting the whole force of the German Empire behind the wedge that Austria was driving into the Balkans and by acquiring for Germany a dominant influence in Constantinople and thus throughout the Turkish Empire. That this would mean war with Russia was fully understood, but such a war was not feared. The "Slav peril," so far as Germany was concerned, was

a bugbear that might advantageously be employed in domestic politics, but it was not taken seriously by the German General Staff or by the German Foreign Office.

In his belief that Germany should regard its position in Europe and in the world as substantially satisfactory, Lichnowsky was again, from the point of view of Berlin, hopelessly old-school. He was not in touch with the Pan-German movement. He did not understand that Germany must obtain an absolutely dominant position in Europe, in order later to oust Great Britain from its leading position in the world.

Given this complete antithesis between Lichnowsky's antiquated views and the "new course" which the German imperial authorities had followed since 1890, the Prince may well wonder why, in 1912, he was exhumed from his Silesian estates and sent to London. Quite characteristically he seeks the explanation in his personal relations with the Emperor, the chancellor, and the foreign secretary; and quite frankly he tells us that he cannot find it there. An explanation, however, does not seem difficult. Pending the outbreak of the long planned war for German hegemony on the continent, it was desirable that British suspicions of Germany's intentions should be quieted. When the war should come, it would be highly desirable that Great Britain should not intervene, at least not at the outset. British intervention, it was thought, would come more rapidly if Great Britain were already in a state of acute suspicion, less rapidly, and probably too late to be of value to France or to Russia, if Great Britain were taken by surprise. For this reason it was obviously politic

that Germany should be represented in London by an ambassador who was not aware of Germany's real purposes, who was peacefully minded and friendly to Great Britain, and whose efforts to concentrate British attention on colonial negotiations and a *rapprochement* between the Triple Alliance and the Entente Powers might be successful precisely because they were sincere. It was to secure these advantages that the Prince was, as he complains, kept uninformed of the most important matters. In the meantime, as has been intimated both in France and in England by persons familiar with German diplomacy and its methods, the Berlin government had in Great Britain agents who were in sympathy with its real designs and who were kept fully informed of all relevant facts and events. These agents controlled the spy system and discharged all the obscure and devious duties which could not be entrusted to a diplomat of Lichnowsky's rank, traditions, and character. It has been suggested that the representative of Germany's real policy was Herr von Kühlmann, then chief counselor of the London embassy, and now (1918) imperial foreign secretary.* If this were the case, von Kühlmann was clever enough to play his part without exciting any suspicion in the mind of his chief; for Lichnowsky speaks of him always with the highest appreciation.

II

The chief value of Prince Lichnowsky's memorandum lies in the fact that he rejects and helps to disprove every plea in justification of Germany's conduct that has been advanced since the outbreak of the World War by Germany's official apologists. His

* *Journal des Débats, édition hebdomadaire*, March 29, 1918.

testimony is of especial value in refuting the German assertion that, for a long period before the war, France, Russia, and Great Britain had been united in efforts to check German commercial expansion and to deny to Germany, a newcomer among the Great Powers, its just share in the exploitation of the world's undeveloped resources. By their intrigues Germany was hemmed in or, as the Germans put it, "encircled." In this conspiracy of encirclement Great Britain, as the nation most seriously menaced in its economic interests by German competition, was the arch-conspirator. For its selfish purposes it supported the French desire to recover Alsace-Lorraine and the Russian desire to gain access to the Mediterranean— desires described as French lust for revenge and Russian lust for conquest.

We see today that the encirclement theory was one of the most valued drugs in Berlin's political medicine closet. It was at once an anodyne, by which the German people were made to bear more quietly the growing burden of armaments, and a stimulant adapted to fire them with a sense of wrong and a conviction that by war alone could they obtain satisfaction. Germany's encirclement could also be represented, and was represented, as a prelude to aggressive action by the encircling Powers. Failing to stifle German competition by diplomatic wiles, these Powers would sooner or later seek to crush Germany in war. Thus the German people were prepared to look upon a European war either as necessary, in order to gain a free field for their industry and trade, or as inevitable for the defense of the Fatherland. And, since these different notions were simultaneously presented to them, and were not disassociated

in their minds, the German people were adroitly prepared to regard an aggressive war, whenever it should please Berlin to start it, either as a "preventive" war—that is, a war to anticipate attack—or as a war of defense.

When war should come, the encirclement plea could of course be used, as in fact it was used, to influence neutral opinion. The theory was primarily constructed, however, for domestic use.

Lichnowsky attacks the encirclement theory on two sides. He asserts, in the first place, and adduces new evidence to prove, that the *rapprochement* between Great Britain and France and, later, between Great Britain and Russia was no offensive conspiracy, but a defensive *entente*. The provocative policy pursued by Germany during the years preceding the World War had awakened general distrust of Germany's intentions. It was this distrust, more than anything else, that brought Great Britain into closer touch with France and with Russia. Germany was not isolated by the wiles of its neighbors; it isolated itself by its own conduct.*

* In his preface to an edition of Prince Lichnowsky's memorandum printed in Zurich, the Swiss Professor Nippold puts this point very clearly and very neatly: "Public opinion is regarded in Germany as a thing that is made from above; and since the press and the people consciously or unconsciously accept this situation as a matter of course, it is precisely those views which are regarded as desirable by the powers that be that are dominant in Germany in all questions of foreign policy. Under these circumstances it was of course not difficult to divert the attention of the German public from the mistakes which its own statesmen had made in the last decades. This of course was most easily done by rolling off these mistakes upon others. Thus the self-*ex*circlement of Germany, for which German policy was responsible, was artfully converted into an *en*circlement (*so wurde aus der Selbstauskreisung Deutschlands die eine Schuld der deutschen Politik war, künstlich eine Einkreisung gemacht*)."

Lichnowsky shows, in the second place—and here his testimony is of the greatest value because of the position he held in London during the two years immediately preceding the war—that English jealousy of Germany's commercial and industrial development had come to be outweighed, in the minds of English manufacturers and merchants, by their recognition that Germany had become England's best customer. He testifies that Sir Edward Grey's policy, supported by the English premier, did not aim to exclude Germany from competition in the world's markets or even to arrest Germany's colonial development. On the contrary, Grey was anxious to adjust all disputes between Great Britain and Germany in the field of world politics, as he had previously adjusted all such disputes between Great Britain and France and, later, between Great Britain and Russia. He was ready to accord to Germany spheres of economic influence and of eventual political control in those parts of the world in which the competition of the Great Powers was keenest. Not only was he willing to meet Germany half way, but he was even disposed to accord to Germany, notably as regards the Congo, opportunities and expectancies which, to the German ambassador's surprise, Berlin hesitated to grasp.

The African and the Bagdad treaties which Lichnowsky negotiated gave substantial advantages, as he points out, to German commerce, industry, and finance. They also gave the German Empire important colonial expectations. Why were these treaties not welcomed in Berlin? Why was the Bagdad treaty not concluded? Why was the African treaty accepted only after long delay, and only on the eve of war, when its ratification was no longer possible? Lichnowsky's explana-

tion, that his rivals in German governmental circles grudged him successes so conspicuous, is equally characteristic and unconvincing.

The chief point in controversy, he tells us, was (at least as regards the African treaty) that of publication. Sir Edward Grey insisted that the treaty should be published; Berlin insisted that it should be kept secret. The most plausible argument for secrecy advanced by Berlin, namely, that the partition of the Portuguese colonies into spheres of influence and of pre-emption would so offend Portuguese feeling that German *entrepreneurs* would be unable to obtain concessions, is rightly characterized by Lichnowsky as a pretext. England, as he points out, held Portugal in the hollow of its hand. He might have added that, under the circumstances, any Portuguese resentment would probably direct itself primarily against Great Britain, and that, if Great Britain could take the risk, Germany surely could. Even more absurd (although von Jagow still endorses it) is the pretext that, if the German people had learned that Great Britain was conceding rights of pre-emption in the colonies of Portugal, there would have been an outcry against British "perfidy" which would have embarrassed the German government and (as von Jagow now suggests) would have vitiated the "good atmosphere" which the Berlin Foreign Office desired to create in Anglo-German relations. It is, however, not easy to believe that in the Germany of the 20th century there would have been a general ethical revolt against any British action that was advantageous to Germany.

The probable explanation—the probable reason why Berlin was willing to ratify the treaty but unwilling

to publish it—was that its publication would have shaken, and might even have destroyed, the fiction of encirclement. If the German people had been permitted, in 1913 or in 1914, to read treaties by which Great Britain accorded to Germany the economic control of Mesopotamia and of important parts of Africa, the belief in Germany's encirclement which the German government had created, and which it needed for the coming war, would have been seriously undermined.

Von Jagow's reply to Lichnowsky shows that the opposition on which the African and Bagdad treaties were wrecked was neither made nor supported in the Berlin Foreign Office. The Berlin foreign secretary also desired a *rapprochement* with Great Britain and favored the ratification of the Grey-Lichnowsky treaties. This leaves but one possible conclusion. The opposition was higher up, in the militarist-Junker *entourage* of the Emperor. That in these circles there could be little enthusiasm for arrangements which would primarily subserve the interests of German commerce is quite intelligible. For decades the Junkers had witnessed with growing distaste and apprehension the rapidly increasing wealth of the middle classes. This new wealth was lessening the relative power and the prestige of their own order. Least of all were they disposed to welcome arrangements which would further enrich German merchants, manufacturers, and bankers, if these arrangements tended to avert or even to postpone war; for it was to war they looked to re-establish their threatened prestige and to assure their dominant influence in Prussia and in the Empire.

When Lichnowsky reviews the fateful events of July, 1914, he rejects with the same candor the construction which his government has given to these events and which the German people have, for the most part, blindly accepted.

For the official German theory that Serbia had inflicted upon Austria's honor a stain that could be washed out only by blood, he substitutes the statement that Serbia had to be "massacred" because it stood in the way of Austria's ambitions.

The official German statement that Russian mobilization was an act of war he dismisses with contempt. He does not attempt to disprove it, because it is a purely military theory that has never had the least recognition in the diplomatic world. He reminds us only that the Czar had pledged his word that no Russian soldier should march so long as negotiations continued.*

Against the theory formally advanced by Chancellor von Bethmann-Hollweg in his speech of December 2, 1914, before the Reichstag, that Great Britain was responsible for the war because it assured France, and therefore Russia also, of unconditional support against Germany—a theory fully disproved by the documents—Lichnowsky insists upon Grey's earnest desire and persistent efforts to prevent the outbreak of a European war. He expresses his own conviction that Grey's proposed conference with the German, Italian, and French ambassadors in London, for the purpose of devising an adjustment of the issue raised

* Telegram of the Czar to King George August 1, 1914: "I have given most categorical assurances to the Emperor William that my troops would not move so long as mediation negotiations continued." *Collected Diplomatic Documents* (London, 1915), part ix, no. 2, page 537.

between Austria and Russia, would undoubtedly have averted the war, had Germany wished to avert it.

To justify Germany's refusal to take part in such a conference, von Jagow now argues that "Italy was Serbophil and, with its Balkan interests, stood rather opposed to Austria." Has Herr von Jagow forgotten that, when he first heard of the proposed conference, he told the French ambassador, Jules Cambon, that he was "disposed to join in," and that it was only when he was instructed, from above, that the conference would be "a court of arbitration," that he changed his attitude? If the conference were to have been a court, Germany might properly have challenged Italy's participation on the ground now first suggested by von Jagow. In fact, however, it was not proposed that the conference should attempt to decide anything; it was simply to suggest a settlement; and Bethmann-Hollweg's deliberate misconstruction of Grey's proposal was simply a link in the chain of lies with which Berlin dragged Europe into war. Von Jagow's record is so much better than that of his superiors that it is painful to find him still countenancing a misrepresentation for which he was not primarily responsible.

On the more important question of Great Britain's alleged responsibility for the war, von Jagow supports Lichnowsky's view. Britain did not contrive the war; "on the contrary," von Jagow writes, "I believe in Sir Edward Grey's love of peace and in his earnest wish to arrive at an agreement with us."

Perhaps the most valuable feature of Lichnowsky's memorandum for the future historian, certainly its most interesting feature for us today, is his characterization of Sir Edward Grey. After two years' close

association, Lichnowsky was assuredly in a position to form a just estimate of the man as well as of the statesman. Not only is he thoroughly convinced of Grey's love of peace, he is also profoundly impressed by Grey's complete honesty and unmistakable sincerity. Seldom, if ever, in the history of the world has a diplomat of one nation paid such a tribute to a colleague of another nation as Lichnowsky pays to Grey. Never has such a tribute been paid at a moment when the two nations concerned were locked in a desperate struggle.

In the light of subsequent events, many Englishmen have found that Grey was too peaceful. They have criticized him for his readiness to make concessions to a rival power which, as we now see, was unlikely to be satisfied with any concessions, because its appetite was insatiable. Grey has also been criticized because in his negotiations with predatory Balkan principalities, after the outbreak of the war, he was too scrupulous to be successful. There remains, however, to his credit one achievement that far outweighs any errors or failures, an achievement that was due to his love of peace, his honesty, and his scrupulous honor. He carried Great Britain into the greatest of all its wars with spotlessly clean hands.

III

The value of such evidence as Prince Lichnowsky gives us depends of course not alone on the witness's knowledge of men and of events, but also on his personal characteristics.

It would be an exaggeration to describe the Prince as a subtle man or even as a very acute man. He is possessed, however, of good sound understanding.

His description of the public men with whom he came in contact in England shows discernment. His analysis of the relations between society and government in England, as England was before this war, is substantially correct. His truthfulness is apparently beyond question; he is too much of a grand seigneur to say anything that he does not believe.

His chief foible is that to which the grand seigneur is most liable, an exaggerated sense of his own importance. It is because he is so self-centered that he is inclined to ascribe to the envy of rivals all opposition to his policies. This illusion finds an extreme expression in his belief that one reason, at least, why the authorities in Berlin clung to a policy that must lead to war was their disinclination to give to him and to Grey the credit of keeping the peace.

It is on this weakest point that the German press, taking its cue as always from the German government, dwells with especial insistence. It should be noted, however, that Lichnowsky's vanity appears to mislead him only in the explanation of facts. It does not anywhere appear that it has led him to misstate the facts themselves. He is very proud of his African and Bagdad treaties, but his summary of their provisions is confirmed by other testimony. In general, so far as his assertions can be controlled by other evidence—and most of them can—that evidence is confirmatory.

If we accept the statement which Lichnowsky made to the imperial chancellor, in his letter of March 15, 1918, that he wrote his memorandum "with regard to the future" and for the sake of "noting the details of my experiences and impressions before they van-

ished from my memory"—that is, that he wrote for his family archives and for history—the trustworthiness of the document is enhanced. There is, apparently, no reason to doubt the sincerity of this statement. The Prince had, indeed, urgent motives to desire that the living world as well as the future historian should appreciate his diplomatic activity. Even a more modest and more judicious man might well have found it unendurable to be made, as Lichnowsky was made from the moment Great Britain entered the war, the chief scapegoat for the disastrous results of a policy which he had consistently opposed. Even such a man would probably have defended himself with equal energy and frankness in private conversation with his friends. Such a man, however, would hardly have put his defense into writing, much less have put several typewritten copies into circulation, as Lichnowsky did, while the war was still raging. A less self-centered and more judicious man would have seen clearly that a document of such interest, thus made current, could hardly be kept secret; and he would not have characterized as "unprecedented" the breach of confidence through which it became public. That Lichnowsky foresaw such an outcome and was not unwilling that his defense should be published, provided this happened without his sanction, is conceivable indeed but highly improbable. Such a hypothesis is improbable, not only because so underhand a way of attaining an object would have been repugnant to a man of his rank and character, but also because the inconveniences which even an unauthorized publication would draw upon the writer would have been fully realized.

IV

Lichnowsky's memorandum was written in the summer of 1916. According to German statements which have reached neutral and allied countries, and which, in spite of minor variations, are in the main accordant, a copy of the memorandum was lent by Privy Councillor Witting, a brother-in-law of Maximilian Harden, to Captain von Beerfelde, who was employed in the political section of the General Staff. Von Beerfelde is described as an idealist and a pacifist. A man who was neither might well desire, in the interest of Germany itself, an early conclusion of peace. Such a man might well have thought, as Captain von Beerfelde is said to have thought, that one great obstacle to peace was the conviction prevailing in Germany that Great Britain was responsible for the war, and might well have believed that the publication of Lichnowsky's memorandum would tend to remove this misconception and lessen the resulting hatred. Since the publication of the memorandum a similar view has been expressed by Captain Persius, military expert of the Berlin *Tageblatt*, who is apparently neither an idealist nor a pacifist. Captain von Beerfelde, without the authorization of Prince Lichnowsky, had a number of copies made and sent them to some of his friends and acquaintances. Early in February, 1918, the New Fatherland Alliance (a society formed in the autumn of 1914, which is neither socialist nor pacifist but is opposed to autocracy and has protested eloquently against annexations) had 2,000 copies printed in South Germany and sent to Berlin, where they were seized by the police. Such a seizure, of course, is seldom complete: there are usually copies, or at least proof sheets,

which the police do not find. About the middle of March, 1918, a portion of the memorandum appeared at Stockholm in *Politiken*, the leading organ of the Swedish socialists. Publication of further instalments was temporarily arrested by the Swedish government; but on March 21, 1918, the complete text of the memorandum was published in the Berlin *Börsen-Courier*. After this, the German government ceased to oppose further publication in Germany. Efforts were still made, however, to prevent printed copies from passing the frontier, and not until May was any copy of the German text available in this country.

Captain von Beerfelde was placed under arrest and, according to the Bernese *Freie Zeitung*, which usually is well informed, he has been confined in an insane asylum. No such measures have been taken against the author of the memorandum. At a meeting of the main committee of the Reichstag, on March 16, Vice-Chancellor von Payer read to the deputies Lichnowsky's letter of explanation, already cited, and stated that as the Prince had been guilty of imprudence only and had resigned his diplomatic rank, no further steps would be taken against him. Since that time many German writers have demanded that he be placed on trial and be sent either to prison or to a sanatorium; and a movement was started in the Prussian Upper House to expel him from membership in that body. The most vehement demands for Lichnowsky's punishment very naturally came from leading militarists and annexationists who knew that his statements were substantially true. The imperial and Prussian governments, however, evidently wish to leave the matter where von Payer left it. Under

governmental suggestion the German press has almost unanimously treated the memorandum as unimportant. Not only is the Prince described as a discredited diplomat, but his narrative and his conclusions are alleged to be so colored by his extreme vanity as to be valueless.

As far as the German people are concerned, this view seems to be generally accepted. Upon some intelligent German readers the memorandum has undoubtedly made a strong impression; but most of these were already fully aware that the official explanations of the causes of the war were false. The effect of the memorandum was doubtless sensibly lessened by the absorbing anxiety with which all Germans were following their great offensive movement on the western front. This, it will be remembered, was started at the very moment when the memorandum began to circulate freely in Germany.

In a Germany sobered by defeat, the Lichnowsky memorandum, with the Mühlon letters and many other pieces of evidence that demonstrate the guilt of Berlin, will doubtless attract increasing attention, and it may be anticipated that the truth will slowly filter into the German mind, as it seems already to be filtering into the minds of many Americans of German descent who have heretofore accepted the German official legends. In the social-political struggles that will follow the conclusion of peace, all this mass of evidence will be re-examined, if only because it will be valuable campaign material.

Among the peoples of the allied countries and among neutrals the importance of the memorandum was promptly appreciated. Its revelations did not surprise them nor change their views, for they had

long known the truth. Nearly all intelligent Americans had understood the events of July, 1914, before the end of that year, as soon as the evidence then accessible was laid before them. We and our allies, however, welcome every new piece of corroborative testimony, and we rightly attach the highest importance to evidence that comes from Germany itself. Especial value attaches, of course, to the testimony given by men of political standing, like Lichnowsky, or of prominence in the industrial world, like Mühlon. From a lawyer's point of view, perhaps the greatest importance is to be attached to the admissions of the chief witness called by the German government for its defense, its former foreign secretary, von Jagow.

The German text that follows is that published in the Berlin *Börsen-Courier*, March 21, 1918, with no changes except corrections of typographical errors. Every such change is indicated. For control of the accuracy of the Berlin text, the editor has had at his disposal a text published in Germany in pamphlet form and reproduced in photographic facsimile in London, and a text published in Zurich, also in pamphlet form. These three texts are identical, except for typographical errors. As no one of the errors occurs in all three texts, it has been easy, with the aid of an excellent French translation published in the Paris *Journal des Débats*, to establish in every case the correct reading. The French translation, which is faithful as well as felicitous, is of value for this purpose, because it is based on a fourth German text, published in the *Münchner Post*.

COLUMBIA UNIVERSITY   MUNROE SMITH
    June, 1918

True translation filed with the Postmaster at New York, N. Y., on June 26, 1918, as required by the Act of October 6, 1917.

MEINE LONDONER MISSION

1912–1914

Von

Fürst Lichnowsky
ehemaliger deutscher Botschafter in England [1]

Meine Berufung

Im September 1912 starb Baron Marschall, der nur wenige Monate auf dem Londoner Posten gewesen war. Seine Ernennung, die wohl hauptsächlich wegen seines Alters und der nach London gerichteten Wünsche seines jüngeren Beamten erfolgte, gehörte [2] zu den vielen Missgriffen unserer Politik.

Trotz eindrucksvoller Persönlichkeit und grossem Ansehen zu alt und zu müde, um sich noch in die ihm völlig fremde angelsächsische Welt einzuleben, war er mehr Beamter und Jurist als Diplomat und Staatsmann. Er war sofort eifrig bestrebt, die Engländer von der Harmlosigkeit unserer Flotte zu überzeugen, wodurch natürlich nur der gegenteilige Eindruck erstarkte.

Zu meiner grossen Überraschung wurde mir im Oktober der Posten angeboten. Ich hatte mich nach mehrjähriger Tätigkeit als Personalreferent auf das Land zurückgezogen, da auch ein geeigneter Posten nicht zu meiner Verfügung war, und die Zeit zwischen

---

[1] *Börsen-Courier* heading reads: "Die Aufzeichnungen des Fürsten Lichnowsky: Die vollständige Denkschrift."

[2] B.-C. has "gehören."

MY LONDON MISSION

1912–1914

By

PRINCE LICHNOWSKY

Former German Ambassador in England

My Nomination

Baron Marschall, who had held his post in London for a few months only, died in September, 1912. His appointment, which was due, probably, mainly to his age and the desire of a younger subordinate to get to London, was one of the many mistakes made in our foreign policy.

In spite of his impressive personality and great reputation, he was too old and too tired to adapt himself to the Anglo-Saxon world, with which he was wholly unfamiliar. He was rather an official and lawyer than a diplomat and statesman. He made prompt and earnest efforts to convince the English of the harmless character of our fleet—efforts which naturally had no result except to strengthen the opposite impression.

To my great surprise the post was offered me in October. After several years' service in draughting despatches [in the Foreign Office], I had withdrawn to the country, as no suitable post had been found for me; and I spent my time between flax and beets, or on horseback in the fields, reading much also, and occasionally publishing political articles.

[25]

Flachs und Rüben und auf Pferden und Wiesen ver-
bracht, dabei auch manches gelesen und gelegentlich
politische Aufsätze veröffentlicht.

So waren acht Jahre vergangen und dreizehn,
seitdem ich Wien als Gesandter verliess. Meine letzte
politische Wirksamkeit war eigentlich dort gewesen,
da man damals im Amte zu keiner Betätigung [3] gelangen konnte, ohne nach den Weisungen eines Mannes, der an Wahnvorstellungen litt, schrullenhafte
Erlasse mit krausen Instruktionen zu verfassen.

Auf wen eigentlich meine Berufung nach London
zurückzuführen war, weiss ich nicht. Auf S. M. allein
keinesfalls, denn ich gehörte nicht zu seinen Intimen,
wenn er mir auch stets mit Wohlwollen begegnete.
Aus Erfahrung weiss ich auch, dass seine Kandidaten
meist mit Erfolg bekämpft werden. Herr von Kiderlen
wollte eigentlich Herrn von Stumm nach London
schicken! Er begegnete mir sofort mit unverkenn-
barem Übelwollen und suchte mich durch Unhöflich-
keit einzuschüchtern. Herr von Bethmann Hollweg
brachte mir damals freundschaftliche Gesinnungen
entgegen und hatte mich kurz vorher in Grätz besucht.
So glaube ich, dass man sich auf mich einigte, weil kein
anderer Kandidat augenblicklich zur Verfügung
stand. Wäre nicht Baron Marschall unerwartet
gestorben, so wäre ich damals ebensowenig hervorge-
holt worden, wie in den vielen vergangenen Jahren.

Marokkopolitik

Der Augenblick war zweifellos günstig für einen
neuen Versuch, um mit England auf besseren Fuss zu
gelangen. Unsere rätselhafte Marokkopolitik hatte
wiederholt das Vertrauen in unsere friedlichen Gesin-

[3] B.-C.: "Bestätigung."

Thus eight years passed—thirteen since I had left Vienna with the title of envoy. That was my last really political employment, for in the [Foreign] Office there was at that time no chance to do anything, unless one drew up crotchety orders with crabbed instructions, in accordance with the directions of a man who was subject to insane delusions.[1] . . . .

To whom my appointment in London was really due, I do not know. Certainly not to His Majesty alone, for I was not one of his intimate associates, although he always gave me a cordial reception. I know, too, by experience that in most instances his candidates were successfully opposed. Herr von Kiderlen's real desire was to send Herr von Stumm to London! He met me at once with unmistakable illwill, and tried to intimidate me by rudeness. Herr von Bethmann Hollweg was at that time on friendly terms with me; he had visited me shortly before at Grätz. I am therefore inclined to think that they settled on me because, at the moment, no other candidate was available. Had Baron Marschall not died unexpectedly, I should have been left where I had lain for many years, on the shelf.

The Morocco Question

The moment was undoubtedly favorable for a new effort to establish better relations with England. Our enigmatic policy in Morocco [2] had repeatedly shaken confidence in our peaceful intentions; it had at least

[1] See Appendix, note i.
[2] *Ibid.*, note vii.

nungen erschüttert, zum mindesten aber den Verdacht erregt, dass wir nicht recht wussten, was wir wollten, oder dass wir beabsichtigten, Europa in Atem zu erhalten und die Franzosen gelegentlich zu demütigen. Ein österreichischer Kollege, der lange in Paris war, sagte mir: „Wenn die Franzosen anfingen, die Revanche zu vergessen, dann habt Ihr sie regelmässig durch kräftige Tritte dran erinnert."

Nachdem wir die Versuche des Herrn Delcassé, sich mit uns über Marokko zu verständigen, zurückgewiesen und vorher feierlich erklärt hatten, keine politischen Interessen dort zu besitzen—eine Haltung, die wohl den Überlieferungen der Bismarckschen Politik entsprach—entdeckten wir plötzlich in Abdul Asis einen zweiten Krüger. Auch ihm verhiessen wir, wie den Buren, den Schutz des mächtigen deutschen Reiches mit demselben Aufwand und dem gleichen Erfolge. Denn beide Kundgebungen endeten, wie sie enden mussten: mit dem Rückzug, falls wir nicht entschlossen waren, schon damals den Weltkrieg zu führen. Daran vermochte auch der traurige Kongress in Algeciras nichts zu ändern, noch weniger der Sturz des Herrn Delcassé.

Unsere Haltung förderte die russisch-japanische und später die russisch-britische Annäherung. Gegenüber der deutschen Gefahr—*"the German peril"*—traten alle anderen Gegensätze in den Hintergrund. Die Möglichkeit eines neuen deutsch-französischen Krieges war augenfällig geworden, und ein solcher konnte, anders wie anno 70, weder Russland noch England unberührt lassen.

Die Wertlosigkeit des Dreibundes hatte sich bereits in Algeciras gezeigt, die der dortigen Vereinbarungen aber bald danach durch den Zusammenbruch des

aroused the suspicion that we did not quite know what we wanted or that our purpose was to keep Europe on edge and, on occasion, to humiliate the French. An Austrian colleague, who had been long in Paris, said to me: "If the French begin to forget *la revanche*, you regularly remind them of it by a good hard kick or two."

After we had repelled M. Delcassé's efforts to come to an understanding with us regarding Morocco and, before that, had solemnly declared that we had no political interests there—an attitude which was in harmony with the traditions of Bismarckian policy—we suddenly discovered in Abdul Aziz a second Krü-ger.[3] To him, as to the Boers, we promised the protection of the mighty German Empire, at the same cost to ourselves and with the same outcome. Both demonstrations ended, as they were bound to end, in a retreat, so long as we had not yet decided to wage the World War at that time. The pitiable Congress of Algeciras could not modify this fact; still less could the fall of M. Delcassé.[4]

Our attitude furthered the Russo-Japanese and, later, the Russo-British *rapprochement*. In face of "the German peril" all other antagonisms slid into the background. The possibility of a new Franco-German war had become evident, and, as had not been the case in 1870, such a war could not leave either Russia or England unconcerned.

The worthlessness of the Triple Alliance had already been demonstrated at Algeciras. The equal worthlessness of the agreements there made was

[3] See Appendix, note v.
[4] *Ibid.*, note vii.

Sultanats, der natürlich nicht zu verhindern war. Im deutschen Volke jedoch verbreitete sich der Glaube, dass unsere Auslandspolitik schwächlich sei und vor der „Einkreisung" zurückweiche, und dass hochtönenden Gebärden kleinmütige Nachgiebigkeit folge.

Es bleibt das Verdienst des Herrn von Kiderlen, der als Staatsmann sonst überschätzt wird, dass er die marokkanische Erbschaft liquidierte und sich mit den Tatsachen abfand, an denen nichts mehr zu ändern war. Ob freilich die Welt durch den Coup von Agadir erschreckt werden musste, lasse ich dahingestellt. In Deutschland wurde das Ereignis lebhaft begrüsst, in England aber hatte es um so mehr beunruhigt, als die Regierung durch drei Wochen vergeblich auf Aufklärung über unsere Absichten wartete. Die Rede Mr. Lloyd Georges, die uns warnen sollte, war die Folge. Vor dem Sturze Delcassés und vor Algeciras wären Hafen und Gebiet an der Westküste zu haben gewesen, nachher aber nicht mehr.

Sir Ed. Greys Programm

Als ich nach London kam im November 1912, hatte man sich über Marokko beruhigt, da inzwischen in Berlin eine Vereinbarung mit Frankreich erfolgt war. Die Mission Haldanes war zwar gescheitert, da wir die Zusage der Neutralität verlangten, statt uns mit einem Vertrage zu begnügen, der uns vor britischen Angriffen und vor Angriffen mit britischer Unterstützung sichern sollte.

Sir Ed. Grey aber hatte den Gedanken, mit uns zu einer Verständigung zu gelangen, nicht aufgegeben und versuchte es zunächst auf kolonialen und wirtschaft-

shown soon afterward, by the collapse of the sultanate—a result which it was of course impossible for us to prevent. Among the German people, however, the belief was spreading that our foreign policy was feeble, that we were yielding ground to the "encirclement," and that ringing assertions were followed by pusillanimous concessions.

It stands to the credit of Herr von Kiderlen, otherwise overrated as a statesman, that he liquidated the Moroccan inheritance and adapted himself to circumstances which could not be altered. Whether, indeed, it was necessary to alarm the world by the Agadir *coup* is a question I leave unanswered.[5] In Germany this occurrence was warmly welcomed; in England, on the other hand, it aroused the more uneasiness because the government waited in vain for three weeks for an explanation of our intentions. Mr. Lloyd George's speech, intended to warn us, was the consequence. Before Delcassé's fall and before Algeciras we could have obtained harbors and territory on the West Coast, but not afterwards.

Sir Edward Grey's Program

When I came to London in November, 1912, anxiety regarding Morocco had subsided, for in Berlin, in the meantime, an agreement had been reached with France. Haldane's mission had indeed failed, because we demanded a promise of neutrality instead of contenting ourselves with a treaty which was to insure us against British attacks and against attacks with British support.[6]

Sir Edward Grey, however, had not given up the idea of coming to an understanding with us, and made

[5] See Appendix, note viii.
[6] *Ibid.*, note xvi.

lichen Gebieten. Durch Vermittelung des befähigten und geschäftskundigen Botschaftrats [4] von Kühlmann waren Besprechungen über eine Erneuerung des portugiesischen Kolonialvertrages und über Mesopotamien (Bagdadbahn) im Gange, die das unausgesprochene Ziel verfolgten, sowohl die genannten Kolonien, wie Kleinasien in Interessensphären zu teilen.

Der britische Staatsmann wollte, nachdem sowohl mit Frankreich wie mit Russland die alten Streitfragen geregelt waren, auch mit uns zu ähnlichen Abmachungen gelangen. Nicht uns zu vereinsamen, sondern uns möglichst zu Teilnehmern an der bestehenden Genossenschaft zu machen, war seine Absicht. Wie es gelang, britisch-französische und britisch-russische Gegensätze zu überbrücken, so wollte er auch die britisch-deutschen möglichst beseitigen und durch ein Netz von Verträgen, zu denen schliesslich wohl auch eine Vereinbarung über die leidige Flottenfrage gehört hätte, den Weltfrieden sichern, nachdem unsere frühere Politik zu einer Genossenschaft, der Entente, geführt hatte, die eine gegenseitige Versicherung gegen Kriegsgefahr darstellte.

Das war das Programm Sir Ed. Greys. In seinen eigenen Worten: unbeschadet der bestehenden Freundschaften (zu Frankreich und Russland), die keinerlei agressive Zwecke verfolgen und keinerlei bindende Verpflichtungen für England in sich schliessen, mit Deutschland zu einer freundschaftlichen Annäherung und Verständigung zu gelangen. *"To bring the two groups nearer"* (die beiden Gruppen einander näher bringen).

Es gab damals in England wie bei uns in dieser Hinsicht zwei Richtungen: die der Optimisten, die an

[4] B.-C.: "Botschafters."

such an attempt first in the colonial and economic fields. Through the agency of the capable and experienced counselor of the embassy, von Kühlmann, discussions were under way concerning a renewal of the Portuguese colonial treaty and concerning Mesopotamia (Bagdad railway). The tacit aim of these negotiations was to divide not only the above-mentioned colonies but also Asia Minor into spheres of interest.

It was the desire of the British statesman, now that the old matters of dispute had been settled both with France and with Russia,[7] to come to similar arrangements with us. His intention was not to isolate us but to make us in so far as possible partners in the association already established. Just as he had succeeded in bridging over British-French and British-Russian differences, so he wished as far as possible to get rid of causes of controversy between Great Britain and Germany, and by a network of treaties—which in the end would probably have included an agreement on the troublesome naval question—to secure the peace of the world. Our previous policy had already led to the formation of an association, the Entente, which represented a mutual assurance against the risk of war.

This was Sir Edward Grey's program. As he himself put it: Without impairing the existing friendships (with France and Russia), which have no aggressive purposes and involve no binding obligations for England, to attain a friendly *rapprochement* and understanding with Germany—"to bring the two groups nearer."

In this matter there were then in England, as with us, two currents of opinion: that of the optimists, who

[7]See Appendix, notes vi and ix.

die Verständigung glaubten, und die der Pessimisten, die den Krieg früher oder später für unvermeidlich hielten.

Zur erstern gehörten die Herren Asquith, Grey, Lord Haldane und die meisten Minister des radikalen Kabinetts, sowie die führenden liberalen Organe, wie "Westminster Gazette", "Manchester Guardian", "Daily Chronicle." Zu den Pessimisten namentlich konservative Politiker, wie Mr. Balfour, der mir dies wiederholt zu verstehen gab, dann führende Militärs, wie Lord Roberts, die auf die Notwendigkeit der allgemeinen Wehrpflicht hinwiesen. (*"The Writing on the Wall."*) Ferner die Northcliffepresse und der bedeutende englische Journalist Mr. Garvin ("Observer"). Während meiner Amtszeit haben sie sich jedoch aller Angriffe enthalten und persönlich wie politisch eine freundliche Haltung eingenommen. Unsere Flottenpolitik und unsere Haltung in den Jahren 1905, 1908 und 1911 hatten bei ihnen aber den Glauben erweckt, dass es doch einmal zum Kriege kommen werde. Erstere werden heute in England gerade so, wie es auch bei uns geschieht, der Kurzsichtigkeit und Einfalt geziehen, letztere gelten als die wahren Propheten.

Albanische Frage

Der erste Balkankrieg hatte damals zum Zusammenbruch der Türkei und damit zu einer Niederlage unserer Politik geführt, die sich mit den Türken seit Jahren identifizierte. Nachdem die Türkei in Europa nicht mehr zu retten war, gab es zwei Möglichkeiten gegenüber der Regelung ihrer Hinterlassenschaft: entweder wir erklärten unser völliges Desinteressement an der Gestaltung der Grenzen auf dem Balkan und

believed in an understanding, and that of the pessimists, who considered war inevitable, sooner or later.

In the first group were Messrs. Asquith, Grey, Lord Haldane, and most of the ministers in the Radical Cabinet, as well as the leading Liberal organs, such as the *Westminster Gazette*, the *Manchester Guardian*, and the *Daily Chronicle*. In the pessimist group were, in particular, Conservative politicians like Mr. Balfour, who repeatedly indicated to me that this was his attitude; also leading military men, like Lord Roberts, who insisted on the necessity of universal military service ("The Writing on the Wall"); further, the Northcliffe press, and that influential English journalist, Mr. Garvin of the *Observer*. During my term of office, however, they abstained from all attacks and took up, personally and politically, a friendly attitude. Our naval policy and our attitude in the years 1905, 1908, and 1911 [8] had, however, convinced them that some day or other it would come to war. Just as with us, so in England today, those who belonged to the first group are censured as shortsighted and simple-minded, while the others are regarded as the true prophets.

The Albanian Question

At that time, the First Balkan War [9] had led to the collapse of Turkey and, consequently, to a defeat of our policy, which for years had tied itself up with the Turks. Now that European Turkey was past saving, two possible courses were open to us as regarded the settlement of its estate. Either we declared that we were in no wise interested in the determination of

[8] See Appendix, notes vii, iv (last paragraph), and viii.
[9] *Ibid.*, note xi.

überliessen die Regelung den Balkanvölkern, oder aber wir unterstützten unsere „Bundesgenossen", trieben Dreibundpolitik im Orient und traten dadurch aus der Rolle des Vermittlers heraus.

Ich befürwortete von Anfang an die erstere Lösung, das Auswärtige Amt aber vertrat um so entschiedener die letztere.

Der springende Punkt war die albanische Frage. Unsere Bundesgenossen wünschten die Gründung eines selbständigen Staates Albanien, da Österreich die Serben nicht an die Adria und Italien die Griechen nicht nach Valona, ja, nicht einmal nördlich von Korfu gelangen lassen wollte. Im Gegensatz hierzu förderte bekanntlich Russland die serbischen und Frankreich die griechischen Wünsche.

Mein Rat ging nun dahin, diese Frage als ausserhalb des Bündnisses stehend zu betrachten und weder die österreichischen noch die italienischen Wünsche zu unterstützen. Ohne unsere Förderung aber wäre die Errichtung Albaniens, dessen Lebensunfähigkeit vorauszusehen war, unmöglich gewesen. Serbien wäre an das Meer gelangt und der jetzige Weltkrieg vermieden. Frankreich und Italien hätten sich über Griechenland ernstlich entzweit und die Italiener, falls sie nicht gegen Frankreich allein kämpfen wollten, sich mit der Ausdehnung Griechenlands bis nördlich von Durazzo abfinden müssen. Die Zivilisation in dem grössten Teil Albaniens ist griechisch. Die Städte sind es im Süden vollkommen, und während der Botschafterkonferenz kamen Abordnungen aus grösseren Städten nach London, um die Angliederung an Griechenland durchzusetzen. Auch im heutigen Griechenland leben albanische Volksteile und die sogenannte griechische Nationaltracht sogar ist al-

boundaries in the Balkan Peninsula, and left their adjustment to the Balkan peoples, or we supported our allies, pursued a Triple Alliance policy in the East, and thus abandoned the rôle of mediator.

I advocated from the outset the first of these solutions, but our Foreign Office gave its support all the more decidedly to the second.

The salient point was the Albanian question. Our allies desired the establishment of an independent state of Albania, because Austria was unwilling to permit the Serbs to gain access to the Adriatic, and Italy did not wish the Greeks to push their boundary to Valona, or even to the north of Corfu. On the other hand, Russia, as is known, favored the Serbian, and France the Greek desires.

My advice was to consider this question as one lying outside the alliance, and to support neither the Austrian nor the Italian desires. Without our support, however, the Albanian state, whose incapacity to exist might have been foreseen, could not possibly have been established. Serbia would have pushed forward to the sea, and the present world war would have been avoided. Between France and Italy there would have been a serious dispute as to Greece, and unless the Italians had been willing to fight France singlehanded, they would have been obliged to accept the expansion of Greece to a point north of Durazzo. In the greater part of Albania the civilization is Greek. The southern towns are entirely Greek, and when the conference of ambassadors was in session, deputations from the larger towns came to London for the purpose of securing annexation to Greece. In Greece today there are still Albanian groups, and the so-called Greek national dress itself is of Albanian origin.

[37]

banischen Ursprungs. Die Einverleibung der überwiegend orthodoxen und islamitischen Albaner in den
griechischen Staat war daher die beste Lösung, die
natürlichste wenn man etwa Skutari und den Norden
den Serben und den Montenegrinern überliesse. Für
diese Lösung war auch S. M. aus dynastischen
Gründen. Als ich den Monarchen brieflich in dieser
Richtung bestärkte, erhielt ich vom Reichskanzler
erregte Vorwürfe, ich gälte als „Gegner Österreichs"
und er müsste sich solche Eingriffe und die direkte
Korrespondenz verbitten.

Orient und Dreibundpolitik

Wir mussten uns von der verhängnisvollen Über-
lieferung endlich lossagen, Dreibundpolitik auch im
Orient zu treiben, und den Irrtum erkennen, der darin
lag, uns im Süden mit den Türken und im Norden mit
den Austro-Madjaren zu identifizieren. Denn die
Fortsetzung dieser Politik, die wir beim Berliner
Kongress begonnen und seither mit Eifer gepflegt
hatten, musste mit der Zeit und namentlich, wenn die
nötige Gewandtheit an leitender Stelle fehlte, zum
Zusammenstoss mit Russland und zum Weltkriege
führen. Statt uns mit Russland auf Grundlage der
Unabhängigkeit des Sultans, den man auch in Petro-
grad nicht aus Konstantinopel entfernen wollte, zu
einigen und uns, unter Verzicht auf militärische und
politische Eingriffe, auf wirtschaftliche Interessen im
Orient zu beschränken und mit der Zerlegung Kleinasiens in Interessensphären zu begnügen, ging unser
politischer Ehrgeiz dahin, am Bosporus zu dominieren.
In Russland entstand die Meinung, der Weg nach
Konstantinopel bzw. ins Mittelländische Meer führe

The incorporation of the Albanians, of whom the great majority are either Orthodox Christians or Mussulmans, in the Greek state was, therefore, the best solution. It was also the most natural, if, let us say, Skutari and the northern part had been assigned to the Serbs and Montenegrins. His Majesty also was in favor of this solution on dynastic grounds. When I wrote to the monarch in support of these views, I received from the imperial chancellor agitated reproaches: I was taken to be an "enemy of Austria," and he must beg me to refrain from such interferences and from all direct correspondence.

The East and the Triple Alliance Policy

We should have abandoned definitively the fatal tradition of pushing Triple Alliance policies in the Near East; we should have recognized that it was a mistake to make ourselves solidary with the Turks in the south and with the Austro-Magyars in the north; for the continuance of this policy, which we had started at the Berlin Congress and had afterwards zealously developed,[10] was bound in time, and particularly in case the requisite adroitness should be found wanting in the supreme directing agencies, to lead to the collision with Russia and the World War. Instead of coming to an understanding with Russia on the basis of the independence of the Sultan, whom even the St. Petersburg government did not wish to drive out of Constantinople; instead of renouncing military and political interference, confining ourselves to economic interests in the Near East, and contenting ourselves with a division of Asia Minor into spheres of interest, our political ambition was directed to the

[10] See Appendix, notes iii and iv.

über Berlin. Statt die kräftige Entwicklung der Balkanstaaten zu fördern, die, einmal befreit, alles eher sind als russisch, und mit denen wir die besten Erfahrungen machten, stellten wir uns auf Seite der türkischen und madjarischen[5] Unterdrücker.

Der verhängnisvolle Irrtum unserer Dreibund- und Orientpolitik, die Russland, unseren naturgemässen besten Freund und Nachbar, in die Arme Frankreichs und Englands gedrängt und von der asiatischen Ausbreitungspolitik abgedrängt hatte, war umso augenfälliger, als ein russisch-französischer Überfall, die *einzige* Hypothese, die eine Dreibundpolitik rechtfertigte, aus unserer Berechnung ausscheiden konnte.

Über den Wert des italienischen Bündnisses erübrigt sich ein weiteres Wort. Italien braucht unser Geld und unsere Touristen auch nach dem Kriege mit oder ohne Bündnis. Dass letzteres im Kriegsfalle versagen würde, war vorauszusehen. Das Bündnis war daher *wertlos.* Österreich braucht unseren Schutz in Krieg und Frieden und hat keine andere Anlehnung. Die Abhängigkeit von uns beruht auf politischen, nationalen und wirtschaftlichen Erwägungen und ist umso grösser, je intimer unsere Beziehungen zu Russland sind. Das hat die bosnische Krise gelehrt. Seit dem Grafen Beust ist noch kein Wiener Minister so selbstbewusst gegen uns aufgetreten, wie Graf Ährenthal in den letzten Jahren seines Lebens. Bei richtig geleiteter deutscher Politik, die die Fühlung mit Russland pflegt, ist Österreich-Ungarn unser Vasall und auf uns angewiesen, auch ohne Bündnisse und Gegenleistungen, bei falsch geleiteter sind wir auf Österreich angewiesen. Das Bündnis war daher *zwecklos.*

[5] B.-C.: "majarischen."

[40]

attainment of a dominant position on the Bosporus. In Russia the opinion arose that the way to Constantinople and so into the Mediterranean ran *via* Berlin. Instead of furthering the development of strong Balkan states, which, once set free, are anything but Russian, and with which our experiences were most satisfactory, we placed ourselves on the side of the Turkish and Magyar oppressors.

The fatal mistake of our Triple Alliance and Eastern policy, by which Russia, naturally our best friend and neighbor, was driven into the arms of France and England, and diverted from the policy of Asiatic expansion, was the more obvious, as a Franco-Russian attack, the sole hypothesis justifying a Triple Alliance policy, could be eliminated from our calculations.

As to the value of the Italian alliance, words may be spared. Italy needs our money and our tourists, and will need them after the war, with or without an alliance. That the alliance would fail to hold in the event of war was to be foreseen. The alliance, consequently, was worthless. Austria needs our protection both in war and in peace, and there is no other Power on which it can lean. Its dependence on us is based on political, national, and economic grounds. This dependence increases in proportion to the intimacy of our relations with Russia. This was proved in the Bosnian crisis. Since Count Beust,[11] no Vienna minister has assumed toward us so independent an attitude as was displayed by Count Ährenthal during the last years of his life. Given a properly conducted German policy, which keeps us in touch with Russia, Austria-Hungary is our vassal, and must

[11] See Appendix, note ii.

[41]

Ich kannte Österreich zu genau, um nicht zu wissen, dass eine Rückkehr zur Politik des Fürsten Felix Schwarzenberg [6] oder des Grafen Moritz Esterhazy dort undenkbar war. So wenig die dortigen Slawen uns lieben, so wenig wollen sie in ein deutsches Kaiserreich zurückkehren, selbst mit Habsburg-Lothringer Spitze. Sie streben den Föderalismus innerhalb Österreichs an auf nationaler Grundlage, ein Zustand, der im Rahmen des Deutschen Reiches noch viel weniger Aussicht auf Verwirklichung hätte wie unter dem Doppeladler. Die Deutschen Österreichs aber erkennen in Berlin den Mittelpunkt deutscher Macht und Kultur, und wissen, dass Österreich niemals wieder Präsidialmacht werden kann. Sie wünschen einen möglichst intimen Anschluss an das Reich, nicht aber eine antideutsche Politik.

Seit den siebziger Jahren hatte sich die Lage von Grund aus verändert in Österreich wie etwa in Bayern. Wie hier eine Rückkehr zum grossdeutschen Partikularismus und zur altbayerischen Politik nicht zu befürchten ist, so war dort ein Wiederaufleben der Politik des Fürsten Kaunitz und Schwarzenberg nicht zu gewärtigen. Unsere Interessen aber würden durch einen staatsrechtlichen Anschluss Österreichs, das auch ohne Galizien und Dalmatien nur etwa zur Hälfte von Germanen bewohnt ist, also etwa ein grosses Belgien darstellt, ebenso leiden wie andererseits durch Unterordnung unserer Politik unter Wiener und Pester Gesichtspunkte—*d'épouser les querelles de l'Autriche* (sich mit den österreichischen Zwistigkeiten zu vermählen).

[6] B.-C.: "Schwanenberg."

come our way even without an alliance and without reciprocal services. Under a misdirected policy, we must go Austria's way. Consequently the alliance served no purpose.

I was too thoroughly acquainted with Austria not to know that a return to the policy of Prince Felix Schwarzenberg or to that of Count Moritz Esterhazy was unthinkable. The Slavs living there have little love for us, and equally little desire to come back into a German Empire, even with a Hapsburg-Lorraine at its head. They are striving to develop in Austria a federal system based on nationality—a state of things which there would be far less chance of establishing within the framework of the German Empire than under the two-headed Eagle. The Germans in Austria, on the other hand, recognize that Berlin is the center of German power and culture, and they know that Austria can never recover the presidency of the German states. They desire as close a connection as possible with the Empire but do not favor a policy directed against [the existing organization of] the German Empire.

Since the seventies there has been a radical change of position in Austria—a change resembling that which has taken place in Bavaria. Just as here a return to the particularism of the Great German party and to the old Bavarian policy is not to be apprehended, so in Austria there was no prospect of a revival of the policy of Prince Kaunitz and Prince Schwarzenberg.[12] Our interests, however, would be as injuriously affected by a constitutional union with Austria, which even without Galicia and Dalmatia is inhabited only to the extent of, say, one-half by Germans, and which accord-

[12] See Appendix, note ii.

[43]

Wir brauchten daher keine Rücksichten auf die Wünsche unserer „Bundesgenossen" zu nehmen, sie waren nicht nur unnötig, sondern auch gefährlich, weil sie zum Zusammenstoss mit Russland führten, wenn wir orientalische Fragen durch österreichische Brillen betrachteten. Die Ausgestaltung des Bündnisses aus einem unter einer einzigen Voraussetzung geschlossenen „Zweckverbande" zu einer „Gesamtgemeinde", zu einer Interessengemeinschaft auf allen Gebieten, war geeignet, eben dasjenige herbeizuführen, was das Rechtsgeschäft verhindern sollte—den Krieg. Eine solche Bündnispolitik musste ausserdem den Verlust der Sympathien junger, kräftiger, aufstrebender Gemeinwesen auf dem Balkan nach sich ziehen, die bereit waren, sich an uns zu wenden und uns ihre Märkte zu öffnen.

Der Gegensatz zwischen Hausmacht und Nationalstaat, zwischen dynastischer und demokratischer Staatsidee musste zum Austrag kommen, und wir standen wie gewöhnlich auf falscher Seite.

König Karol hat zu einem unserer Vertreter gesagt, er habe das Bündnis mit uns unter der Voraussetzung geschlossen, dass *wir* die Führung behielten, ginge diese aber an Österreich über, so ändere das die Grundlage des Verhältnisses, und er werde unter solchen Umständen nicht weiter mitmachen können.

Ähnlich lagen die Dinge in Serbien, wo wir gegen unsere eigenen wirtschaftlichen Interessen die österreichische Erdrosselungspolitik unterstützten.

Wir haben stets auf das Pferd gesetzt, dessen Niederbruch vorauszusehen war, auf Herrn Krüger, auf Abdul Asis, auf Abdul Hamid, Wilhelm Wied und—

ingly is something like a larger Belgium, as, on the other hand, by a subordination of our policy to the points of view of Vienna and Budapest, with the obligation *"d'épouser les querelles de l'Autriche."*

We, therefore, had no need to consider the desires of our allies. Such considerations were not only unnecessary but also dangerous, inasmuch as they would lead to a collision with Russia if we looked at Eastern questions through Austrian glasses. The development of our alliance from a partnership with a definite purpose, formed in view of a single contingency, into a solidary union, with community of interests in every field, was adapted to produce the very result which the original treaty[13] was intended to prevent—war. Moreover, an alliance policy of this sort could not but entail the loss of the sympathies of the young, strong, and growing communities in the Balkan Peninsula, which were ready to turn to us and open to us their markets.

The conflict between family power and the national state, between the dynastic and the democratic theory of the state, had to be definitively settled, and, as usual, we stood on the wrong side.

King Charles [of Rumania] told one of our representatives that he had made an alliance with us on the assumption that we were to keep the control of affairs. If that control passed to Austria, the basis on which his relations with us rested would be changed, and under such conditions he could no longer act with us.

The situation was similar in Serbia, where against our own economic interests we were supporting the Austrian policy of strangulation.

[13] Literally, "legal transaction."

der verhängnisvollste von allen Irrtümern—schliesslich den grossen *plunge* auf den Stall Berchtold gemacht!

Botschafterkonferenz

Bald nach meiner Ankunft in London Ende 1912 regte Sir Ed. Grey eine zwanglose Besprechung an, um zu vermeiden, dass aus dem Balkankriege sich ein europäischer entwickelt, nachdem wir leider die Aufforderung der französischen Regierung, einer Desinteressementserklärung beizutreten, bei Ausbruch des Krieges abgelehnt hatten. Der britische Staatsmann nahm von Anfang an die Haltung ein, dass England an Albanien kein Interesse habe, wegen dieser Frage also nicht gewillt sei, es auf einen Krieg ankommen zu lassen. Er wollte als „ehrlicher Makler" lediglich zwischen den beiden Gruppen vermitteln und Schwierigkeiten beilegen. Er stellte sich daher keineswegs auf Seite der Ententegenossen und hat während der Dauer der etwa achtmonatlichen Unterhandlungen durch guten Willen und seinen massgebenden Einfluss nicht unwesentlich zur Einigung beigetragen. Statt dass wir eine der englischen analoge Haltung einnahmen, vertraten wir ohne Ausnahme den Standpunkt, der uns von Wien aus vorgeschrieben wurde. Graf Mensdorff führte den Dreibund in London, ich war sein „Sekundant". Meine Aufgabe bestand darin, seine Vorschläge zu unterstützen. In Berlin schaltete der kluge und erfahrene Graf Szögyenyi. Sein Refrain war: „Und dann tritt der *casus fœderis* (der Bündnisfall) ein", und als ich die Richtigkeit dieses Schlusses einmal anzuzweifeln

We have always bet on the horse whose breakdown might have been foreseen, on Krüger, on Abdul Aziz, on Abdul Hamid, on Wilhelm of Wied,[14] and—the most disastrous of all our mistakes—we finally made our great plunge on the Berchtold stable!

The Conference of Ambassadors[15]

Soon after my arrival in London, at the close of the year 1912, Sir Edward Grey suggested an informal discussion to prevent a European war from growing out of the Balkan war. We had unfortunately already declined the request of the French government, made at the outbreak of the war, to join in a declaration of disinterestedness. From the outset the British statesman took the position that England had no interest in Albania and therefore did not mean to let war come on this issue. It was his purpose simply to act as a mediator, an "honest broker," between the two groups and to try to smooth away difficulties. Accordingly, he by no means placed himself on the side of his Entente associates; and during the negotiations, which lasted some eight months, by force of his good will and his controlling influence he made no slight contributions to an understanding. Instead of taking a position like the English, we invariably defended the point of view which was prescribed to us by Vienna. Count Mensdorff led the Triple Alliance in London, I was his second. My task was to support his proposals. In Berlin it was the shrewd and experienced Count Szögyenyi who ran the affair. His refrain was: "Here the *casus foederis* comes in"; and when on one occasion I ventured to dispute the correctness of this conclu-

14 See Appendix, notes v, vii and xi.
15 *Ibid.*, note xi.

wagte, wurde ich wegen „Austrophobie" ernstlich verwarnt. Unter Anspielung auf meinen Vater hiess es auch, ich sei „erblich belastet!"

Bei allen Anlässen: Albanien, serbischer Adriahafen, Skutari, ferner bei der Bestimmung der Grenzen Albaniens stellten wir uns auf den Standpunkt Österreichs und Italiens, während Sir Ed. Grey fast niemals den französischen oder den russischen unterstützte. Er trat vielmehr meist für unsere Gruppe ein, um keinen Vorwand zu schaffen, wie ihn später ein toter Erzherzog liefern sollte. So gelang es mit seiner Hilfe, den König Nikita aus Skutari wieder herauszulocken. Schon über diese Frage wäre es sonst zum Weltkrieg gekommen, da wir sicher nicht gewagt hätten, „unseren Bundesgenossen" zur Nachgiebigkeit zu veranlassen.

Sir Ed. Grey leitete die Verhandlungen mit Umsicht, Ruhe und Takt. Wenn eine Frage sich zu verwickeln drohte, entwarf er eine Einigungsformel, die das Richtige traf und auch stets Annahme fand. Seine Persönlichkeit genoss bei allen Teilnehmern gleiches Vertrauen.

Wir hatten tatsächlich wieder einmal eine der vielen Kraftproben, die unsere Politik kennzeichnen, glücklich überstanden. Russland hatte überall vor uns zurückweichen müssen, da es niemals in der Lage war, den serbischen Wünschen Erfolg zu verschaffen. Albanien war als österreichischer Vasallenstaat errichtet und Serbien vom Meere verdrängt. Der Verlauf der Konferenz war daher eine neue Demütigung für das russische Selbstbewusstsein. Wie 1878 und 1908 hatten wir uns schon dem russischen Programm entgegengestellt, ohne dass *deutsche* Interessen im Spiele waren. Bismarck wusste den Fehler des Kongresses durch den geheimen Vertrag und durch seine

sion, I received a serious warning on the ground of my "Austrophobia." It was also asserted, alluding to my father, that I was under an "hereditary burden."

On every issue—Albania, a Serbian harbor on the Adriatic, Skutari, also in drawing the boundaries of Albania—we took the point of view of Austria and of Italy, while Sir Edward Grey almost never supported that of France or of Russia. On the contrary, in most instances he lent his support to our group, in order to give no pretext for war, such as was subsequently furnished by a dead archduke. It was thus with his help that we succeeded in coaxing King Nikita out of Skutari. Otherwise the World War might have been started on this question, since we surely would not have ventured to urge our ally to make any concession.

Sir Edward Grey conducted the negotiations with prudence, calmness and tact. As often as a question threatened to become complicated, he suggested a formula of agreement that met the case and was invariably accepted. His personality won him equal confidence among all who took part in the conference.

So far as [immediate] results were concerned, we had again passed successfully through one of those many tests of power which were characteristic of our policy. Russia had been obliged to give way to us all along the line; in no instance was it able to attain satisfaction of the Serbian desires. Albania was set up as an Austrian vassal state, and Serbia was thrust back from the sea. The outcome of the conference was therefore a new humiliation of Russian national sentiment. As in 1878 and in 1908 we had placed ourselves in opposition to the Russian program, although no German interests were involved. Bismarck contrived to minimize the mistake made at the Congress [of

Haltung in der Battenbergfrage zu mildern; die in der bosnischen Frage wieder betretene abschüssige Bahn wurde in London weiter verfolgt und später, als sie zum Abgrund führte, nicht rechtzeitig verlassen.

Die Misstimmung, die damals in Russland herrschte, kam während der Konferenz durch Angriffe gegen meinen russischen Kollegen und die russische Diplomatie in den russischen Blättern zum Ausdruck. Seine deutsche Herkunft und katholische Konfession, sein Ruf als Deutschenfreund, und der zufällige Umstand, dass er sowohl mit dem Grafen Mensdorff, wie mit mir verwandt ist, kamen den unzufriedenen Kreisen zu statten. Ohne eine sehr bedeutende Persönlichkeit zu sein, besitzt Graf Benckendorff eine Reihe von Eigenschaften, die einen guten Diplomaten kennzeichnen: Takt, gesellschaftliches Geschick, Erfahrung, verbindliches Wesen, natürlichen Blick für Menschen und Dinge. Er war stets bestrebt, eine schroffe Stellungnahme zu vermeiden und wurde durch die Haltung Englands und Frankreichs auch darin bestärkt.

Ich sagte ihm später einmal: Die Stimmung in Russland ist wohl sehr antideutsch. Er entgegnete: Es gibt auch sehr starke und einflussreiche prodeutsche Kreise, man ist aber allgemein antiösterreichisch!

Es erübrigt sich, hinzuzufügen, dass unsere *Austrophilie à outrance* (Österreich-Freundschaft bis zur äussersten Grenze) nicht gerade geeignet war, die Entente zu lockern und Russland seinen asiatischen Interessen zuzuführen!

Balkankonferenz

Gleichzeitig tagte in London die Balkankonferenz, und ich hatte Gelegenheit, mit den Leitern der Balkan-

Berlin] through the secret treaty [with Russia] and through the attitude he took in the Battenberg question; the dangerous slope down which we started again in the Bosnian question was followed further in London and was not abandoned later in time to save us from falling into the abyss.[16]

The dissatisfaction which prevailed at the time in Russia found expression during the conference in attacks in Russian journals upon my Russian colleague and upon the Russian diplomacy. Count Benckendorff's German origin and Catholic faith, his reputation as a friend of the Germans, and the accidental circumstance that he was related both to Count Mensdorff and to me, were exploited in the discontented circles. Although not a man of great force, Count Benckendorff possesses a number of qualities that are essential to a good diplomatist: tact, social adaptability, experience, pleasant manners and an instinctive appreciation of men and of things. It was always his effort to avoid taking an uncompromising position, and this disposition on his part was strengthened by the attitude of England and of France.

I said to him once, on a later occasion: "The feeling in Russia, I suppose, is very anti-German." He replied: "There are also very strong and influential pro-German circles, but everybody is anti-Austrian."

It is almost needless to add that our extreme Austrophil attitude was not precisely adapted to loosen the Entente or to direct Russia's attention to its Asiatic interests!

The Balkan Conference [17]

At the same period the Balkan conference was sitting in London, and I had opportunity to get in touch

[16] See Appendix, notes iii and iv.
[17] Ibid., note xi.

staaten in Fühlung zu treten. Die bedeutendste Persönlichkeit war wohl Herr Venizelos. Er war damals nichts weniger als deutschfeindlich, besuchte mich wiederholt und trug mit Vorliebe und sogar auf der französischen Botschaft das Band des Roten Adlerordens. Von gewinnender Liebenswürdigkeit, mit weltmännischem Auftreten, wusste er sich Sympathien zu verschaffen. Neben ihm spielte Herr Danew, der damalige bulgarische Ministerpräsident und Vertrauensmann des Grafen Berchtold, eine grosse Rolle. Er machte den Eindruck eines verschlagenen und energischen Mannes, und es ist wohl nur dem Einfluss seiner Wiener und Pester Freunde zuzuschreiben, über deren Huldigungen er sich gelegentlich belustigte, dass er sich zu der Torheit des zweiten Balkankrieges verleiten liess und die russische Vermittelung ablehnte.

Auch Herr Take Jonescu war öfters in London und besuchte mich dann regelmässig. Ich kannte ihn von der Zeit her, da ich Sekretär in Bukarest war. Er gehörte auch zu den Freunden des Herrn von Kiderlen. In London war er bestrebt, durch Verhandlungen mit Herrn Danew Zugeständnisse für Rumänien zu erreichen und wurde dabei von dem sehr befähigten rumänischen Gesandten Nisu unterstützt. Dass diese Verhandlungen an dem Widerstande Bulgariens scheiterten, ist bekannt. Graf Berchtold (und wir natürlich mit ihm) war ganz auf Seiten Bulgariens, sonst wäre es wohl gelungen, den Rumänen die gewünschte Genugtuung durch einen Druck auf Herrn Danew zu verschaffen und uns Rumänien zu verpflichten, das durch die Haltung Österreichs während des zweiten Balkankrieges und danach den Mittelmächten endgültig entfremdet wurde.

with the leading men of the Balkan states. Quite the most significant personality was that of M. Venizelos. At that time he was anything but hostile to Germany. He paid me repeated visits, and he wore by preference, even at the French embassy, the ribbon of the order of the Red Eagle. With winning and kindly ways and the manners of a man of the world, he made himself generally liked. M. Danef, at that time prime minister of Bulgaria and confidant of Count Berchtold, also played a leading rôle. He impressed one as a subtle and energetic man; and the mistake he made in permitting himself to be drawn into the unwise venture of the Second Balkan War, refusing Russian mediation, is probably to be ascribed solely to the influence of his friends at Vienna and at Budapest, by whose homage he sometimes showed himself amused.

M. Take Jonescu also was frequently in London and on such occasions always called on me. I had known him since the time when I was secretary at Bucharest. He was also one of Herr von Kiderlen's friends. In London he was trying to gain concessions for Rumania by negotiations with M. Danef, and he was supported in these efforts by the very able Rumanian envoy, M. Nisu. These negotiations, it is known, failed in consequence of the resistance of Bulgaria. Count Berchtold—and we of course with him—was altogether on the side of Bulgaria. But for this it would probably have been possible, by putting some pressure on M. Danef, to obtain for the Rumanians the concessions they desired, and thus to place Rumania under obligations to us. As it was, in consequence of the attitude of Austria during the Second Balkan War and afterwards, Rumania was completely estranged from the Central Powers.

Die Niederlage Bulgariens im zweiten Balkankriege und der Sieg Serbiens sowie der rumänische Einmarsch bedeuteten naturgemäss für Österreich eine Blamage. Der Gedanke, diese durch einen Waffengang gegen Serbien auszugleichen, scheint bald in Wien Eingang gefunden zu haben. Die italienischen Enthüllungen beweisen es, und es ist anzunehmen, dass Marquis San Giuliano, der den Plan als eine „pericolosissima aventura" (äusserst gefährliches Abenteuer) sehr treffend kennzeichnete, uns davor bewahrt hat, schon im Sommer 1913 in einen Weltkrieg verwickelt zu werden.

Bei der Vertrautheit der russisch-italienischen Beziehungen wird die Wiener Anregung auch wohl in Petersburg bekannt geworden sein. Jedenfalls hat Herr Sasonow in Konstanza, wie Herr Take Jonescu mir erzählte, offen gesagt, dass ein Angriff Österreichs auf Serbien für Russland den Kriegsfall bedeutet.

Als einer meiner Herren im Frühjahr 1914 von Urlaub aus Wien zurückkehrte, erzählte er, Herr von Tschirschky erklärte, es gäbe bald Krieg. Da ich aber über wichtige Vorgänge stets in Unkenntnis gelassen wurde, hielt ich diesen Pessimismus für unbegründet.

Seit dem Bukarester Frieden scheint tatsächlich in Wien die Absicht bestanden zu haben, eine Revision dieses Vertrages auf eigene Faust durchzuführen, und man wartete anscheinend nur auf einen günstigen Anlass. Auf unsere Unterstützung konnten die Wiener Staatsmänner selbstverständlich rechnen. Das wussten sie, denn es war ihnen schon wiederholt „Schlappheit" vorgeworfen worden. Man drängte in Berlin sogar auf eine „Rehabilitierung" Österreichs.

The Second Balkan War [18]

The defeat of Bulgaria in the Second Balkan War the victory of Serbia and the Rumanian march into Bulgaria meant for Austria a loss of prestige. The idea of offsetting this loss by a campaign against Serbia seems to have been entertained in Vienna shortly afterward. This is proved by the Italian revelations; and it is to be assumed that Marquis di San Giuliano, who quite appropriately characterized the plan as a "very risky adventure," saved us from being involved in a world war in the summer of 1913.[19]

In view of the intimacy of the relations between Italy and Russia, it may be assumed that the Viennese overture was known in St. Petersburg. At all events, M. Sazonof declared openly in Constanza, as M. Take Jonescu informed me, that an attack of Austria on Serbia would amount to a *casus belli* for Russia.

When, in the spring of 1914, one of the members of my embassy returned from a leave of absence in Vienna, he told me that Herr von Tschirschky had declared that there would soon be war. But as I was systematically kept in ignorance of important occurrences, I regarded this pessimistic view as baseless.

Ever since the Peace of Bucharest, Vienna seems really to have intended to secure a revision of this treaty by its own independent action and to have been waiting only for a favorable occasion. On our support the Vienna statesmen could reckon as a matter of course. They knew this, for they had been repeatedly reproached for "flabbiness." In Berlin there was actual insistence that Austria be "rehabilitated."

[18] See Appendix, note xii.
[19] *Ibid.*, note xiv.

Liman von Sanders

Als ich im Dezember 1913 nach längerem Urlaub nach London zurückkehrte, hatte die Frage Liman von Sanders zu einer neuen Verschärfung unserer Beziehungen zu Russland geführt. Sir Edward Grey machte mich nicht ohne Besorgnis auf die Erregung aufmerksam, die darüber in Petersburg herrsche! *"I have never seen them so excited"* (ich habe sie niemals so aufgeregt gesehen).

Ich wurde von Berlin aus beauftragt, den Minister zu bitten, in mässigendem Sinne in Petersburg zu wirken und uns bei Beilegung des Streites behilflich zu sein. Sir Edward war hierzu gern bereit, und seine Vermittlung hat nicht wenig dazu beigetragen, die Angelegenheit zu ebnen. Meine guten Beziehungen zu Sir Edward und sein grosser Einfluss in Petersburg wurden auf ähnliche Weise wiederholt benutzt, wenn es galt, dort etwas durchzusetzen, da unsere Vertretung sich hierzu als völlig ungeeignet erwies.

In den kritischen Tagen des Juli 1914 sagte mir Sir Edward: „Wenn Sie etwas in Petersburg erreichen wollen, wenden Sie sich regelmässig an mich, wenn ich aber einmal Ihren Einfluss in Wien anrufe, so versagen Sie mir Ihre Unterstützung."

Kolonialvertrag

Die guten und vertrauensvollen Beziehungen, die es mir gelang, nicht nur in der Gesellschaft und mit den einflussreichsten Persönlichkeiten, wie Sir Ed. Grey und Mr. Asquith, sondern auch bei *public dinners* (bei öffentlichen Dîners) mit der Öffentlichkeit anzuknüpfen, hatten eine merkliche Besserung unseres Verhältnisses zu England herbeigeführt. Sir Edward

Liman von Sanders [20]

When, after a lengthy leave of absence, I returned
to London in December, 1913, the Liman von Sanders
question had led to renewed tension in our relations
with Russia. Sir Edward Grey called my attention,
not without anxiety on his part, to the widespread
agitation which this matter had aroused in St. Petersburg, saying: "I have never seen them so excited."

I received instructions from Berlin to ask the minister to work in favor of moderation in St. Petersburg
and to assist us in settling the dispute. Sir Edward
was quite willing to do this, and his mediation contributed in no small degree to smoothing the matter
over. My good relations with Sir Edward and his
great influence in St. Petersburg were repeatedly utilized in a like manner when it was a question of carrying
any point there; for our representative proved quite
unfit for any such purpose.

During the critical days of July, 1914, Sir Edward
said to me: "If you wish to get anything in St. Petersburg, you always come to me, but if once I ask for
your influence in Vienna, you refuse me your support."

Colonial Treaty

The excellent and confidential relations I succeeded
in establishing, not only in society and with the most
influential personalities, such as Sir Edward Grey and
Mr. Asquith, but also at public dinners with [the
agencies of] publicity, had brought about a noticeable
improvement in our relations with England. It was

[20] See Appendix, note xv.

war aufrichtig bemüht, diese Annäherung weiter zu befestigen, und seine Absichten traten besonders in zwei Fragen hervor: dem Kolonial- und dem Bagdadvertrag.

Im Jahre 1898 war zwischen dem Grafen Hatzfeld und Herrn Balfour ein geheimes Abkommen unterzeichnet worden, das die portugiesischen Kolonien in Afrika in wirtschaftspolitische [7] Interessensphären zwischen uns und England teilte. Da die portugiesische Regierung weder die Macht noch die Mittel besass, ihren ausgedehnten Besitz zu erschliessen oder sachgemäss zu verwalten, hatte sie sich früher bereits mit dem Gedanken getragen, ihn zu veräussern und ihre Finanzen dadurch zu sanieren. Eine Einigung zwischen uns und England war zustande gekommen, welche die beiderseitigen Interessen begrenzte, und die um so grösseren Wert besass, als Portugal sich bekanntlich in völliger Abhängigkeit von England befindet.

Dieser Vertrag sollte wohl äusserlich die Unversehrtheit und Unabhängigkeit des portugiesischen Reiches sichern, und er sprach nur die Absicht aus, den Portugiesen finanziell und wirtschaftlich behilflich zu sein. Er stand daher dem Wortlaut nach nicht im Widerspruch zu dem alten englisch-portugiesischen Bündnis aus dem 15. Jahrhundert, das zuletzt unter Karl II. erneuert wurde und den gegenseitigen Besitzstand verbürgte.

Trotzdem war auf Bestreben des Marquis Soveral, der vermutlich über die deutsch-englischen Abmachungen nicht in Unkenntnis blieb, ein neuer Vertrag, der sogenannte Windsorvertrag, im Jahre 1899, zwischen England und Portugal geschlossen worden,

[7] B.-C.: "wirtschaftspolitischen."

Sir Edward's honest endeavor to place this *rapprochement* on a firmer basis. His aims were most clearly manifested in two matters: the colonial and the Bagdad treaties.

In the year 1898 a secret convention had been signed by Count Hatzfeldt and Mr. Balfour, which divided the Portuguese colonies in Africa [21] into economic-political spheres of interest as between us and England. As the Portuguese government possessed neither the power nor the means to open up its extensive possessions or to administer them suitably, it had already at an earlier date entertained the idea of selling them and thereby putting its finances on a sound basis. An agreement had been reached between us and England, delimiting the interests of the two parties. Its value was enhanced by the fact that Portugal, as is well known, is completely dependent upon England.

On its face, of course, this treaty was designed to secure the integrity and independence of the Portuguese realm, and the only purpose it expressed was to give to the Portuguese financial and economic assistance. In its wording, accordingly, it did not contravene the old Anglo-Portuguese alliance, dating from the fifteenth century, which was last renewed under Charles II and which contained a reciprocal guaranty of existing territorial possessions.[22]

Nevertheless, at the instance of Marquis Soveral, who presumably was not left uninformed regarding the Anglo-German agreements, a new treaty, the so-called Windsor Treaty, was concluded in 1899 between England and Portugal, confirming the old agreements, which had never been put out of force.

[21] See Appendix, note xvii.
[22] *Ibid.*, note xviii.

welcher die alten, niemals ausser Kraft gesetzten Vereinbarungen bestätigte.

Die Unterhandlungen zwischen uns und England, die bereits vor meiner Ankunft begonnen hatten, bezweckten, unseren Vertrag von 1898, der auch hinsichtlich der geographischen Abgrenzung manche Unzuträglichkeiten aufwies, umzugestalten und zu verbessern. Dank der entgegenkommenden Haltung der britischen Regierung gelang es mir, dem neuen Vertrag eine unseren Wünschen und Interessen durchaus entsprechende Form zu geben. Ganz Angola bis an den 20. Längengrad wurde uns zugesprochen, so dass wir an das Kongogebiet von Süden gelangten, ausserdem noch die wertvollen Inseln San Thomé und Principe, die nördlich des Äquators liegen und dadurch eigentlich dem französischen Interessengebiet zufielen, eine Tatsache, die meinen französischen Kollegen zu lebhaften, wenn auch vergeblichen Gegenvorstellungen veranlasste.

Ferner erhielten wir den nördlichen Teil von Mosambik; der Licango bildete die Grenze.

Unseren Interessen und Wünschen wurde seitens der britischen Regierung das grösste Entgegenkommen gezeigt. Sir Ed. Grey beabsichtigte, uns seinen guten Willen zu bekunden, er wünschte aber auch unsere koloniale Entwicklung überhaupt zu fördern, da England die deutsche Kraftentfaltung von der Nordsee und von Westeuropa nach dem Weltmeer und Afrika abzulenken hoffte. *"We don't want to grudge Germany her colonial development"* (Wir wollen Deutschland seine koloniale Entwicklung nicht missgönnen), sagte mir ein Mitglied des Kabinetts.

Der Kongostaat sollte auf britische Anregung ursprünglich auch in den Vertrag einbezogen werden,

The object of the negotiations between us and England, which had begun before my arrival, was to revise and amend our treaty of 1898, which contained a number of impracticable provisions, even as regarded geographical delimitation. Thanks to the conciliatory attitude of the British government, I succeeded in giving to the new treaty a form which entirely corresponded to our wishes and interests. All Angola, as far as the 20th degree of longitude, was assigned to us, so that we reached the Congo territory from the south. Moreover the valuable islands of San Thomé and Principe, which lie north of the equator and therefore really belonged to the French sphere of interest, were allotted to us—a fact which caused my French colleague to enter energetic but unavailing protests.

Further, we obtained the northern part of Mozambique; the Licango formed the boundary.

The British government showed the utmost readiness to meet our interests and wishes. Sir Edward Grey intended to prove his good will to us, but he also desired to promote our colonial development as a whole, because England hoped to divert the German output of energy from the North Sea and Western Europe to the ocean and to Africa. "We don't want to grudge Germany her colonial development," a member of the Cabinet said to me.

Originally, at the British suggestion, the Congo State also was to have been included in the treaty, which would have given us a right of preëmption and would have enabled us to penetrate it economically. But we refused this offer, out of alleged respect for Belgian sensibilities! Perhaps the idea was to economize our successes? Furthermore, as regarded the

was uns ein Vorkaufsrecht und die Möglichkeit gegeben hätte, ihn wirtschaftlich zu durchdringen. Angeblich mit Rücksicht auf belgische Empfindlichkeiten lehnten wir aber dieses Angebot ab! Vielleicht sollte mit Erfolgen gespart werden? Auch hinsichtlich der praktischen Verwirklichung des eigentlichen unausgesprochenen Zweckes des Vertrages, der späteren tatsächlichen Teilung des portugiesischen Kolonialbesitzes, bot die neue Fassung wesentliche Vorteile und Fortschritte gegen die alte. Es waren nämlich Fälle vorgesehen, die es uns ermöglichten, zur Wahrung unserer Interessen auf den uns zugewiesenen Gebieten einzuschreiten. Diese Voraussetzungen wurden so weit gefasst, dass es eigentlich uns überlassen blieb, selbst zu bestimmen, wenn „vitale" Interessen vorlagen, so dass es bei der völligen Abhängigkeit Portugals von England nur darauf ankam, die Beziehungen zu England weiter zu pflegen, um mit englischer Zustimmung unsere beiderseitigen Absichten später zu verwirklichen.

Die Aufrichtigkeit der britischen Regierung in ihrem Bestreben, unsere Rechte zu achten, zeigte sich darin, dass Sir Ed. Grey, noch ehe der Vertrag fertiggestellt oder unterzeichnet war, englische Unternehmer, die in dem uns durch den neuen Vertrag zugewiesenen Gebieten Kapitalanlagen suchten, und dafür die britische Unterstützung wünschten, an uns verwies, mit dem Bemerken, dass das betreffende Unternehmen in unsere Interessensphäre gehöre.

Der Vertrag war schon zur Zeit des Königsbesuches in Berlin, also im Mai 1913, im wesentlichen fertig. In Berlin fand damals unter dem Vorsitz des Herrn Reichskanzlers eine Besprechung statt, an der auch ich teilnahm, und bei der noch einzelne Wünsche

practical execution of the real but unexpressed purpose of the treaty—the actual partition at a later date of the Portuguese colonial possessions—the new formulation, as compared with the old, offered us important advantages and represented a distinct advance. Thus it was provided that in certain cases we should be authorized to intervene in the territories assigned to us for the protection of our interests. These conditional clauses were so broad that it was really left to us to decide whether "vital" interests were concerned; so that, Portugal being completely dependent on England, it was necessary only to cultivate further our relations with England in order, later on, with English assent, to realize our respective intentions.

The sincerity of the British government in its effort to respect our rights was proved by the fact that, even before the treaty was completed or signed, English *entrepreneurs* who wished to invest capital in the districts assigned to us under the new treaty, and who desired British support for their undertaking, were referred by Sir Edward Grey to us, with the information that the enterprise in question belonged in our sphere of interest.

The treaty was substantially complete at the time of the King's visit to Berlin in May, 1913. At that time a discussion took place in Berlin, under the presidency of the imperial chancellor, in which I took part, and at which some further desires of ours were defined. On my return to London I succeeded, with the help of the counselor of the embassy, Herr von Kühlmann, who was working with Mr. Parker upon the details of the treaty, in putting through our last proposals also; so that in August, 1913, before I

[63]

festgelegt wurden. Bei meiner Rückkehr nach London gelang es mir mit Hilfe des Botschaftsrats, Herrn von Kühlmann, der mit Mr. Parker die Einzelheiten des Vertrages bearbeitete, auch unsere letzten Vorschläge durchzusetzen, so dass der ganze Vertrag schon im August 1913, vor Antritt meines Urlaubs, von Sir Ed. Grey und mir paragraphiert werden konnte.

Nun sollten aber neue Schwierigkeiten entstehen, die die Unterzeichnung verhinderten, und erst nach einem Jahre, also kurz vor Kriegsausbruch, konnte ich die Ermächtigung erhalten zum endgültigen Abschluss. Zur Unterzeichnung aber ist es nicht mehr gekommen.

Sir Ed. Grey wollte nämlich nur unterzeichnen, *falls der Vertrag mitsamt den beiden Verträgen von 1898 und 1899 veröffentlicht würde.* England besitze sonst keine geheimen Verträge, und es sei gegen die bestehenden Grundsätze, bindende Abmachungen zu verheimlichen. Er könne daher keinen Vertrag eingehen, ohne ihn zu veröffentlichen. Über Zeitpunkt und Art der Veröffentlichung sei er aber bereit, unseren Wünschen Rechnung zu tragen, vorausgesetzt, dass die Veröffentlichung in längstens Jahresfrist nach Unterzeichnung erfolge.

Im Auswärtigen Amt aber, wo meine Londoner Erfolge zunehmendes Missvergnügen erregten, und wo eine einflussreiche Persönlichkeit, die die Rolle des Herrn von Holstein spielte, den Londoner Posten für sich in Anspruch nahm, erklärte man, die Veröffentlichung gefährde unsere Interessen in den Kolonien, da die Portugiesen uns alsdann keine Konzessionen mehr geben würden.

Die Nichtigkeit des Einwandes erhellt aus der Erwägung, dass der alte Vertrag den Portugiesen höchst wahrscheinlich ebenso längst bekannt war, wie

went on leave, Sir Edward Grey and I were able to paragraph the entire treaty.

At this point, however, new difficulties were to arise, which prevented the signing of the treaty; and it was only a year later, shortly before the outbreak of war, that I was able to obtain authorization for its definite conclusion. But it never reached the point of being signed.

The difficulty was that Sir Edward Grey was willing to sign only if the treaty were published, together with the two treaties of 1898 and 1899. England, he said, had no other secret treaties, and it was contrary to existing principles that binding agreements should be kept secret. He could therefore conclude no treaty without publishing it. As regarded time and manner of publication, however, he was ready to take account of our wishes, provided publication took place within one year, at latest, after the signing.

In our Foreign Office, however, where my London successes aroused increasing dissatisfaction, and where an influential personage, who had taken over the rôle previously played by Herr von Holstein,[23] was claiming for himself the post at London, it was explained that the publication would imperil our interests in the colonies, because the Portuguese would then give us no more concessions.

That there was nothing in this objection becomes clear when we consider that in all probability, in view of the intimacy of the Portuguese-English relations, the old treaty had long been known, and the new agreements had likewise been made known, to the Portuguese. It is also to be remembered that, with the influence England has in Lisbon, the Portu-

[23] See Appendix, note i.

[65]

unsere neuen Abmachungen, angesichts der Intimität der portugiesisch-englischen Beziehungen, und dass bei dem Einfluss, den England in Lissabon besitzt, die dortige Regierung einem deutsch-britischen Einverständnisse gegenüber völlig willenlos ist.

Es galt also, einen anderen Vorwand zu finden, um den Vertrag scheitern zu lassen: Die Bekanntgebung[8] des Windsorvertrages, der zur Zeit des Fürsten Hohenlohe geschlossen wurde, und der nur eine Erneuerung des niemals ausser Kraft getretenen Vertrags Karls II. war, könne die Stellung des Herrn von Bethmann Hollweg gefährden, als Beweis britischer Heuchelei und Perfidie!

Ich wies darauf hin, dass die Einleitung zu unseren Verträgen ganz dasselbe besage, wie der Windsorvertrag und wie andere ähnliche Verträge, nämlich, dass wir die souveränen Rechte Portugals wahren, und die Unversehrtheit seines Besitzes schützen wollten. Vergebens! Trotz wiederholter Unterredungen mit Sir Ed. Grey, bei denen der Minister immer neue Vorschläge machte, für die Veröffentlichung, beharrte das Auswärtige Amt auf seinem Standpunkt, und verabredete schliesslich mit Sir Ed. Goschen, dass alles so bleiben sollte, wie es bisher gewesen!

Der Vertrag, der uns ausserordentliche Vorteile bot, das Ergebnis einer mehr als einjährigen Arbeit, war somit gefallen, weil er für mich ein öffentlicher Erfolg gewesen wäre.

Als ich im Frühjahr 1914 gelegentlich eines Dîners[9] auf der Botschaft, an dem Mr. Harcourt teilnahm, den Gegenstand berührte, erklärte mir der Kolonialminister, er befinde sich in Verlegenheit und wisse nicht,

[8] B.-C.: "Bekanntgabe."
[9] B.-C.: "Dîner."

guese government could not think of opposing a German-British understanding.

Consequently, another pretext had to be found for wrecking the treaty. It was urged that the publication of the Windsor Treaty, which was concluded in the time of Prince Hohenlohe—though it was only a renewal of the treaty of Charles II, which had never gone out of force—might jeopard the position of Herr von Bethmann Hollweg, because it would be proof of British hypocrisy and perfidy!

I pointed out that the preamble to our treaties said exactly the same thing as the Windsor Treaty and other similar treaties—namely, that it was our purpose to protect the sovereign rights of Portugal and the integrity of its possessions. In vain! Although Sir Edward Grey, in repeated conversations, kept making fresh proposals concerning publication, our Foreign Office persisted in its attitude, and finally arranged with Sir Edward Goschen that everything should be left as it was before.

So the treaty, which gave us extraordinary advantages and was the result of more than a year's work, perished because it would have been a public success for me.

When in the spring of 1914 I had an opportunity, at a dinner in the embassy at which Mr. Harcourt was present, to touch upon the matter, the colonial secretary explained that he found himself in a perplexing position and did not know what attitude he should take. The present state of affairs was intolerable, because he, Mr. Harcourt, wished to respect our rights, but, on the other hand, was in doubt as to whether he was to be guided by the old treaty or the new. It was therefore urgently desirable to clear

wie sich zu verhalten. Der gegenwärtige Zustand sei unerträglich, da er, Mr. Harcourt, unsere Rechte berücksichtigen wolle, andererseits aber im Zweifel sei, ob er sich nach dem alten Vertrage oder dem neuen zu tichten habe. Es sei daher dringend erwünscht, Klarheit zu schaffen und die Sache, die sich nun schon so lange hinziehe, zum Abschluss zu bringen.

Auf einen diesbezüglichen Bericht erhielt ich einen sehr wenig höflichen, aber um so erregteren Erlass, demzufolge ich mich jeder weiteren Einmischung in der Sache zu enthalten hätte.

Ich bedauere es heute, dass ich nicht daraufhin nach Berlin gefahren bin, um dem Monarchen meinen Posten zur Verfügung zu stellen, und dass ich immer noch den Glauben an die Möglichkeit einer Verständigung zwischen mir und den leitenden Persönlichkeiten nicht verloren hatte, ein verhängnisvoller Irrtum, der sich wenige Monate später in so tragischer Weise rächen sollte!

So wenig ich auch damals das Wohlwollen des obersten Reichsbeamten noch besass, da er fürchtete, ich strebe nach [10] seinem Posten, so muss ich ihm die Gerechtigkeit widerfahren lassen, dass er bei unserer letzten Unterredung vor Kriegsausbruch, Ende Juli 1914, auf die ich später noch zurückkomme, seine Zustimmung zur Unterschrift und Veröffentlichung erteilte. Trotzdem bedurfte es noch wiederholter Anregungen meinerseits, die von Herrn Dr. Solf in Berlin unterstützt wurden, um endlich Juli 1914 die Genehmigung zu erwirken. Da aber die serbische Krisis damals schon den Frieden Europas bedrohte, musste die Vollziehung des Vertrages verschoben werden. Auch er gehört zu den Opfern dieses Krieges.

[10] B.-C.: "nach nach."

matters up and to bring the affair, which had dragged on so long already, to a conclusion.

In reply to a report on this subject I received a dispatch that was far from courteous but was correspondingly excited, to the effect that I was to abstain from any further interference in the matter.

I now regret that I did not go at once to Berlin and place my position at the Emperor's disposal; and that I still clung to the belief that an understanding was not impossible between me and the persons who were directing our policies—a fatal mistake, and one for which vengeance was to be exacted, a few months later, in so tragic a fashion!

Although at that time I was no longer in favor with the highest official of the Empire, since he feared that I aspired to his position, I must do him the justice to say that at the end of June, 1914, in our last conversation before the outbreak of war—a conversation to which I shall again refer later—he gave his consent to the signing and publication [of the treaty]. In spite of this, it still required repeated applications on my part, which were supported in Berlin by Dr. Solf, to obtain finally, in July, 1914, the [necessary formal] approval. Since, however, the Serbian crisis was then already threatening the peace of Europe, the execution of the treaty had to be postponed. It too is one of the victims of this war.

Gleichzeitig unterhandelte ich in London, dabei wirksam unterstützt durch Herrn von Kühlmann, über den sog. Bagdagvertrag. Dieser bezweckte tatsächlich die Einteilung Kleinasiens in Interessensphären, obwohl dieser Ausdruck mit Rücksicht auf die Rechte des Sultans ängstlich vermieden wurde. Sir Ed. Grey erklärte auch wiederholt, dass keine Abmachungen mit Frankreich und Russland beständen, die die Aufteilung Kleinasiens bezweckten.

Unter Zuziehung eines türkischen Vertreters, als welcher Hakki Pascha erschien, wurden alle wirtschaftlichen Fragen, die mit den deutschen Unternehmungen in Verbindung standen, im wesentlichen den Wünschen der Deutschen Bank entsprechend geregelt. Das wichtigste Zugeständnis, das Sir Ed. Grey mir persönlich gemacht hatte, war die Verlängerung der Bahnstrecke bis Basra. Dieser Standpunkt war nämlich unsererseits aufgegeben worden zugunsten des Anschlusses nach Alexandrette; Bagdad bildete bisher den Endpunkt der Bahn. Für die Schiffahrt auf dem Schatt-el-Arab sollte eine internationale Kommission sorgen. Auch an den Hafenbauten in Basra wurden wir beteiligt und erhielten ferner Rechte an der Tigrisschiffahrt, die bisher ein Monopol des Hauses Lynch war.

Durch diesen Vertrag wurde ganz Mesopotamien bis Basra unser Interessengebiet, unbeschadet älterer britischer Rechte an der Tigrisschiffahrt und den Wilcox-Bewässerungsanlagen, ferner das ganze Gebiet der Bagdad- und Anatolischen Eisenbahn.

Als britischer Wirtschaftsbereich galten die Küsten des Persischen Busens und die Smyrna-Aidin-Bahn,

The Bagdad Treaty[24]

During the same period I was carrying on negotiations in London, with the efficient support of Herr von Kühlmann, in reference to the so-called Bagdad Treaty. The real purpose of this treaty was to divide Asia Minor into spheres of influence, although this expression was anxiously avoided, out of regard for the rights of the Sultan. Sir Edward Grey repeatedly stated, moreover, that no agreements existed with France and with Russia aiming at the dismemberment of Asia Minor.

After we had drawn into conference a representative of Turkey, Hakki Pasha, all the economic questions connected with the German enterprises were regulated, in substantial accord with the desires of the German Bank. The most important concession made to me personally by Sir Edward Grey was the prolongation of the railway to Basra. This particular object had been abandoned, on our part, in favor of a connection with Alexandretta. Up to this time Bagdad formed the terminus of the line. Navigation on the Shatt-el-Arab was to be placed under an international commission. We were also admitted to participation in the Basra harbor works and, in addition, we obtained rights in the navigation of the Tigris, which had been previously a monopoly of the firm of Lynch.

By virtue of this treaty all Mesopotamia as far as Basra became our sphere of interest, without prejudice to older British rights in the navigation of the Tigris and in the Wilcox irrigation works. Our sphere further included the whole region of the Bagdad and Anatolian railway.

[24] See Appendix, note xix.

als französischer Syrien, als russischer Armenien. Würden beide Verträge vollzogen und veröffentlicht, so war damit eine Verständigung mit England erreicht, die allen Zweifeln an der Möglichkeit einer *"Anglo-German coöperation"* (eines englisch-deutschen Zusammenwirkens) für immer ein Ende machte.

Flottenfrage

Die heikelste aller Fragen war und blieb die Flottenfrage. Sie wird nicht immer ganz richtig beurteilt.

Die Schaffung einer mächtigen Flotte am anderen Ufer der Nordsee, die gleichzeitige Entwickelung der bedeutendsten Militärmacht des Festlandes zur bedeutendsten Seemacht desselben musste in England zum mindesten als Unbequemlichkeit empfunden werden. Hierüber kann billigerweise kein Zweifel bestehen. Um den nötigen Vorsprung zu behalten und nicht in Abhängigkeit zu geraten und die Herrschaft der Meere zu sichern, die Britannien benötigt, um nicht zu verhungern, musste es zu Rüstungen und Ausgaben schreiten, die schwer auf dem Steuerzahler lasteten. Eine Bedrohung der britischen Weltstellung ergab sich jedoch, wenn unsere Politik die Möglichkeit kriegerischer Entwickelungen gewärtigen liess. Diese Voraussetzung war bei den Marokkokrisen und der bosnischen Frage in sichtbare Nähe getreten.

Mit unserer Flotte *nach den bestehenden Festlegungen* hatte man sich abgefunden, sie war den Briten gewiss nicht willkommen und bildete einen der Gründe, aber nicht den einzigen und vielleicht auch nicht den wichtigsten, für den Anschluss Englands an Frankreich und Russland; aber wegen der Flotte *allein* hätte England ebensowenig zum Schwerte gegriffen, wie

The British economic domain was to include the coasts of the Persian Gulf and the Smyrna-Aidin line; the French, Syria; the Russian, Armenia. Had these two treaties been executed and published, an understanding with England would have been reached which would forever have dissipated all doubts as to the possibility of an Anglo-German coöperation.

The Naval Question [25]

The naval question was and remained the thorniest of all the questions at issue. It is not always quite rightly appreciated.

The creation of a powerful fleet on the other side of the North Sea, the development of the most important military power of the continent into its most important naval power as well, could not but arouse in England a sense at least of discomfort. On this point there can be no reasonable doubt. In order to keep the lead it had gained and needed and not to lose its independence, in order to secure the rule of the sea, which Great Britain requires to avoid starvation, it was forced to proceed to armaments and outlays that weighed heavily on the tax-payer. The British position in the world, however, was threatened if our policy caused possible warlike complications to be anticipated. This anticipation had been brought into the immediate field of vision in the Moroccan crisis and in the Bosnian question.

The development of our fleet in accordance with the plans existing at that time had been accepted. It was certainly not welcome to the Britons, and it was one of the motives, although not the only and perhaps not the most important motive, that had

[25] See Appendix, note xvi.

[73]

etwa wegen unseres Handels, der angeblich den Neid und schliesslich den Krieg gezeitigt hat.

Ich vertrat von Anfang an den Standpunkt, dass es *trotz* der Flotte möglich [11] sei, zu freundschaftlicher Verständigung und Annäherung zu gelangen, wenn wir keine Novelle brächten und eine *zweifelsfreie Friedenspolitik trieben*. Auch vermied ich es, von der Flotte zu sprechen, und zwischen Sir Ed. Grey und mir ist das Wort überhaupt nicht gefallen. Sir Ed. Grey erklärte gelegentlich in einer Kabinettssitzung: *"The present German Ambassador has never mentioned the fleet to me"* (Der gegenwärtige deutsche Botschafter hat vor mir nie die Flotte erwähnt).

Während meiner Amtszeit regte bekanntlich Mr. Churchill, der damalige Erste Lord der Admiralität, den sogenannten *"naval holiday"* (Flottenfeiertag) an und schlug aus finanziellen Gründen und wohl auch um der pazifistischen Richtung in seiner Partei entgegenzukommen, eine einjährige Rüstungspause vor. Amtlich von Sir Ed. Grey wurde der Vorschlag nicht unterstützt, zu mir hat er nie davon gesprochen, Mr. Churchill redete mich aber wiederholt darauf an.

Ich bin überzeugt, dass seine Anregung aufrichtig gemeint war, wie überhaupt Winkelzügigkeit nicht im Wesen des Engländers liegt. Es wäre für Mr. Churchill ein grosser Erfolg gewesen, dem Lande mit Ersparnissen aufzuwarten und den Rüstungsalp, der auf dem Volke lastete, erleichtern zu können.

Ich entgegnete, es würde aus technischen Gründen schwer sein, auf seinen Gedanken einzugehen. Was sollte aus den Arbeitern werden, die für diese Zwecke geworben seien, was aus dem technischen Personal? Unser Flottenprogramm sei einmal festgelegt und

[11] B.-C.: *"unmöglich."*

[74]

led England to establish closer relations with France and with Russia; but England would no more have grasped the sword on account of our fleet alone than on account, say, of our trade, which is alleged to have bred envy and finally war.

From the outset I took the position that, in spite of the fleet, it was possible to reach a friendly understanding and a *rapprochement*, provided we introduced no new naval bill and conducted our policy on indubitably peaceful lines. I also avoided any mention of the fleet and, in the conversations between Sir Edward Grey and me, the word was never uttered. Sir Edward Grey declared incidentally, at a cabinet meeting: "The present German ambassador has never mentioned the fleet to me."

During my term of office Mr. Churchill, at that time first lord of the admiralty, suggested, as is known, the so-called "naval holiday" and, for financial reasons and probably also in order to meet the pacifist tendency in his party, proposed a stay of armaments for one year. This proposal was not officially supported by Sir Edward Grey; he never spoke of it to me; Mr. Churchill, however, repeatedly addressed me on the subject.

I am convinced that his suggestion was honestly intended. Chicane is not natural to the Englishman. It would have been a great success for Mr. Churchill if he could have come before the country with reductions of expenditure and lightened the burden of armament that weighed like a nightmare on the people.

My answer was that for technical reasons it would be difficult to accept his idea. What was to become of the workmen who had been hired for these purposes?

daran liesse sich schwer etwas ändern. Wir beabsichtigten es andererseits auch nicht zu überschreiten. Er kam aber wieder darauf zurück und machte geltend, dass die für ungeheure Rüstungen aufgewendeten Mittel auch besser für andere, nutzbringende Zwecke Verwendung fänden. Ich entgegnete, dass auch diese Ausgaben der heimischen Industrie zugute kämen.

Es gelang mir auch durch Unterredungen mit Sir W. Tyrrell, dem Kabinettschef Sir Edwards, die Frage von der Tagesordnung [12] abzusetzen, ohne zu verstimmen, obwohl sie im Parlamente wiederkehrte, und zu verhindern, dass ein amtlicher Vorschlag erging. Es war aber ein Lieblingsgedanke Mr. Churchills und der Regierung, und ich glaube, dass wir durch Eingehen auf seine Anregung sowie auf die Formel 16:10 für Grosskampfschiffe einen greifbaren Beweis unseres guten Willens geben und die bei der Regierung vorherrschende Tendenz, mit uns in nähere Fühlung zu kommen, wesentlich befestigen und fördern könnten.

Aber wie gesagt, es war möglich, *trotz der Flotte* und auch ohne *"naval holiday"* zu einer Verständigung zu gelangen. In diesem Sinne hatte ich meine Mission von Anfang aufgefasst, und es war mir auch gelungen, mein Programm zu verwirklichen, als der Ausbruch des Krieges alles Erreichte vernichtete.

Handelsneid

Der Handelsneid, von dem bei uns so viel die Rede ist, beruht auf unrichtiger Beurteilung der Verhältnisse. Gewiss bedrohte das Emporkommen Deutsch-

[12] B.-C.: "Tagesornung."

What was to be done with the technical personnel? Our naval program was definitely fixed, and it would be difficult to make any change in it. On the other hand, we did not mean to go beyond it. Nevertheless he came back to the matter and urged that the sums expended for enormous armaments might better be applied to other useful purposes. I answered that even these outlays were of advantage to our home industry.

As a result of conversations with Sir William Tyrrell, Sir Edward Grey's private secretary, I succeeded in eliminating this question from the order of the day, and this without provoking any dissatisfaction, although it came up again in Parliament; and I was able to prevent the submission of any official proposal. It was, however, an idea strongly favored by Mr. Churchill and by the government; and I believe that by accepting his suggestion, and also the rate of sixteen to ten for large steam vessels, we might have given tangible evidence of our good will and sensibly strengthened and furthered the tendency that was dominant in the government to bring the two countries into closer touch.

However, as I have said, it was possible to arrive at an understanding in spite of the fleet and also without a naval "holiday." I had viewed my mission in this sense from the outset, and I had succeeded, too, in carrying out my program, when the outbreak of the war swept away all that had been gained.

Commercial Jealousy

The [theory of] commercial jealousy, of which there has been so much talk in our country, rests on an erroneous view of the situation. Germany's growing importance as a commercial power, after the war of

lands als Handelsmacht nach dem siebziger Kriege und in folgenden Dezennien die Interessen der britischen Handelskreise, die mit ihrer Industrie und mit ihren Exporthäusern eine Art Monopolstellung besassen. Der zunehmende Warenaustausch mit Deutschland aber, das an der Spitze aller britischen Exportländer in Europa [13] stand, eine Tatsache, auf die ich in meinen öffentlichen Reden immer hinwies, hatte den Wunsch, mit dem besten Kunden und Geschäftsfreund in guten Beziehungen zu bleiben, gezeitigt und alle andern Erwägungen allmählich zurückgedrängt.

Der Brite ist *matter of fact*, er findet sich mit Tatsachen ab und kämpft nicht gegen Windmühlen. Gerade in den kaufmännischen Kreisen fand ich das lebhafteste Entgegenkommen und das Bestreben, die gemeinsamen wirtschaftlichen Interessen zu fördern. Tatsächlich interessierte sich niemand dort für den russischen, italienischen, österreichischen, ja nicht einmal für den französischen Vertreter, trotz seiner bedeutenden Persönlichkeit und seiner politischen Erfolge. Nur der deutsche und der amerikanische Botschafter erregte die öffentliche Aufmerksamkeit.

Ich habe, um mit den wichtigen Handelskreisen Fühlung zu bekommen, den Einladungen der vereinigten Handelskammern sowie der Londoner und Bradforder Kammer entsprochen und war Gast der Städte Newcastle und Liverpool. Überall war ich der Gegenstand herzlicher Huldigungen. Manchester, Glasgow und Edinburg hatten mich gleichfalls geladen und ich wollte später dorthin gehen.

Es wurde mir von Leuten, die britische Verhältnisse nicht kennen, und die Bedeutung der "*public dinners*" nicht würdigen, und auch von solchen, denen meine

[13] B.-C.: omits "in Europa."

1870 and in the following decades, undoubtedly menaced the interests of British trade circles, since with their industry and their export houses these had a sort of monopoly. On the other hand, the increasing exchange of goods with Germany, to which Great Britain exported more merchandise than to any other country in Europe—a fact to which I invariably alluded in my public speeches—had created a desire to maintain good relations with their best customer and business friend and had gradually supplanted all other considerations.

The Briton is a matter-of-fact person, he adjusts himself to conditions and does not tilt against windmills. It was precisely in commercial circles that I found the liveliest disposition to establish good relations and to promote common economic interests. As a matter of fact there was in these circles no particular interest in the Russian, the Italian, the Austrian or even the French representative, in spite of the latter's marked personality and political successes. Only the German and the American ambassadors attracted public attention.

In order to get in touch with the most important trade circles, I accepted invitations from the United Chambers of Commerce and also from the London and Bradford Chamber. I was also entertained by the cities of Newcastle and of Liverpool. I received everywhere cordial tributes of respect. Manchester, Glasgow and Edinburgh had also sent me invitations, and I intended to visit these cities later.

People who do not understand British conditions and who do not appreciate the importance of "public dinners," and also persons to whom my successes were unwelcome, accused me of doing harm by my

Erfolge unerwünscht waren, der Vorwurf gemacht, ich habe durch meine Reden geschadet. Ich glaube vielmehr, dass mein öffentliches Auftreten und die Betonung gemeinsamer wirtschaftlicher Interessen nicht unwesentlich zur Besserung der Beziehungen beigetragen hat, abgesehen davon, dass es ungeschickt und unhöflich gewesen wäre, alle Einladungen abzulehnen.

Auch in allen andern Kreisen habe ich die liebenswürdigste Aufnahme und ein warmes Entgegenkommen gefunden, bei Hof wie in der Gesellschaft und bei der Regierung.

Hof und Gesellschaft

Der König, wenn auch nicht gerade sehr gebildet und bedeutend, aber ein harmloser und wohlwollender Mann mit einfachem, gesundem Sinn, *common sense*, war bestrebt, mir Wohlwollen zu zeigen und aufrichtig gewillt, meine Aufgabe zu fördern. Trotz der geringen Macht, die die englische Verfassung der Krone lässt, vermag der Monarch, kraft seiner Stellung, die Stimmung doch sehr zu beeinflussen, sowohl in der Gesellschaft, wie auch bei der Regierung. Die Krone ist die Spitze der Gesellschaftspyramide, von ihr geht der Ton aus. Die Gesellschaft, überwiegend unionistisch (konservativ), befasst sich, mit Einschluss der Damen, von jeher eifrig mit Politik. Sie ist im *House of Lords* (Oberhaus), wie bei den *Commons* (Haus der Gemeinen), und daher auch im Kabinett vertreten. Der Engländer gehört entweder zur *Society* (Gesellschaft) oder möchte zu ihr gehören. Sein Streben ist und bleibt: ein vornehmer Mann, ein *Gentleman* zu sein, und selbst Leute bescheidener Herkunft, wie Mr. Asquith, verkehren mit Vorliebe in der Gesellschaft und mit schönen, eleganten Damen.

speeches. I am convinced, on the contrary, that my public appearances and my insistence on common economic interests contributed in no slight degree to improving our relations, apart from the fact that it would have been awkward and discourteous to refuse all invitations.

In all other circles I was most kindly received and warmly welcomed, at court as well as in society and on the part of the government.

Court and Society

The King, although not highly educated or of very marked personality, but yet an inoffensive and kindly man, with simple, sound sense—common sense—made a point of indicating his good will to me and was honestly desirous to further the accomplishment of my task. However slight the power that the English constitution leaves in the crown, the King is still able, by virtue of his position, to exercise much influence on opinion, not only in society but also within the government. The crown is the apex of the social pyramid; it sets the fashion. Society, which is for the most part Unionist (conservative) has always taken a very active interest, the women no less than the men, in politics. It is represented not only in the House of Lords, but also in the Commons, and for this reason in the Cabinet as well. The Englishman is either in society or wishes to get into society. It is his constant effort to be a man of distinction, a gentleman; and even men of modest origin, such as Mr. Asquith, wish to move in society and prefer to meet handsome and fashionable women.

Der britische Gentleman beider Parteien geniesst die gleiche Erziehung, besucht dieselben Colleges und Universitäten, betreibt die nämlichen Sports, sei es nun Golf, Cricket, Lawn-Tennis oder Polo. Alle haben in der Jugend Cricket und Fussball gespielt, sie haben dieselben Lebensgewohnheiten und verbringen das *week-end* (Ende der Woche) auf dem Lande. Keine soziale Kluft trennt die Parteien, sondern nur eine politische, die sich in den letzten Jahren nur insofern zu einer sozialen entwickelte, als die Politiker beider Lager sich gesellschaftlich mieden. Man durfte selbst auf dem neutralen Boden einer Botschaft beide Lager nicht mischen, da die Unionisten seit der Veto- und Homerulebill die Radikalen ächteten. Als wenige Monate nach meiner Ankunft das Königspaar bei uns speiste, verliess Lord Londonderry nach Tisch das Haus, um nicht mit Sir Ed. Grey zusammen zu bleiben. Aber es ist kein Gegensatz, der in der Kaste und Erziehung liegt, wie in Frankreich; es sind nicht zwei getrennte Welten, sondern dieselbe Welt, und das Urteil über einen Ausländer ist ein gemeinsames und nicht ohne Einfluss auf seine politische Stellung, ob nun Mr. Asquith regiert oder Lord Lansdowne.

Ein Gegensatz der Kaste besteht in England nicht mehr, seit der Zeit der Stuarts und nachdem die Welfen und die Whigoligarchie im Gegensatz zu dem toristischen Landadel die bürgerlich-städtischen Kreise emporkommen liessen. Es ist vielmehr ein Gegensatz der politischen Meinungen über staatsrechtliche Fragen oder über Steuerpolitik. Gerade Aristokraten, die sich der Volkspartei, den Radikalen anschliessen, die Grey, Churchill, Harcourt, Crewe, wurden von der unionistischen Aristokratie am meisten gehasst. Niemals begegnete man einem dieser Herren in den

The British gentleman, no matter to which party he belongs, enjoys the same education, goes to the same colleges and universities, engages in the same sports, whether it be golf, cricket, tennis or polo. They have all played cricket and football in their youth; they have the same habits of life, and they spend the week-end in the country. The cleavage between the parties is not social but purely political. In the last few years it has become a social cleavage only in so far as the politicians of the two camps avod social intercourse with one another. Even on the neutral territory of an embassy the two camps could not be brought together, for, since the Home Rule and Veto Bills, the Unionists have put the Radicals under a ban. When, a few months after my arrival, the King and Queen dined with us, Lord Londonderry left the house after dinner in order not to remain in company with Sir Edward Grey. There is, however, no barrier based on caste and education, such as exists in France. There are not two separate worlds, it is the same world, and its judgment regarding a foreigner is a common judgment and is not without influence on his political position, whether Mr. Asquith is governing or Lord Lansdowne.

There has been no barrier of caste in England since the time of the Stuarts, since the Guelphs and the Whig oligarchy, in opposition to the Tory landed gentry, promoted the rise of the urban middle classes. There is rather a difference of political opinions regarding constitutional questions or regarding tax policies. The bitterest hatred of the Unionist aristocracy is directed precisely against aristocrats, such as Grey, Churchill, Harcourt and Crewe, who attach themselves to the popular party, to the Radicals. One never

grossen aristokratischen Häusern, ausser bei den wenigen Parteifreunden.

Wir wurden in London mit offenen Armen aufgenommen und beide Parteien überboten sich in Zuvorkommenheit. Es wäre fehlerhaft, gesellschaftliche Beziehungen bei dem engen Verhältnis, das in England zwischen Politik und Gesellschaft besteht, zu unterschätzen, selbst wenn die grosse Mehrheit der obern Zehntausend sich in Opposition zur Regierung befindet.

Zwischen Herrn Asquith und dem Duke of Devonshire [14] besteht eben nicht die unüberbrückbare Kluft wie etwa zwischen Herrn Briand und dem Duc de Doudeauville. Sie verkehren zwar in Zeiten erregter Spannung nicht miteinander, sie gehören zwei gesonderten gesellschaftlichen Gruppen an, es sind aber doch Teile *derselben* Gesellschaft, wenn auch verschiedener Stufen, deren Mittelpunkt der Hof ist, sie haben gemeinsame Freunde und Lebensgewohnheiten, sie kennen sich meist von Jugend an und sind auch oft verwandt und verschwägert.

Erscheinungen wie Mr. Lloyd George, der Mann des Volkes, kleiner Advokat und Selfmademan, sind Ausnahmen. Selbst Mr. Burns, Sozialist, Arbeiterführer und Autodidakt, suchte Fühlung in der Gesellschaft. Bei dem verbreiteten Bestreben, als Gentleman zu gelten, als dessen unerreichtes Vorbild der grosse Aristokrat noch immer erscheint, ist das Urteil gerade der Gesellschaft und ihre Haltung nicht zu unterschätzen.

Nirgends spielt daher die gesellschaftliche Eignung eines Vertreters eine grössere Rolle wie in England. Ein gastreiches Haus mit freundlichen Wirten ist

[14] B.-C.: "Devoshire."

[84]

met any of these gentlemen in the great aristocratic houses, except in those of their few party friends.

We were received in London with open arms, and the two parties outbid each other in attentions. Given the close relation that exists in England between politics and society, it would be a mistake to undervalue social connections, even though the great majority of the upper ten thousand are in opposition to the government.

Between Mr. Asquith and the Duke of Devonshire there is nothing like the unbridgeable gulf that exists, let us say, between M. Briand and the Duc de Doudeauville. In periods of acute tension, indeed, they do not meet each other. They are members of two separate social groups; but these, although on different levels, are nevertheless parts of the same society, of which the court is the center. They have common friends and common ways of living. For the most part they have known each other from their youth and are often related or connected by marriage.

Phenomena such as Mr. Lloyd George, a man of the people, a lawyer in a small way and a self-made man, are exceptional. Even Mr. Burns, a socialist, a labor leader, and a self-educated man, tried to get in touch with society. Given the general desire to rank as a gentleman, whose unattained prototype is still the great aristocrat, the judgment of society and its attitude are by no means to be undervalued.

Nowhere in the world, accordingly, does the social adaptability of a [diplomatic] representative play a more important part than in England. An open house with friendly hosts counts for more than the profoundest scientific attainments, and a savant with

[85]

mehr wert als die profundesten wissenschaftlichen Kenntnisse, und ein Gelehrter mit provinziellem Wesen und allzu kargen Mitteln würde trotz alles Wissens keinen Einfluss gewinnen.

Was der Brite hasst, ist *a bore*, a *schemer*[15] a *prig* (ein langweiliger Kerl, ein Ränkeschmied, ein Fant), was er liebt, ist *a good fellow* (ein guter Gesell)!

Sir Edward Grey

Sir Ed. Greys Einfluss war in allen Fragen der auswärtigen Politik nahezu unbeschränkt. Zwar sagte er bei wichtigen Anlässen: *"I must first bring it before the Cabinet"* (Ich muss das erst im Ministerrat vorbringen), doch schloss dieses sich seinen Ansichten regelmässig an. Seine Autorität war unbestritten. Obwohl er das Ausland gar nicht kennt und ausser einer kurzen Reise nach Paris niemals England verlassen hatte, beherrschte er alle wichtigen Fragen durch langjährige parlamentarische Erfahrung und natürlichen Überblick. Französisch versteht er, ohne es zu sprechen. In jungen Jahren in das Parlament gewählt, hatte er bald angefangen, sich mit Auslandspolitik zu befassen. Unter Lord Rosebery parlamentarischer Unterstaatssekretär des Auswärtigen, wurde er 1906 unter Mr. Campbell-Bannermann Staatssekretär und bekleidet diesen Posten nunmehr seit zehn Jahren.

Aus einer alten, im Norden Englands begüterten Familie stammend, die bereits den bekannten Staatsmann Grey geliefert hatte, schloss er sich dem linken Flügel seiner Partei an und sympatisierte mit Sozialisten und Pazifisten. Man kann ihn einen Sozialisten im idealsten Sinne nennen, denn er überträgt die Theorie auch auf sein Privatleben, das sich durch die

[15] B.-C.: "Shemer."

provincial manners and too limited means would, despite all his knowledge, gain no influence.

What the Briton hates is a bore, a schemer, a prig; what he loves is a good fellow.

Sir Edward Grey

In all questions of foreign policy Sir Edward Grey's influence was almost unlimited. On important occasions he used indeed to say: "I must first bring it before the Cabinet," but this body regularly accepted his views. His authority was undisputed. Although he was wholly unacquainted with foreign countries and, except for one short journey to Paris, had never left England, he was competent to deal with all important questions by reason of many years of parliamentary experience and a natural breadth of vision. He understands French, although he does not speak it. Elected to parliament at an early age, he soon began to occupy himself with foreign affairs. Parliamentary under-secretary of state for foreign affairs under Lord Rosebery, he became secretary of state under Mr. Campbell-Bannermann, and has now [1916] held this post for ten years.

Sprung from an old family, possessing estates in the north of England—a family which had already produced the well-known statesman Earl Grey—he attached himself to the left wing of his party and exhibited sympathy with socialists and pacifists. He may be described as a socialist in the most ideal sense of the term; for he carries the theory of socialism even into his private life, which is marked by the

[87]

grösste Einfachheit und Anspruchslosigkeit auszeichnet, obwohl er über reichliche Mittel verfügt. Jede Repräsentation liegt ihm fern. Er hatte in London nur ein kleines Absteigequartier, gab niemals Dîners, ausserdem einen amtlichen im *Foreign Office* (Auswärtigen Amt) zu Königs Geburtstag. Wenn er ausnahmsweise einige Gäste bei sich sah, so war es zu einem einfachen Essen oder Frühstück in ganz kleinem Kreise und mit weiblicher Bedienung. Auch mied er grosse Geselligkeiten und Feste.

Das *week-end* verbringt er, wie seine Kollegen, regelmässig auf dem Lande, doch nicht mit eleganten, grossen Parties. Meist bleibt er allein in seinem *Cottage* im Newforest, wo er lange Spaziergänge macht, um Vögel zu beobachten als leidenschaftlicher Naturfreund und Ornithologe. Oder aber er ging nach Norden auf sein Gut, wo er Eichhörnchen fütterte, die den Weg durch das Fenster fanden, und verschiedene Arten Wasservögel züchtete.

Mit Vorliebe setzte er sich gelegentlich nach Norfolk in die Sümpfe, um seltene Reiherarten beim Brüten zu beobachten, die nur dort nisten.

In seiner Jugend ein berühmter Cricket- und Racketspieler, treibt er jetzt als Hauptsport das Angeln nach Lachs und Forellen in den schottischen Gewässern—in Begleitung seines Freundes Lord Glenconner, des Bruders von Mr. Asquith. *"All the rest of the year I am looking forward to it"* (Das ganze Jahresende warte ich darauf). Er hat ein Buch über den Angelsport herausgegeben.

Als wir ein *week-end* mit ihm allein bei Lord Glenconner in der Nähe von Salisbury verbrachten, kam er auf dem Zweirad angefahren und kehrte ebenso

greatest simplicity and absence of all pretension, although he is possessed of ample means. Display of any sort is foreign to him. He had in London modest quarters only, and gave no dinners except the one official dinner in the Foreign Office on the King's Birthday. If, exceptionally, he asked a few people to his house, it was to a simple meal or to a small luncheon served by a maid. He shunned large gatherings and celebrations.

Like his colleagues, he regularly spends his weekends in the country, but not at large, fashionable house parties. For the most part he lives alone, in his cottage in the New Forest, where he takes long walks to watch the ways of birds, being a devoted lover of nature and an ornithologist. Or, on the other hand, he goes north, to his property, where he feeds squirrels that make their way in through the window and breeds different kinds of water-fowl.

He was specially fond of occasional excursions to the Norfolk marshes, to watch during the breeding season some rare varieties of heron that nest only in that region.

In his youth he was a noted cricketer and tennis player. Now his chief sport is salmon and trout fishing, in Scotch waters, in the company of his friend Lord Glenconner, Mr. Asquith's brother-in-law. "All the rest of the year I am looking forward to it." He has published a book on fishing.

When on one occasion we spent a week-end with him alone, at Lord Glenconner's, near Salisbury, he arrived on a bicycle and returned in the same way to his cottage, some thirty miles distant.

The simplicity and sincerity of his character won for him the esteem even of his opponents, who were to be

nach seinem etwa dreissig englische Meilen ent-
fernten *Cottage* zurück.

Die Einfachheit und Lauterkeit seines Wesens
verschafften ihm auch die Achtung seiner Gegner, die
mehr auf dem Gebiete der innern als der auswärtigen
Politik zu suchen waren. Lügen und Intrigen sind
ihm gleichmässig fern.

Seine Frau, die er zärtlich liebte, trotzdem sie angeblich nicht eigentlich seine Gattin war, und von der
er sich niemals trennte, starb infolge eines Sturzes aus
einem Wagen, den sie selbst lenkte. Einer seiner
Brüder wurde bekanntlich durch einen Löwen getötet.

Wordsworth ist sein Lieblingsdichter, und er konnte
ihn auswendig vortragen.

Der kühlen Ruhe seines britischen Wesens fehlt
nicht der Sinn für Humor. Als er bei uns frühstückte
in Gesellschaft der Kinder, und deren deutsche Unter-
haltung hörte, meinte er: *"I can't help thinking how
clever these children are to talk German so well"* (Ich muss
immer denken, wie klug sind diese Kinder, dass sie so
gut deutsch sprechen) und freute sich über den Witz.

So sieht der Mann aus, der als Lügen-Grey und als
Anstifter des Weltkrieges verschrien wird.

Mr. Asquith

Mr. Asquith ist ganz anderer Art. Jovialer Lebe-
mann, Freund der Damen, namentlich der jungen und
hübschen, liebt er heitere Gesellschaft und gute
Küche, und wird dabei von seiner lebenslustigen
Gattin unterstützt. Ehemals bekannter Advokat mit
reichem Einkommen und langjähriger Parlamentarier,
dann Minister unter Mr. Gladstone, Pazifist wie sein
Freund Grey, und Freund einer Verständigung mit
Deutschland, behandelte er alle Fragen mit der

found rather in the field of domestic politics than in that of foreign affairs. Falsehood and intrigue are equally foreign to him.

His wife, whom he loved tenderly (in spite of gossip that they did not live as man and wife) and from whom he was inseparable, was killed by being thrown from a trap which she herself was driving. One of his brothers, as is known, was killed by a lion.

Wordsworth is his favorite poet, and he is able to recite long passages from memory.

Under the cool repose of his British manner there is no lack of a sense of humor. When, on one occasion, he took lunch in our house in the company of the children and heard their German conversation, he said: "I can't help thinking how clever these children are to talk German so well," and he showed himself pleased with the joke.

This is a true picture of the man who is denounced as "Liar Grey" and as instigator of the World War.

Mr. Asquith

Mr. Asquith is quite a different sort of man. Jovial, a *bon vivant*, a friend of the ladies, especially of those who are young and good looking, he loves cheerful society and good cooking. His social tastes are shared by his vivacious wife. Formerly a well-known barrister, with a large income, he was for many years a member of Parliament and then, under Mr. Gladstone, a minister. Like his friend Grey, a pacifist and inclined to an understanding with Germany, he

heiteren Ruhe und Sicherheit eines erfahrenen Geschäftsmannes, dessen gute Gesundheit und vortreffliche Nerven durch fleissiges Golfspiel gestählt sind.

Seine Töchter gingen in deutsche Pensionate und sprachen fliessend Deutsch. Wir waren nach kurzer Zeit mit ihm und seiner Familie befreundet und seine Gäste auf dem Lande in dem kleinen Hause an der Themse.

Um auswärtige Politik kümmerte er sich nur in seltenen Fällen, wenn wichtige Fragen vorlagen; dann war natürlich die letzte Entscheidung bei ihm. In den kritischen Tagen des Juli kam Mrs. Asquith wiederholt zu uns, um zu warnen, und war schliesslich ganz verzweifelt über die tragische Wendung. Auch Herr Asquith war am 2. August, als ich ihn besuchte, um einen letzten Versuch im Sinne einer abwartenden Neutralität zu machen, ganz gebrochen, wenn auch vollkommen ruhig. Die Tränen liefen ihm über die beiden Wangen hinunter.

Nicolson

Im *Foreign Office* (Auswärtigen Amt) hatten neben dem Minister Sir A. Nicolson und Sir W. Tyrrell [16] den stärksten Einfluss.

Ersterer war nicht unser Freund, aber seine Haltung gegen mich war immer durchaus korrekt und zuvorkommend. Unsere persönlichen Beziehungen waren die besten. Auch er wollte den Krieg nicht, als wir aber gegen Frankreich zogen, hatte er zweifellos im Sinne des sofortigen Anschlusses gearbeitet. Er war der Vertrauensmann meines französischen Kollegen, mit dem er in dauernder Fühlung stand; auch wollte er Lord Bertie in Paris ablösen.

[16] B.-C.: "Tyrell."

treated all questions with the cheerful calmness and the sure touch of an experienced man of affairs. His sound health and excellent nerves are strengthened by assiduous golf-playing.

His daughters studied in German boarding schools and spoke German fluently. We were soon on friendly terms with him and with his family, and visited him in the country, at his little house on the Thames.

With foreign affairs he occupied himself only on rare occasions, when important questions came up; at such times naturally the final decision lay with him. During the critical days of July Mrs. Asquith came repeatedly to our house to warn us, and in the end she was quite in despair over the tragic turn of events. Mr. Asquith, also, when on the second of August I called on him to make a last attempt to obtain a neutral and waiting attitude, was completely broken, although quite calm. Tears were rolling down his cheeks.

Nicholson

In the Foreign Office the men of greatest influence, aside from the minister, were Sir Arthur Nicholson and Sir William Tyrrell.

Nicholson was not our friend, but his attitude towards me was always perfectly correct and courteous. Our personal relations could not have been better. He also had no desire for war; but when we marched against France, he undoubtedly worked for immediate intervention. He was the confidant of my French colleague, with whom he kept in constant touch; he hoped, moreover, to succeed Lord Bertie in Paris.

Bekanntlich war Sir Arthur vorher Botschafter in Petersburg und hatte den Vertrag des Jahres 1907 abgeschlossen, der es Russland ermöglichte, sich dem Westen und dem nahen Orient wieder zuzuwenden.

Tyrrell [16]

Viel grösseren Einfluss als der permanente Unterstaatssekretär besass der Kabinettschef oder *"private secretary"* Sir Edwards: Sir Tyrrell.[16] Dieser hochintelligente Mann hatte in Deutschland das Gymnasium besucht und sich nachher der Diplomatie zugewandt, war aber nur kurze Zeit im Ausland gewesen. Zunächst schloss er sich der damals unter den jüngeren britischen Diplomaten modernen antideutschen Richtung an, um später ein überzeugter Befürworter der Verständigung zu werden. In diesem Sinne hat er auch Sir Ed. Grey beeinflusst, mit dem er sehr intim war. Seit Ausbruch des Krieges hat er das Amt verlassen und im *Home Office* (Ministerium des Innern) Anstellung gefunden, wohl infolge der gegen ihn wegen seiner germanophilen Richtung erhobenen Kritik.

Haltung des Amtes

Die Wut gewisser Herren über meine Londoner Erfolge und über die Stellung, die ich mir in kurzer Zeit machen konnte, war unbeschreiblich. Schikanöse Erlasse wurden ersonnen, um mein Amt zu erschweren; ich blieb in völliger Unkenntnis der wichtigsten Dinge und wurde auf die Mitteilung belangloser, langweiliger Berichte beschränkt. Geheime Agentennachrichten über Dinge, die ich ohne Spionage und die nötigen Fonds nicht erfahren konnte, waren mir niemals

[16] B.-C.: "Tyrell."

Sir Arthur, as everyone knows, was formerly ambassador in St. Petersburg. He concluded the treaty of 1907, which enabled Russia to direct its attention again to the West and the Near East.

Tyrrell

An influence much greater than that of the permanent under-secretary of state was exercised by Sir Edward Grey's private secretary, Sir William Tyrrell. This exceptionally intelligent man had studied in a German preparatory school and had then entered the diplomatic service, but was abroad for only a short time. At the outset, he associated himself with the anti-German tendencies which at that time were up-to-date among the younger British diplomats; later, he became a convinced advocate of an understanding. His influence with Sir Edward Grey, with whom he was on a very intimate footing, was exercised in this direction. After the outbreak of the war he left the Foreign Office and obtained a position in the Home Office. This change was probably made on account of the criticism directed against him on account of his Germanophil tendencies.

Attitude of the Berlin Foreign Office

The rage excited among certain gentlemen by my successes in London, and by the position which I had been able to gain for myself in a short time, was indescribable. Captious orders were devised to make my position difficult; I was kept in complete ignorance of the most important matters; and I was restricted to sending unimportant and tiresome reports. The information acquired by secret agents, regarding things which I could not ascertain without spies

[95]

zugänglich, und erst in den letzten Tagen des Juli [17]
1914 erfuhr ich zufällig durch den Marine-attaché die
geheimen englisch-französischen Abmachungen über
das Zusammenwirken beider Flotten im Falle eines
Krieges. Auch andere wichtige und dem Amt längst
bekannte Vorgänge wie der Briefwechsel Grey-Cambon
wurden mir vorenthalten.

Kriegsfall

Ich hatte bald nach meiner Ankunft die Überzeugung gewonnen, dass wir unter *keinen* Umständen
einen englischen Angriff oder eine englische Unterstützung eines fremden Angriffes zu befürchten hätten,
dass aber *unter allen Umständen England die Franzosen schützen würde*. Diese Ansicht habe ich in
wiederholten Berichten und mit ausführlicher Be-
gründung und grossem Nachdruck vertreten, ohne
jedoch Glauben zu finden, obwohl die Ablehnung der
Neutralitätsformel durch Lord Haldane und die
Haltung Englands während der Marokkokrise recht
deutliche Winke waren. Dazu kamen noch die bereits
erwähnten und dem Amte bekannten geheimen
Abmachungen.

Ich wies immer darauf hin, dass England als
Handelsstaat bei jedem Kriege zwischen europäischen
Grossmächten ausserordentlich leiden, ihn daher mit
allen Mitteln verhindern würde, andererseits aber eine
Schwächung oder Vernichtung Frankreichs im Interesse des europäischen Gleichgewichts und um eine
deutsche Übermacht zu verhindern niemals dulden

[17] B.-C.: "Jahres."

and the necessary funds, was never placed at my
disposal; and it was not until the last days of July,
1914, that I learned by chance from the naval attaché
of the secret Anglo-French agreements concerning
the coöperation of the two fleets in case of a war.
Moreover, other important correspondence, long known
to the Foreign Office, such as the Grey-Cambon correspondence, was withheld from me.[26]

The Casus Belli

Soon after my arrival I became convinced that
under no circumstances had we to apprehend an
English attack or any English support of an attack
by a third power, but that under any circumstances
England would protect the French. I advanced this
opinion in repeated reports, with detailed statement
of my reasons and with great emphasis, but without
obtaining any credence, although Lord Haldane's refusal of the proposed neutrality clause [27] and England's
attitude during the Morocco crisis gave us very clear
hints. Besides all this, there were those secret agreements which I have already mentioned and which
were known to the Foreign Office.

I always pointed out that, in any war between
European Great Powers, England, as a commercial
state, would suffer enormously, and that it would
therefore make every effort to prevent such a war, but
that, on the other hand, because of its interest in maintaining the European balance of power and in preventing Germany from gaining a dominant position,
England could never tolerate a weakening or annihila-

[26] See Appendix, note x.
[27] *Ibid.*, note xvi.

könne. Das hatte mir bald nach meiner Ankunft
Lord Haldane gesagt. In ähnlichem Sinne äusserten
sich alle massgebenden Leute.

Serbische Krise

Ende Juni begab ich mich auf Allerhöchsten Befehl
nach Kiel, nachdem ich wenige Wochen vorher in
Oxford Ehrendoktor geworden war, eine Würde, die
vor mir kein deutscher Botschafter seit Herrn von
Bunsen bekleidet hatte. An Bord des „Meteor"
erfuhren wir den Tod des Erzherzogthronfolgers.
S. M. bedauerte, dass dadurch seine Bemühungen, den
hohen Herrn für seine Ideen zu gewinnen, vergeblich
waren. Ob der Plan einer aktiven Politik gegen Serbien schon in Konopischt festgelegt wurde, kann ich
nicht wissen.

Da ich über Wiener Ansichten und Vorgänge nicht
unterrichtet war, mass ich dem Ereignisse keine
weitgehende Bedeutung bei. Ich konnte später nur
feststellen, dass bei österreichischen Aristokraten ein
Gefühl der Erleichterung andere Empfindungen über-
wog. An Bord des „Meteor" befand sich auch als
Gast S. M. ein Österreicher, Graf Felix Thun. Er
hatte die ganze Zeit wegen Seekrankheit, trotz herr-
lichen Wetters, in der Kabine gelegen. Nach Ein-
treffen der Nachricht war er aber gesund. Der
Schreck oder die Freude hatte ihn geheilt!

In Berlin angekommen, sah ich den Reichskanzler
und sagte ihm, dass ich unsere auswärtige Lage für
sehr befriedigend hielt, da wir mit England so gut
ständen, wie schon lange nicht. Auch in Frankreich
sei ein pazifistisches Ministerium am Ruder.

Herr von Bethmann Hollweg schien meinen Opti-
mismus nicht zu teilen und beklagte sich über rus-

tion of France. Lord Haldane had told me this shortly after my arrival. All the influential people expressed themselves in the same sense.

The Serbian Crisis

At the end of June I went to Kiel, by command of the Emperor. A few weeks earlier I had received an honorary doctorate at Oxford, a distinction which had not been conferred on any German ambassador since Herr von Bunsen. On board the *Meteor* we learned of the death of the archducal heir to the throne. His Majesty regretted that his efforts to win that prince's support for his ideas had thus been rendered vain. Whether the plan of an active policy against Serbia had already been decided on at Kono-pischt, I am not in a position to know.

As I was not kept posted regarding views and proceedings in Vienna, I did not attach very great importance to this event. All that I could ascertain later was that among Austrian aristocrats a feeling of relief outweighed other sentiments. On board the *Meteor*, also as a guest of His Majesty, was an Austrian, Count Felix Thun. In spite of the splendid weather, he had remained in his cabin all the time, suffering from sea-sickness. After receiving the news, however, he was well. Alarm or joy had cured him!

On my arrival in Berlin I saw the imperial chancellor. I told him that I considered our foreign situation very satisfactory, since we were on better terms with England than we had been for a long time. In France, too, a pacifist ministry was at the helm.

Herr von Bethmann Hollweg did not seem to share my optimism and complained about Russian armaments. I tried to calm him, emphasizing in particular

sische Rüstungen. Ich suchte ihn zu beruhigen und betonte namentlich, dass Russland gar kein Interesse habe, uns anzugreifen, und dass ein solcher Angriff auch niemals die englisch-französische Unterstützung finden würde, da beide Länder den Frieden wollten. Darauf ging ich zu Herrn Dr. Zimmermann, der Herrn von Jagow vertrat, und erfuhr von ihm, dass Russland im Begriff sei, 900,000 Mann neuer Truppen aufzustellen. Aus seinen Worten ging eine unverkennbare Misstimmung gegen Russland hervor, das uns überall im Wege sei. Es handelte sich auch um handelspolitische Schwierigkeiten. Dass General von Moltke zum Krieg drängte, wurde mir natürlich nicht gesagt. Ich erfuhr aber, dass Herr von Tschirschky einen Verweis erhalten, weil er berichtete, er habe in Wien Serbien gegenüber zur Mässigung geraten.

Auf meiner Rückreise aus Schlesien auf dem Wege nach London hielt ich mich nur wenige Stunden in Berlin auf und hörte, dass Österreich beabsichtigte,[18] gegen Serbien vorzugehen, um unhaltbaren Zuständen ein Ende zu machen.

Leider unterschätzte ich in dem Augenblick die Tragweite der Nachricht. Ich glaubte, es würde doch wieder nichts daraus werden und, falls Russland drohte, leicht beizulegen sein. Heute bereue ich, nicht in Berlin geblieben zu sein und sogleich erklärt zu haben, dass ich eine derartige Politik nicht mitmache.

Nachträglich erfuhr ich, dass bei der entscheidenden Besprechung in Potsdam am 5. Juli die Wiener Anfrage die unbedingte Zustimmung aller massgebenden Persönlichkeiten fand, und zwar mit dem Zusatze, es werde auch nichts schaden, wenn daraus ein Krieg mit Russland entstehen sollte. So heisst

[18] B.-C.: "beabsichtige."

[my belief] that Russia had no interest whatever in attacking us, and that such an attack would in no case receive Anglo-French support, since both countries desired peace. Next I went to Dr. Zimmermann, who was acting for Herr von Jagow, and learned from him that Russia was about to raise 900,000 additional troops. His words revealed unmistakable dissatisfaction with Russia, which he found everywhere in our way. There was question also of difficulties in the field of trade policy. Of course I was not told that General von Moltke was pressing for war. I learned, however, that Herr von Tschirschky had received a reprimand, because he reported that in Vienna he had counselled moderation toward Serbia.

On my return from Silesia, on my way to London, I stopped only a few hours in Berlin, where I heard that Austria intended to take steps against Serbia in order to put an end to an untenable situation.

At the moment, unfortunately, I underestimated the significance of the news. I thought that nothing would come of it, this time either, and that in case Russia made threats the matter would be easily adjusted. I now regret that I did not stay in Berlin and at once declare that I would not coöperate in a policy of this kind.

Subsequently I learned that, at the decisive conference at Potsdam on July 5th,[28] the Vienna inquiry received the unqualified assent of all the controlling authorities, with the further suggestion that it would not be a bad thing if war with Russia should result. At least this statement was made in the Austrian protocol which Count Mensdorff received in London

[28] See Appendix, note xx.

es wenigstens im österreichischen Protokoll, das Graf Mensdorff in London erhielt. Bald darauf war Herr von Jagow in Wien, um mit Graf Berchtold alles zu besprechen.

Dann bekam ich die Weisung, darauf hinzuwirken, dass die englische Presse eine freundliche Haltung einnehme, wenn Österreich der grossserbischen Bewegung den „Todesstoss" versetze, und durch meinen Einfluss möglichst zu verhindern, dass die öffentliche Meinung gegen Österreich Stellung nähme. Die Erinnerungen an die Haltung Englands während der Annexionskrise, wo die öffentliche Meinung für die serbischen Rechte auf Bosnien [19] Sympathie zeigte, sowie auch an die wohlwollende Förderung nationaler Bewegungen zur Zeit Lord Byrons und Garibaldis, dieses und anderes sprach so sehr gegen die Wahrscheinlichkeit einer Unterstützung der geplanten Strafexpedition gegen die Fürstenmörder, dass ich mich veranlasst sah, dringend zu warnen. Ich warnte aber auch vor dem ganzen Projekt, das ich als abenteuerlich und gefährlich bezeichnete, und riet, den Österreichern *Mässigung* anzuempfehlen, da ich nicht an Lokalisierung des Konfliktes glaubte.

Herr von Jagow antwortete mir, Russland sei nicht bereit, etwas Gepolter würde es wohl geben, aber je fester wir zu Österreich ständen, um so mehr würde Russland zurückweichen. Österreich beschuldigte uns schon so der Flaumacherei und so dürften wir nicht kneifen. Die Stimmung in Russland würde anderseits immer deutschfeindlicher, und da müssten wir es eben riskieren.

Angesichts dieser Haltung, die, wie ich später erfuhr, auf Berichten des Grafen Pourtalès fusste, dass

[19] B.-C.: "Bosniens."

Soon afterwards Herr von Jagow was in Vienna, to talk everything over with Count Berchtold.

Next I received instructions to try to induce the English press to adopt a friendly attitude, should Austria administer the "death blow" to the Pan-Serbian movement, and to use my influence so far as possible to prevent public opinion from becoming hostile to Austria. Recollections of the English attitude during the annexation crisis, when public opinion showed sympathy for the rights of Serbia to Bosnia, and of the benevolent furtherance of national movements in the days of Lord Byron and of Garibaldi—these and other considerations argued so strongly against the probability of any support of the intended punitive expedition against the regicides that I found myself moved to give an urgent warning. I added a warning against the whole plan, which I characterized as adventurous and dangerous; and I advised that moderation be recommended to the Austrians, as I did not believe that the conflict could be localized.

Herr von Jagow replied to me that Russia was not ready. There would probably be some blustering, but the more firmly we stood by Austria the more certainly would Russia give way. Already Austria was accusing us of flabbiness, and for this reason we must not hold back. Public opinion in Russia, on the other hand, was becoming more and more anti-German, so we must just risk it.

In view of this attitude (which, as I found later, was based on reports from Count Pourtalès that Russia would not move under any circumstances—[reports] that caused us to incite Count Berchtold to the utmost energy) I hoped for rescue through English mediation,

Russland unter keinen Umständen sich rühren werde, und die uns veranlassten, den Grafen Berchtold zu möglichster Energie anzufeuern, erhoffte ich die Rettung von einer englischen Vermittlung, da ich wusste, dass Sir Ed. Greys Einfluss in Petersburg im Sinne des Friedens zu verwerten war. Ich benutzte daher meine freundschaftlichen Beziehungen zum Minister, um ihn vertraulich zu bitten, in Russland zur Mässigung zu raten, falls Österreich, wie es schien, von den Serben Genugtuung verlangte.

Zunächst war die Haltung der englischen Presse ruhig und den Österreichern freundlich, da man den Mord verurteilte. Allmählich aber wurden immer mehr Stimmen laut, welche betonten, dass, so sehr eine Ahndung des Verbrechens nötig sei, eine Ausbeutung desselben zu politischen Zwecken nicht zu rechtfertigen wäre. Österreich wurde eindringlich zur Mässigung aufgefordert.

Als das Ultimatum erschien, waren alle Organe, mit Ausnahme des stets notleidenden und von den Österreichern anscheinend bezahlten "Standard" einig in der Verurteilung. Die ganze Welt, ausser in Berlin und Wien, begriff, dass es den Krieg, und zwar den Weltkrieg bedeutete. Die britische Flotte, welche zufällig zu einer Flottenschau versammelt war, wurde nicht demobilisiert.

Ich drängte zunächst auf eine möglichst entgegenkommende Antwort Serbiens, da die Haltung der russischen Regierung keinen Zweifel mehr an dem Ernst der Lage liess.

Die serbische Antwort entsprach den britischen Bemühungen, denn tatsächlich hatte Herr Paschitsch alles angenommen, bis auf zwei Punkte, über die er sich bereit erklärte zu unterhandeln. Wollten Russ-

as I knew that Sir Edward Grey's great influence in St. Petersburg could be utilized in favor of peace. I therefore availed myself of my friendly relations with the minister to request him in confidence to advise moderation in Russia, in case Austria, as seemed likely, should demand satisfaction from Serbia.

At first the attitude of the English press was calm and friendly to the Austrians, because the murder was generally condemned. But gradually more and more voices were raised, insisting that, however much the crime merited punishment, its exploitation for political purposes could not be justified. Austria was earnestly exhorted to show moderation.

When the ultimatum was published, all the papers, with the exception of the *Standard*, which was always in financial difficulties and was apparently paid by the Austrians, were unanimous in condemnation. The whole world, except in Berlin and Vienna, realized that it meant war, and what was more, world war. The British fleet, which by chance was assembled for a naval review, was not demobilized.

I urged, in the first place, that as conciliatory a reply as was possible be obtained from Serbia, since the attitude of the Russian government left room for no further doubt as to the gravity of the situation.

Serbia's answer was in accord with the British efforts; M. Pashitch in fact agreed to everything, except two points, about which he declared his willingness to negotiate. Had Russia and England wished for war, in order to fall upon us unawares, a hint to Belgrade would have been enough, and the unprecedented [Austrian] note would have been left unanswered.

land und England den Krieg, um uns zu überfallen, so genügte ein Wink nach Belgrad, und die unerhörte Note blieb unbeantwortet.

Sir Ed. Grey ging die serbische Antwort mit mir durch und wies auf die entgegenkommende Haltung der Regierung in Belgrad. Wir berieten dann seinen Vermittlungsvorschlag, der eine beiden Teilen annehmbare Auslegung dieser beiden Punkte vereinbaren sollte. Unter seinem Vorsitz wären Herr Cambon, Marquis Imperiali[20] und ich zusammengetreten, und es wäre leicht gewesen, eine annehmbare Form für die strittigen Punkte zu finden, die im wesentlichen die Mitwirkung der k. u. k. Beamten bei den Untersuchungen Belgrad betrafen. In einer oder zwei Sitzungen war alles bei gutem Willen zu erledigen, und schon die blosse Annahme des britischen Vorschlages hätte eine Entspannung bewirkt und unsere Beziehungen zu England weiter verbessert. Ich befürwortete ihn daher dringend, da sonst der Weltkrieg bevorstehe, bei dem wir alles zu verlieren und nichts zu gewinnen hätten. Umsonst! Es sei gegen die Würde Österreichs, auch wollten wir uns in die serbische Sache nicht mischen, wir überliessen sie unserem Bundesgenossen. Ich solle auf „Lokalisierung des Konfliktes" hinwirken.

Es hätte natürlich nur eines Winkes von Berlin bedurft, um den Grafen Berchtold zu bestimmen, sich mit einem diplomatischen Erfolg zu begnügen und sich bei der serbischen Antwort zu beruhigen. Dieser Wink ist aber nicht ergangen. Im Gegenteil, es wurde zum Kriege gedrängt. Es wäre ein so schöner Erfolg gewesen.

Nach unserer Ablehnung bat Sir Edward uns, mit einem Vorschlag hervorzutreten. Wir bestanden auf

[20] B.-C.: "Imperioli."

Sir Edward Grey went through the Serbian reply with me and pointed out the conciliatory attitude of the Belgrade government. Thereupon we discussed his proposal of mediation, which was to establish by agreement an interpretation of the two points which should be acceptable to both parties. M. Cambon, Marquis Imperiali and I were to meet under his presidency; and it would have been easy to find an acceptable formula for the points at issue, which in substance concerned the coöperation of Austrian officials in the investigations at Belgrade. Given good will, everything could have been settled at one or two sittings, and the mere acceptance of the British proposal would have brought about a relaxation of the tension and would have further improved our relations with England. I therefore strongly supported the proposal, because otherwise the World War was in sight, in which we would have everything to lose and nothing to gain. In vain! It was declared to be derogatory to the dignity of Austria; moreover we did not intend to interfere in the Serbian affair; we were leaving this to our ally. I was to work for the "localization of the conflict."

It would of course have required only a hint from Berlin to induce Count Berchtold to content himself with a diplomatic success and quietly accept the Serbian answer. This hint, however, was not given. On the contrary, pressure was exercised in favor of war. It would have been so fine a success.

After our refusal, Sir Edward Grey begged us to come forward with a proposal of our own. We insisted on war. I could not obtain any reply except that Austria was showing itself enormously "concili-

dem Kriege. Ich konnte keine andere Antwort erhalten, als dass es ein kolossales „Entgegenkommen" Österreichs sei, keine Gebietserwerbungen zu beabsichtigen.

Sir Edward wies mit Recht darauf hin, dass man auch ohne Gebietserwerbung ein Land zum Vasallen erniedrigen kann, und dass Russland hierin eine Demütigung erblicken und es daher nicht dulden werde.

Der Eindruck befestigte sich immer mehr, dass wir den Krieg unter allen Umständen wollten. Anders war unsere Haltung in einer Frage, die uns doch direkt gar nichts anging, nicht zu verstehen. Die inständigen Bitten und bestimmten Erklärungen des Herrn Sasonow, später die geradezu demütigen Telegramme des Zaren, die wiederholten Vorschläge Sir Edwards, die Warnungen des Marquis San Giuliano und des Herrn Bollati, meine dringenden Ratschläge, alles nützte nichts, in Berlin blieb man dabei, Serbien muss massakriert werden!

Je mehr ich drängte, um so weniger wollte man einlenken, schon weil ich nicht den Erfolg haben sollte, mit Sir Edward Grey den Frieden zu retten!

Da entschloss sich letzterer am 29. zu der bekannten Warnung. Ich entgegnete, dass ich stets berichtet hätte, wir würden mit der englischen Gegnerschaft rechnen müssen, falls es zum Kriege mit Frankreich käme. Wiederholt sagte mir der Minister: *"If war breaks out, it will be the greatest catastrophe the world has ever seen"* (wenn ein Krieg ausbricht, gibt es die grösste Katastrophe, die die Welt je erlebt hat).

Die Ereignisse überstürzten sich bald darauf. Als endlich Graf Berchtold, der bis dahin auf Berliner Weisungen den starken Mann spielte, sich zum Einlenken entschloss, beantworteten wir die russische

atory" in that it aimed at no annexation of territory.

Sir Edward rightly pointed out that, without annexation of territory, it was possible to reduce a country to vassalage, and that Russia would see in this a humiliation and therefore would not suffer it.

The impression grew continually stronger that we desired war under any circumstances. In no other way was it possible to interpret our attitude on a question which, after all, did not directly concern us. The urgent requests and explicit declarations of M. Sazonof, followed by the Czar's positively humble telegrams; the repeated proposals of Sir Edward Grey; the warnings of Marquis di San Giuliano and of Signor Bollati; my own urgent counsels—all were of no avail. Berlin would not budge; Serbia must be massacred.

The more I pressed, the less inclination there was to turn back, if only that I might not have, together with Sir Edward Grey, the credit of preserving peace.

Then, on the 29th, Sir Edward decided to give his famous warning.[29] I replied that I had invariably reported that we should have to reckon with English opposition if it came to a war with France. Repeatedly the minister said to me: "If war breaks out, it will be the greatest catastrophe the world has ever seen."

Soon after this events were precipitated. Until this time, following the directions he received from Berlin, Count Berchtold had played the part of the strong man. When at last he decided to change his course, and after Russia had negotiated and waited

[29] See Appendix, note xxi.

Mobilmachung, nachdem Russland eine ganze Woche vergeblich unterhandelt und gewartet hatte, mit dem Ultimatum und der Kriegserklärung.

Englische Kriegserklärung

Noch immer sann Sir Edward Grey nach neuen Auswegen. Am 1. August vormittags kam Sir W. Tyrrell[21] zu mir, um zu sagen, sein Chef hoffe noch immer, einen Ausweg zu finden. Ob wir neutral bleiben wollten, falls Frankreich es auch täte? Ich verstand, dass wir dann bereit sein sollten, Frankreich zu schonen, er hatte aber gemeint, dass wir überhaupt, also auch gegen Russland, neutral bleiben. Das war das bekannte Missverständnis. Sir Edward hatte mich für den Nachmittag bestellt. Da er sich gerade in einer Kabinettsitzung befand, rief er mich an das Telephon, nachdem Sir W. Tyrrell[21] gleich zu ihm geeilt war. Nachmittags aber sprach er nur mehr von der belgischen Neutralität und von der Möglichkeit, dass wir und Frankreich uns bewaffnet gegenüber ständen, ohne uns anzugreifen.

Es war also überhaupt kein Vorschlag, sondern eine Frage ohne Verbindlichkeit, da, wie ich früher schon gemeldet, bald darauf unsere Besprechung stattfinden sollte. Die Nachricht wurde aber in Berlin, ohne erst die Unterredung abzuwarten, zur Grundlage einer weitgehenden Aktion gemacht. Dann kam der Brief des Herrn Poincaré, der Brief Bonar Laws, das Telegramm des Königs Albert. Die Schwankenden wurden im Kabinett bis auf drei Mitglieder, die austraten, umgestimmt.

Ich hatte bis zum letzten Augenblick auf eine abwartende Haltung Englands gehofft. Auch mein französischer Kollege fühlte sich keineswegs sicher,

[21] B.-C.: "Tyrell."

a whole week in vain, we answered the Russian mobilization with the ultimatum and the declaration of war.

The English Declaration of War

Even then Sir Edward Grey continued to search for new expedients. On the morning of August 1st, Sir William Tyrrell called on me, to tell me that his chief still hoped to find a way out. Would we remain neutral in case France did the same? I understood that we were to declare ourselves ready, in such case, to spare France; but his meaning was that we should remain altogether neutral, that is, toward Russia also. That was the well-known misunderstanding. Sir Edward had an appointment with me for that afternoon. At the moment he was at a meeting of the Cabinet, and, Sir William Tyrrell having hurried to him at once, he called me up on the telephone. In the afternoon, he talked only about Belgian neutrality and the possibility that we and France might face one another in arms without attacking.

There was accordingly no proposal at all, but a question that carried with it no binding engagement, since, as I have already stated, our interview was to take place soon afterwards. Berlin, however, without waiting for the interview, made the news the basis of far-reaching [diplomatic] activity. Then came M. Poincaré's letter, Bonar Law's letter, King Albert's telegram.[30] The waverers in the Cabinet—excepting three members who resigned—were converted.

Till the very last moment I had hoped for a waiting attitude on the part of England. My French colleague, too, as I learned from a private source, felt far

[30] See Appendix, notes xxii–xxiv.

wie ich aus privater Quelle erfuhr. Noch am 1. August hatte der König dem Präsidenten ausweichend geantwortet. In dem Telegramm aus Berlin, das die drohende Kriegsgefahr ankündigte, war aber England schon als Gegner mitgenannt. Man rechnete also bereits in Berlin mit dem Kriege gegen England.

Vor meiner Abreise empfing mich am 5. Sir Edward Grey in seiner Wohnung. Auf seinen Wunsch war ich hingegangen. Er war tief bewegt. Er sagte mir, er werde stets bereit sein, zu vermitteln: *"We don't want to crush Germany"* (Wir wollen Deutschland nicht zerschmettern). Diese vertrauliche Unterredung ist leider veröffentlicht worden. Damit hat Herr von Bethmann Hollweg die letzte Möglichkeit zerstört, über England den Frieden zu erlangen.

Unsere Abreise vollzog sich durchaus würdig und ruhig. Vorher hatte der König seinen *Equerry* (Stallmeister) Sir E. Ponsonby zu mir gesandt, um sein Bedauern über meine Abreise auszusprechen und dass er mich nicht selbst sehen könnte. Prinzess Louise schrieb mir, die ganze Familie betrauere unseren Fortgang. Mrs. Asquith und andere Freunde kamen zum Abschied in die Botschaft.

Ein Extrazug brachte uns nach Harwich. Dort war eine Ehrenkompagnie für mich aufgestellt. Ich wurde wie ein abreisender Souverän behandelt. So endete meine Londoner Mission. Sie scheiterte nicht an den Tücken der Briten, sondern an den Tücken unserer Politik.

Auf dem Bahnhof in London hatte sich Graf Mensdorff mit seinem Stabe eingefunden. Er war vergnügt und gab mir zu verstehen, dass er vielleicht dort bliebe, den Engländern aber sagte er, Österreich habe den Krieg nicht gewollt, sondern wir.

from sure [that England would intervene]. As late as August 1st the King had given the President an evasive reply.[31] In the telegram from Berlin announcing imminent danger of war,[32] England however was already included in the list of adversaries. Berlin was therefore already reckoning on war with England.

Before my departure, Sir Edward Grey received me, on the 5th, at his house. I had called at his request. He was deeply moved. He told me he would always be ready to mediate. "We don't want to crush Germany." Unfortunately this confidential interview was made public, and thus Herr von Bethmann Hollweg destroyed the last possibility of gaining peace through England.

Our departure was put through in a thoroughly dignified, quiet way. The King had previously sent his equerry, Sir E. Ponsonby, to express his regret that I was leaving and that he could not himself see me. Princess Louise wrote to me that the whole family was sorry that we were going away. Mrs. Asquith and other friends came to the embassy to take leave.

A special train took us to Harwich. There a guard of honor was drawn up for me. I was treated like a departing sovereign. Such was the end of my London mission. It was wrecked, not by the wiles of the British, but by the wiles of our policy.

Count Mensdorff had come with his staff to the station in London. He was cheerful, and gave me to understand that perhaps he would remain there. He told the English that we, and not Austria, had desired the war.

[31] See Appendix, note xxii.
[32] July 31st. See German White Book, No. 25.

Rückblick

Wenn ich jetzt nach zwei Jahren mir alles rückwärts schauend vergegenwärtige, so sage ich mir, dass ich zu spät erkannte, dass kein Platz für mich war in einem System, das seit Jahren nur von Tradition und Routine lebte und das nur Vertreter duldet, die so berichten, wie man es lesen will. Vorurteilslosigkeit und unabhängiges Urteil werden bekämpft, Unfähigkeit und Charakterlosigkeit gepriesen und geschätzt. Erfolge aber erregen Missgunst und Beunruhigung.

Ich hatte den Widerstand gegen die wahnsinnige Dreibund politik aufgegeben, da ich einsah, dass es zwecklos war, und dass man meine Warnungen als *Austrophobie* (Feindschaft gegen Österreich), als fixe Idee hinstellte. In der Politik, die nicht Akrobatentum oder Aktensport ist, sondern das Geschäft der Firma, gibt es keine *Philie* oder *Phobie* (Freundschaft oder Feindschaft), sondern nur das Interesse des Gemeinwesens. Eine Politik aber, die sich bloss auf Österreicher, Madjaren und Türken stützt, muss in Gegensatz zu Russland geraten und schliesslich zur Katastrophe führen.

Trotz früherer Irrungen war im Juli 1914 noch alles zu machen. Die Verständigung mit England war erreicht. Wir mussten einen wenigstens das Durchschnittsmass politischer Befähigung erreichenden Vertreter nach Petersburg senden und Russland die Gewissheit geben, dass wir weder die Meerengen beherrschen, noch die Serben erdrosseln wollten. *"Lâchez l'Autriche et nous lâcherons les Français"* (lasst Österreich fallen, und wir werden die Franzosen fallen lassen), sagte uns Herr Sasonow. Und Mr. Cambon sagte Herrn von Jagow: *"Vous n'avez pas besoin de*

Retrospect

When now, after two years, I review the whole course of events, I tell myself that I realized too late that there was no place for me in a system that for years has lived on traditions and routine alone, and that tolerates no representatives save those who report what [their superiors] wish to read. Absence of prejudice and an independent judgment arouse hostility; incapacity and want of character are praised and esteemed; successes, on the other hand, beget disfavor and awaken disquietude.

I had given up my opposition to the insane Triple Alliance policy, because I realized that it was useless and that my warnings were attributed to an incurable Austrophobia. In politics, which are neither acrobatics nor a game played with documents, but the business of the firm, there is no "philia" or "phobia," but only the interest of the community. A policy, however, which leans only on Austrians, Magyars, and Turks, must come into conflict with Russia and finally lead to a catastrophe.

In spite of former mistakes, all might still have been put right in July, 1914. An understanding with England had been attained. We ought to have sent to St. Petersburg a representative who was at least of average political capacity, and to have convinced Russia that we wished neither to control the Straits nor to strangle Serbia. *"Lâchez l'Autriche et nous lâcherons les Français"* ("Drop Austria and we will drop the French") M. Sazonof said to us. And M. Cambon told Herr von Jagow, *"Vous n'avez pas besoin de suivre l'Autriche partout"* ("You need not follow Austria everywhere").

suivre l'Autriche partout" (Ihr braucht mit Österreich nicht alles mitzumachen).

Weder Bündnisse noch Kriege, sondern nur Verträge brauchten wir, die uns und andere schützten und einen wirtschaftlichen Aufschwung sicherten, der in der Geschichte ohne Vorgang war. War Russland aber im Westen entlastet, so konnte es sich wieder nach Osten wenden, und der anglo-russische Gegensatz trat alsdann automatisch und ohne unsere Mitwirkung hervor, nicht minder aber der russisch-japanische.

Wir konnten auch der Frage der Rüstungsbeschränkung näher tretenhund brauchten uns um österreichische Wirrnisse nicht mehr zu kümmern. Österreich-Ungarn war dann der Vasall des Deutschen Reiches und ohne Bündnis und namentlich ohne Liebesdienste, die schliesslich zum Kriege führten für die Befreiung Polens und die Vernichtung Serbiens, obwohl die deutschen Interessen gerade das Gegenteil heischten.

Ich hatte in London eine Politik zu unterstützen, deren Irrlehre ich erkannte. Das hat sich an mir gerächt, denn es war eine Sünde wider den heiligen Geist.

Ankunft

In Berlin angekommen, sah ich sofort, dass ich zum Sündenbock für die Katastrophe gemacht werden sollte, die unsere Regierung im Gegensatz zu meinen Ratschlägen und Warnungen verschuldet hatte.

Von amtlicher Seite wurde geflissentlich verbreitet, ich hätte mich durch Sir Ed. Grey täuschen lassen, denn wenn er den Krieg nicht gewollt, würde Russland nicht mobilisiert haben. Graf Pourtalès, auf dessen Berichterstattung man sich verlassen konnte, sollte geschont werden, schon wegen seiner Verwandtschaft.

We needed neither alliances nor wars; we needed only treaties protecting us and others and affording security to an economic progress that was without precedent in history. If Russia had been freed from pressure in the West, it could again have turned to the East, and the Anglo-Russian rivalry would then have reappeared automatically and without our help, and not less certainly also the Russo-Japanese rivalry.

We could also have considered the question of the limitation of armaments, and we need no longer have troubled ourselves about Austrian complications. Austria would then have been the vassal of the German Empire, and this without an alliance and, what is most important, without the gratuitous services which finally led us into war—a war for the liberation of Poland and the annihilation of Serbia, although German interests demanded the exact opposite.

I had to support in London a policy, the heresy of which I recognized. For this I have been justly punished, for it was a sin against the Holy Ghost.

My Arrival

As soon as I arrived in Berlin, I saw that I was to be made the scapegoat for the catastrophe which our government had brought upon itself against my counsels and warnings.

A report, proceeding from official sources, was industriously circulated, that I had allowed myself to be deceived by Sir Edward Grey, since if he had not desired war Russia would not have mobilized. Count Pourtalès, whose reports could be relied on, was to be protected, not least on account of his family

Er habe sich „grossartig" benommen, er wurde begeistert gelobt, ich um so schärfer getadelt.

„Was geht denn Serbien Russland an?" sagte mir dieser Staatsmann nach achtjähriger Amtszeit in Petersburg. Die ganze Sache sollte eine britische Tücke sein, die ich nicht gemerkt. Im Amte erklärte man mir auch, im Jahre 1916 wäre es doch zum Kriege gekommen, dann wäre Russland „fertig", daher sei es besser jetzt.

Schuldfrage

Wir haben, wie aus allen amtlichen Veröffentlichungen hervorgeht und auch durch unser Weissbuch nicht widerlegt wird, das durch seine Dürftigkeit und Lückenhaftigkeit eine schwere Selbstanklage darstellt,

1. den Grafen Berchtold ermutigt, Serbien anzugreifen, obwohl kein deutsches Interesse vorlag und die Gefahr eines Weltkrieges uns bekannt sein musste —ob wir den Wortlaut des Ultimatums gekannt, ist völlig gleichgültig;

2. in den Tagen zwischen dem 23. und 30. Juli 1914, als Herr Sasonow mit Nachdruck erklärte, einen Angriff auf Serbien nicht dulden zu können, die britischen Vermittlungsvorschläge abgelehnt, obwohl Serbien unter russischem und britischem Drucke nahezu das ganze Ultimatum angenommen hatte und obwohl eine Einigung über die beiden fraglichen Punkte leicht zu erreichen und Graf Berchtold sogar bereit war, sich mit der serbischen Antwort zu begnügen;

3. am 30. Juli, als Graf Berchtold einlenken wollte und ohne dass Österreich angegriffen war, auf die blosse Mobilmachung Russlands hin ein Ultimatum

connections. He had conducted himself "magnifi-
cently," he was praised enthusiastically, and I was
blamed the more severely.

"What does Serbia matter to Russia?" this statesman said to me, after eight years' service at St.
Petersburg. The whole affair was declared to be a
British trick that I had not noticed. At the Foreign
Office I was told that war would in any case have
come in 1916. Then Russia would have been ready;
therefore it was better now.

The Question of Responsibility

It is shown by all official publications and is not
disproved by our White Book, which, owing to the
poverty of its contents and to its omissions, constitutes
a grave indictment against ourselves, that:

1. We encouraged Count Berchtold to attack Serbia, although no German interest was involved and
the danger of a World War must have been known to
us. Whether we were acquainted with the wording of
the ultimatum is completely immaterial.

2. During the period between the 23d and the 30th
of July, 1914, when M. Sazonof emphatically declared
that he could not tolerate an attack on Serbia,
we rejected the British proposals of mediation, although Serbia, under Russian and British pressure,
had accepted almost the whole of the ultimatum,
and although an agreement about the two points at
issue could easily have been reached and Count Berchtold was even prepared to content himself with the
Serbian reply.

3. On the 30th of July, when Count Berchtold
showed a disposition to change his course, we sent
an ultimatum to St. Petersburg merely because of

nach Petersburg geschickt und am 31. Juli den Russen den Krieg erklärt, obwohl der Zar sein Wort verpfändete, solange noch unterhandelt wird, keinen Mann marschieren zu lassen, also die Möglichkeit einer friedlichen Beilegung geflissentlich vernichtet.

Es ist nicht zu verwundern, wenn angesichts dieser unbestreitbaren Tatsachen ausserhalb Deutschlands die gesamte Kulturwelt uns die alleinige Schuld am Weltkriege beimisst.

Feindlicher Standpunkt

Ist es nicht begreiflich, dass unsere Feinde erklären, nicht eher ruhen zu wollen, bis ein System vernichtet ist, das eine dauernde Bedrohung unserer Nachbarn bildet? Müssen sie nicht sonst befürchten, in einigen Jahren wieder zu den Waffen greifen zu müssen und wieder ihre Provinzen überrannt und ihre Städte und Dörfer vernichtet zu sehen? Haben diejenigen nicht recht behalten, die weissagten, dass der Geist Treitschkes und Bernhardis das deutsche Volk beherrschte, der den Krieg als Selbstzweck verherrlicht und nicht als Übel verabscheut, dass bei uns noch der feudale Ritter und Junker, die Kriegerkaste regiere und Ideale und Werte gestalte, nicht aber der bürgerliche Gentleman, dass die Liebe zur Mensur, die die akademische Jugend beseelt, auch denen erhalten bleibt, die die Geschicke des Volkes leiten? Hatten nicht die Ereignisse in Zabern und die parlamentarischen Verhandlungen des Falles dem Ausland gezeigt, wie staatsbürgerliche Rechte und Freiheiten bei uns bewertet werden, wenn militärische Machtfragen entgegenstehen?

the Russian mobilization and though Austria had not been attacked; and on the 31st of July we declared war against the Russians, although the Czar pledged his word that he would not permit a single man to march as long as negotiations were still going on.[33] Thus we deliberately destroyed the possibility of a peaceful settlement.

In view of these incontestable facts, it is no wonder that the whole civilized world outside of Germany places the sole responsibility for the World War upon our shoulders.

The Enemy Point of View

Is it not comprehensible that our enemies declare that they will not rest until a system which constitutes a permanent menace to our neighbors is destroyed? Must they not otherwise fear that within a few years they will again be obliged to take up arms and again see their provinces overrun and their cities and villages destroyed? Have not those proved to be right who divined that the German people was dominated by the spirit of Treitschke and of Bernhardi, which glorifies war as an end in itself and does not loathe it as an evil; that with us the feudal knight and Junker, the warrior caste, still rules and shapes ideals and values, and not the civilian gentleman; that the love of the duel which animates our academic youth still persists in those who guide the destinies of the nation? Did not the occurrences in Zabern and the parliamentary discussion of this matter show to foreign countries the value we place on the rights and

[33] See *Collected Diplomatic Documents*, p. 537; also German White Book, p. 16.

In die Worte Euphorions kleidete der geistvolle, seither verstorbene Historiker Cramb, ein Bewunderer Deutschlands, die deutsche Auffassung:

> *„Träumt Ihr den Friedenstag?* [22]
> *Träume wer träumen mag,*
> *Krieg ist das Losungswort!*
> *Sieg, und so klingt es fort.“*

Der Militarismus, eigentlich eine Schule des Volkes und ein Instrument der Politik, macht die Politik zum Instrument der Militärmacht, wenn der patriarchalische Absolutismus des Soldatenkönigtums eine Haltung ermöglicht, die eine militärisch-junkerlichen Einflüssen entrückte Demokratie nicht zulassen würde.

So denken unsere Feinde, und so müssen sie denken, wenn sie sehen, dass trotz kapitalistischer Industrialisierung und trotz sozialistischer Organisierung die Lebenden, wie Friedrich Nietzsche sagt, noch von den Toten regiert werden. Das vornehmste feindliche Kriegsziel, die Demokratisierung Deutschlands, wird sich verwirklichen!—

Bismarck

Bismarck, gleich Napoleon, liebte den Kampf als Selbstzweck. Als Staatsmann vermied er neue Kriege, deren Sinnlosigkeit er erkannte. Er begnügte sich mit unblutigen Schlachten. Nachdem er in rascher Folge Christian, Franz Joseph und Napoleon besiegt, kamen Arnim, Pius und Augusta an die Reihe. Das genügte ihm nicht. Gortschakow hatte ihn wiederholt geärgert, der sich für grösser hielt. Er wurde bis hart an den Krieg bekämpft, sogar durch Entziehung des Salonwagens. So entstand der traurige Dreibund.

[22] B.-C.: "Krieg."

liberties of the citizen, if questions of military power stand in the way?

The keen-witted historian Cramb, who has since died, an admirer of Germany, clothed the German conception in the words of Euphorion:

> *Dream ye of peaceful day?*
> *Dream on while dream ye may!*
> *War is the signal cry;*
> *Hark! shouts of victory!* [34]

Militarism, which is properly a school for the nation and an instrument of policy, turns policy into the instrument of military power, if the patriarchal absolutism of a soldier-kingship makes possible an attitude which a democracy, placed beyond the control of militarist-Junker influences, would not permit.

So think our enemies; and so they must think if they see that, in spite of capitalistic industrialization and in spite of socialistic organization, the living, as Friedrich Nietzsche says, are still ruled by the dead. The highest war aim of our enemies, the democratization of Germany, will be realized!

Bismarck

Bismarck, like Napoleon, loved conflict for itself. As a statesman he avoided fresh wars, the folly of which he recognized. He contented himself with bloodless battles. After he had vanquished, in rapid succession, Christian, Francis Joseph, and Napoleon III, it was the turn of Arnim, Pius and Augusta. That did not suffice him. Gortschakof, who thought himself the greater, had repeatedly annoyed him. The conflict was carried almost to the point of war. It was carried even to the point of depriving Gort-

[34] Anna Swanwicks' translation.

Zum Schluss folgte der Kampf gegen Wilhelm, in dem der Gewaltige unterlag, wie Napoleon gegen Alexander.

Politische Ehen auf Tod und Leben geraten nur im staatsrechtlichen, nicht im völkerrechtlichen Verbande. Sie sind um so bedenklicher mit einem brüchigen Genossen. So war das Bündnis von Bismarck auch niemals gemeint.

Die Engländer aber hat er stets schonend behandelt; er wusste, dass es so klüger war. Die alte Viktoria wurde von ihm besonders ausgezeichnet, trotz des Hasses gegen die Tochter und gegen politische Engländerei, der gelehrte Beaconsfield und der welterfahrene Salisbury umworben, und auch der sonderliche Gladstone, den er nicht mochte, hatte sich eigentlich nicht zu beklagen.

Das Ultimatum an Serbien war die Krönung der Politik des Berliner Kongresses, der bosnischen Krise, der Londoner Konferenz; doch noch war die Zeit zur Umkehr.

Was vor allem zu vermeiden war, der Bruch mit Russland und mit England, das haben wir glücklich erreicht.

Unsere Zukunft

Heute nach zweijährigem Kampfe kann es nicht mehr zweifelhaft sein, dass wir auf einen bedingungslosen Sieg über Russen, Engländer, Franzosen, Italiener, Rumänen und Amerikaner nicht hoffen dürfen, mit dem Niederringen unserer Feinde nicht rechnen können. Zu einem Kompromissfrieden gelangen wir aber nur auf Grundlage der Räumung der

schakof of his special railway carriage. Thus arose the lamentable Triple Alliance. At last came the conflict with William, in which the mighty one was vanquished, as the first Napoleon was vanquished in the conflict with Alexander.

Political marriages "until death do us part" are successful only when the union is constitutional, not when it is international. They are all the more questionable when the partner is tottering on the verge of the grave. Bismarck never intended that the alliance with Austria should be such a marriage.

The English, however, he always handled carefully; he knew that this was wiser. He always paid marked respect to the old Victoria, despite his hatred of her daughter and of political anglomania. He courted the learned Beaconsfield and the worldly-wise Salisbury; and even that strange Gladstone, whom he did not like, had no real ground for complaint.

The ultimatum to Serbia was the culminating point of the policy of the Berlin Congress, of the Bosnian crisis [35] and of the London Conference: but there was yet time to turn back.

What above all we should have avoided, the breach with Russia and with England, we have successfully attained.

Our Future

Today, after two years of fighting, it can no longer be doubted that we cannot hope for an unconditional victory over the Russians, English, French, Italians, Rumanians, and Americans, nor count on being able to wear our enemies down. A peace by compromise, however, we can obtain only on the basis of an evacua-

[35] See Appendix, notes iii and iv.

besetzten Gebiete, deren Besitz für uns überdies eine Last und Schwäche und die Gefahr neuer Kriege bedeutet. Daher sollte alles vermieden werden, was denjenigen feindlichen Gruppen, die für den Kompromissgedanken vielleicht noch zu gewinnen wären, den britischen Radikalen und den russischen Reaktionären, ein Einlenken erschwert. Schon von diesem Gesichtspunkte aus ist das polnische Projekt ebenso zu verwerfen, wie jeder Eingriff in belgische Rechte oder die Hinrichtung britischer Bürger, vom wahnwitzigen U-Boot-Plane gar nicht zu reden.

Unsere Zukunft liegt auf dem Wasser. Richtig, also nicht in Polen und Belgien, in Frankreich und Serbien. Das ist die Rückkehr zum heiligen Römischen Reich, zu den Irrungen der Hohenstaufen und Habsburger. Es ist dies die Politik der Plantagenets, nicht die der Drake und Raleigh, Nelson und Rhodes. Dreibundpolitik ist Rückkehr zur Vergangenheit, Abkehr von der Zukunft, dem Imperialismus, der Weltpolitik. Mitteleuropa ist Mittelalter, Berlin-Bagdad eine Sackgasse, nicht der Weg ins Freie, zu unbegrenzten Möglichkeiten, zur Weltmission des deutschen Volkes.

Ich bin kein Gegner Österreichs oder Ungarns oder Italiens und Serbiens oder irgend eines anderen Staates, sondern nur ein Gegner der Dreibundpolitik, die uns von unseren Zielen ablenken und auf die schiefe Ebene der Kontinentalpolitik bringen musste. Sie war nicht deutsche, sondern k. u. k. Hauspolitik. Die Österreicher hatten sich daran gewöhnt, das Bündnis als einen Schirm zu betrachten, unter dessen Schutz sie nach Belieben Ausflüge in den Orient machen konnten.

Und welches Ergebnis des Völkerringens haben wir zu gewärtigen? Die Vereinigten Staaten von Afrika werden britisch sein, wie die von Amerika, Australien

tion of the occupied territories. For this there is the more reason, in that their possession constitutes for us a burden and a cause of weakness and involves the risk of further wars. Therefore everything should be avoided that impedes a change of attitude on the part of those enemy groups which may perhaps still be won over to the idea of a peace by compromise, namely, the British radicals and the Russian reactionaries. Simply from this point of view the Polish scheme is as objectionable as is any interference with Belgian rights, or the execution of British civilians, to say nothing of the insane submarine plan.

"Our future lies on the water."[36] Quite right; therefore it does not lie in Poland and Belgium, in France and Serbia. This is a reversion to the Holy Roman Empire, to the mistakes of the Hohenstaufen and the Hapsburgs. It is the policy of the Plantagenets, not that of Drake and Raleigh, Nelson and Rhodes. The policy of the Triple Alliance turns back to the past; it turns away from the future, from imperialism, from a world-policy. "Middle Europe" is of the middle ages; Berlin-Bagdad is a blind alley and not the way into the open, to unlimited possibilities, to the universal mission of the German nation.

I am no enemy of Austria, or Hungary, or Italy, or Serbia, or of any other state; I am an enemy only of the Triple Alliance policy, which was bound to divert us from our aims and bring us on the downward slope of a continental policy. It was not a German policy, but an imperial and royal [Hapsburg] house policy. The Austrians had accustomed themselves to regard the alliance as a screen, under cover of which they could make excursions into the East whenever they pleased.

[36] Emperor William II, Speech of June 18, 1901.

und Ozeanien. Und die lateinischen Staaten Europas werden, wie ich schon vor Jahren sagte, in dasselbe Verhältnis zu dem Vereinigten Königreich geraten, wie die lateinischen Schwestern Amerikas zu den Vereinigten Staaten. Der Angelsachse wird sie beherrschen. Das durch den Krieg erschöpfte Frankreich wird sich nur noch enger an Grossbritannien anschliessen. Auf die Dauer wird auch Spanien nicht widerstehen.

Und in Asien wird der Russe und der Japaner sich ausbreiten mit seinen Grenzen und Sitten, und der Süden wird den Briten bleiben.

Die Welt wird den Angelsachsen, Russen und Japanern gehören und der Deutsche allein bleiben mit Österreich und Ungarn. Seine Machtherrschaft wird die des Gedankens und des Handels sein, nicht aber die der Bureaukraten und Soldaten. Es war zu spät erschienen, und die letzte Möglichkeit, das Versäumte nachzuholen, ein Kolonialreich zu gründen, hat der Weltkrieg vernichtet.

Denn wir werden die Söhne *Jahwes* [23] nicht verdrängen, das Programm des grossen Rhodes wird sich erfüllen, der in der Ausbreitung des Britentums, im britischen Imperialismus das Heil der Menschheit erblickte.

Tu regere imperio populos, Romane, memento.
Hae tibi erunt artes: pacisque imponere morem,
Parcere subjectis et debellare superbos.

(Du sollst die Völker im Römerreiche regieren. Deine Kunst wird sein, Friedenssitten zu erzwingen, die Unterworfenen zu schonen und die Hochmütigen des Krieges zu entwöhnen.)

[23] B.-C.: *"Ichwes."*

And to what outcome of the struggle of nations have we to look forward? The United States of Africa will be British, like those of America, Australia, and Oceania. And the Latin states of Europe, as I predicted years ago, will come into the same relation to the United Kingdom as their Latin sisters in America to the United States. The Anglo-Saxon will dominate them. France, exhausted by the war, will attach herself all the more closely to Great Britain. Nor will Spain maintain, in the long run, an attitude of resistance.

In Asia, the Russians and the Japanese will extend their frontiers and diffuse their customs, while the south will remain in the hands of the British.

The world will belong to the Anglo-Saxons, the Russians and the Japanese, and the German will be left alone with Austria and Hungary. His dominion will be that of thought and trade, not that of the bureaucrat and the soldier. He made his appearance too late; and his last chance of making up what he had missed, of founding a colonial empire, has been destroyed by the World War.

For we shall not supplant the sons of Jehovah. The future will realize the program of the great Rhodes, who saw the salvation of humanity in the expansion of British influence, in British imperialism.

Roman, be mindful to rule the people with orderly power.
These shall be thine arts: enforcing peace as a custom,
Warring the arrogant down, and sparing those who have yielded.

[129]

Remarks on the article of Prince Lichnowsky

"MY LONDON MISSION"

By Gottlieb Von Jagow

Former Secretary of State for Foreign Affairs

[*From the Norddeutsche Allgemeine Zeitung, March 23, 1918*]

Translation by MUNROE SMITH *

So far as it is possible, in general, I shall refrain from going into the statements that relate to the policy followed before my administration of the Foreign Office.

I should like to make the following remarks about particular points in the article:

When I was appointed secretary of state, in January, 1913, I regarded a German-English *rapprochement* as desirable, and I also believed an agreement attainable on the points where our interests touched or crossed each other. At all events, I wished to try to work in this sense. A principal point for us was the Mesopotamia-Asia Minor question—the so-called Bagdad policy—as this had become for us a question of prestige. If England intended to force us out there, it certainly appeared to me that a conflict could hardly be avoided. In Berlin I began, as soon as it was possible to do so, to negotiate concerning the Bagdad Railroad. We found a favor-

* The editor wishes to acknowledge the courtesy of *The New York Times* in permitting the translation which appeared in the June, 1918, issue of *Current History*, to be used in part as a basis for Professor Munroe Smith's translation.

able disposition on the part of the English government, and the result was the agreement that was almost complete when the World War broke out.

At the same time the negotiations over the Portuguese colonies that had been begun by Count Metternich, continued by Baron Marschall, and reopened by Prince Lichnowsky, were under way. Further negotiations regarding other—for example, East Asiatic—problems I meant to start later, when what was in my opinion the most important question, that of the Bagdad Railroad, should be settled, and an atmosphere of more confidence thus created. I also left the naval question aside, as it would have been difficult to reach an early agreement over that matter, after past experiences.

I can pass over the development of the Albanian question, as it occurred before my term of office began. In general, however, I would like to remark that such far-reaching disinterestedness in Balkan questions as Prince Lichnowsky advocates does not seem possible to me. It would have contradicted the essential character of the alliance if we had completely ignored really vital interests of our ally. We, too, had demanded that Austria should second us at Algeciras, and at that time Italy's attitude had caused serious resentment among us. Russia, too, although she had no interest whatever in Morocco, stood by France. Finally, it was our task, as the third member of the alliance, to support such measures as would render possible an adjustment of the divergent interests of our allies and avoid a conflict between them.

It further appeared impossible to me not to pursue a "Triple Alliance policy" in matters where the interests of the allied powers touched each other. Had no

such policy been pursued, Italy would have been
driven entirely into line with the Entente in Oriental
questions, Austria would have been handed over to
the mercy of Russia, and the Triple Alliance would
thus have really gone to pieces. And we, too, would
have been unable, in the absence of any support, to
safeguard our interests in the Orient. Even Prince
Lichnowsky does not deny that we had there great
economic interests to represent. But today economic
interests are no longer to be separated from political
interests.

That St. Petersburg desired "the independence of
the Sultan" is an assertion that Prince Lichnowsky
will hardly be able to prove; it would contradict
every tradition of Russian policy. If we, furthermore,
had not had at our command the influence at Constantinople established by Baron Marschall, it would
hardly have been possible for us to defend our economic interests in Turkey in the desired way.

When Prince Lichnowsky further asserts that it
was first through "our Triple Alliance and Eastern
policy that Russia, our natural friend and best neighbor, was driven into the arms of France and England,"
he is in conflict with the historical facts. It was
because Prince Gortschakof was guiding Russian policy
toward a *rapprochement* with a France lusting for
revenge that Prince Bismarck was first induced to enter
into the alliance with Austria-Hungary; through the
alliance with Rumania he barred the advance of
Russia toward the south. Prince Lichnowsky con-
demns the basic principles of Bismarck's policy. Our
attempts to draw closer to Russia went to pieces—
Björki proves it—or remained ineffective, like the so-
called Potsdam agreement. Moreover, Russia was

not always our "best neighbor." Under the Empress Elizabeth, as at present, Russia strove for possession of East Prussia to extend its Baltic coasts and to secure for itself the domination of the Baltic Sea. The St. Petersburg "window" has gradually widened, so as to take in Esthonia, Livonia, Courland, and Finland and has stretched over toward Åland. Poland was arranged as a field in which to concentrate troops against us. Pan-Slavism, which was dominating the Russian policy to an ever greater degree, had positive anti-German tendencies.

Nor did we divert Russia "from the policy of Asiatic expansion," but only tried to check its encroachments in European policy and its encirclement of our Austro-Hungarian ally.

Just as little as Sir Edward Grey did we wish war to come over Albania. Therefore, in spite of our unhappy experiences at Algeciras, we agreed to a conference. The credit of an "attitude of mediation" at the conference should not be denied Sir Edward Grey; but that he "by no means placed himself on the side of his Entente associates" is, after all, rather an overstatement. Certainly he often advised yielding in St. Petersburg (as we did in Vienna) and found "formulas of agreement," but in dealing with the other side he represented the Entente, because, like us, he neither would nor could abandon his associates. That we, on the other hand, "uniformly defended the point of view which was prescribed to us by Vienna" is absolutely incorrect. We, like England, played a mediatory rôle, and in Vienna also we advised yielding and moderation far more than Prince Lichnowsky appears, or pretends, to be aware. And then Vienna made far-reaching concessions in several instances

(Dibra, Djakowa). If Prince Lichnowsky, who always wished to be cleverer than the Foreign Office, and who clearly allowed himself to be strongly impressed by the representatives of the Entente, did not know this, he ought now, at any rate, to refrain from making false assertions! If, to be sure, the degree of yielding that was necessary was obtained in Vienna, then of course we had to represent the Austrian standpoint at the conference. Ambassador Szögyenyi himself was not one of the extremists; in Vienna they were by no means always satisfied with his attitude. That the ambassador, with whom I was negotiating almost every day, constantly sounded the refrain of the *casus foederis* is entirely unknown to me. It certainly is true that in Vienna Prince Lichnowsky had been regarded, at an earlier period than this, as no friend of Austria. Nevertheless, complaints about him came oftener to my ears on the part of Marquis di San Giuliano than on the part of Count Berchtold.

King Nikita's seizure of Skutari constituted a mockery of the entire conference and a snub to all the powers taking part in it.

Russia was by no means "obliged to give way to us all along the line;" on the contrary, it obtained "satisfaction of the Serbian desires" in several matters; to such an extent, indeed, that some towns and strips of territory that could have been regarded as purely or mainly Albanian were allotted to Serbia. Prince Lichnowsky says that "the outcome of the conference was a fresh humiliation of Russian national sentiment" and that "dissatisfaction" prevailed in Russia on that account. It cannot be the task of our policy to secure, at the cost of our ally, satisfaction of all the unjustified demands of the exaggerated national

[134]

sentiment of a Power by no means friendly to us. Russia has no vital interests on the Adriatic, but our allies certainly had. If we, as Prince Lichnowsky seems to wish, had completely adopted the Russian point of view, the result would have been a humiliation for Austria-Hungary and thus a weakening of our group. It seems to be Prince Lichnowsky's constant and sole anxiety that Russia be not humiliated; a humiliation of Austria is obviously a matter of indifference to him.

When Prince Lichnowsky says that our "Austrophil attitude" was not adapted "to direct Russia's attention to its Asiatic interests," it is not quite clear to me what this means. After a disastrous diversion towards East Asia—in the Japanese war we had favored Russia without ever being thanked for it!—Russia again took up its policy aimed directly toward the European Orient (the Balkans and Constantinople), and this with increased energy (the Balkan Alliance, Buchlau, Iswolsky, *etc.*).

Venizelos, the cunning Cretan with the "ribbon of the order of the Red Eagle," evidently knew how to throw a little sand into the eyes of our ambassador. He, in contrast to King Constantine and Theototy, was always pro-Entente. His present attitude shows most clearly this tendency on his part. Herr Danef, however, was entirely inclined toward St. Petersburg.

That Count Berchtold displayed certain leanings toward Bulgaria even in its differences with Rumania is true; but that we "of course went with him" is entirely false. With our support, King Charles [of Rumania] had the satisfaction of the Bucharest Peace. If then, in the case of the Bucharest Peace,

in which we favored the wishes and interests of our Rumanian ally, our policy deviated somewhat from that of Vienna, the Austro-Hungarian Cabinet certainly did not believe—as Prince Lichnowsky asserts—that it "could reckon on our support as a matter of course" in securing a revision of this treaty. That Marquis di San Giuliano, by his warning, "saved us from being involved in a world war in the summer of 1913," because at that time "the idea of a campaign against Serbia was entertained in Vienna," is entirely unknown to me. Just as little do I know that Herr von Tchirschky—who, it is true, was naturally, rather inclined to pessimism—is said to have declared in the spring of 1914 that there soon would be war. Of the "important occurrences" that Prince Lichnowsky here suspects I was accordingly just as ignorant as he was himself! Such events as the English visit to Paris—Sir Edward Grey's first to the Continent—surely must have been known to the ambassador, and we informed him about the secret Anglo-Russian naval agreement; to be sure, he was unwilling to believe it!

In the matter of Liman von Sanders, we made an important concession to Russia by renouncing the general's power of command over Constantinople. I am willing to admit that this point in the agreement regarding the military mission was politically not opportune.

When Prince Lichnowsky boasts of having succeeded in giving the colonial treaty a form corresponding to our wishes, this credit is not to be denied him. Strong pressure was necessary, however, on several occasions to induce him to represent some of our desires with more emphasis.

When Prince Lichnowsky says that he received authorization definitely to conclude the colonial treaty, after previously asserting that the treaty "perished," his story contains a contradiction which we may leave to the Prince to explain. Lichnowsky's assertion, however, that we delayed publication because the treaty would have been for him "a public success" that we begrudged him, is an unheard-of insinuation that can be explained only through his egocentric view of things. The treaty would have missed its practical and moral effect—one of its main objects was to create a good atmosphere between us and England—if its publication had been greeted with violent attacks upon "perfidious Albion" in our Anglophobe press and in our Parliament. For such attacks, in view of our internal situation at that time, the simultaneous publication of [the colonial and] the so-called Windsor Treaty would undoubtedly have furnished occasion. And the howl about English perfidy that the internal contradiction between the text of the Windsor Treaty and our treaty would doubtless have evoked could hardly have been so met as to satisfy our public opinion through the assurance of English *bona fides*. With justified precaution, we intended to allow the publication to be made only at a suitable moment, when the danger of hostile criticism was no longer so acute, if possible simultaneously with the announcement of the Bagdad Treaty, which also was on the point of being concluded. The fact that two great agreements had been established between us and England would have materially helped to gain for them a favorable reception and would have made it easier to overlook the aesthetic defects of the Portuguese convention. It

was consideration for the effect of the agreement, through which we wished to obtain an improvement in our relations with England—not to stir up more trouble—that caused our hesitation.

It is true that account was also taken—although in a secondary degree—of the efforts just then being made to acquire economic interests in the Portuguese colonies, which would naturally have been harder to obtain if the terms of the convention had been announced. These conditions Prince Lichnowsky may not have been able to perceive fully from London, but he should have had confidence in our judgment as regarded matters of fact and should have acquiesced in it, instead of replacing his lack of understanding with aspersions and insinuations of personal motives. Particularly in dealing with English statesmen, he would surely have found that our arguments were understood by the English statesmen themselves.

The ambassador's speeches gave much offense in this country. For the creation of a better atmosphere, in which alone the *rapprochement* we were seeking could flourish, it was necessary that confidence in our English policy and in our London representative should be widely established in our own public opinion. Prince Lichnowsky, otherwise so susceptible to public opinion, did not take this factor sufficiently into account, for he saw everything only through his London spectacles. His charges against the attitude of the Foreign Office are too untenable to need discussion. I think it desirable, however, to state that Prince Lichnowsky was not left in ignorance regarding the "most important things," in so far as they were pertinent to his mission. On the contrary, I gave

the ambassadors generally much fuller information than they had usually received under previous administrations. My own experiences as ambassador induced me to do so. But with Lichnowsky there was the inclination to rely more upon his own impressions and conclusions than upon the communications and instructions of the Central Office. To disclose the sources of our information, indeed, I had not always either occasion or authority. Here there were quite definite considerations, particularly anxiety not to compromise our sources. The Prince's memorandum furnishes the best justification for the caution exercised in this regard.

It is not true that in the Foreign Office the reports that England would protect France under all circumstances were not believed.

At Konopischt, on the occasion of the visit of His Majesty the Emperor to the Archduke, heir to the [Austrian] throne, no plan of an active policy against Serbia was laid down. Archduke Franz Ferdinand was not at all the advocate of a policy leading to war for which he has often been taken. During the London conference he advised moderation and the avoidance of war.

Prince Lichnowsky's "optimism" was hardly justified, as he has probably since convinced himself through the revelations of the Sukhomlinof trial. Besides, the secret Anglo-Russian naval agreement (of which, as has been said before, he was informed) should have made him more skeptical. The mistrust voiced by the imperial chancellor and the under secretary of state was, unfortunately, well grounded. How does this agree with the assertion that we, replying upon the reports of Count Pourtalès that

"Russia would not move under any circumstances," had not considered the possibility of a war? Furthermore, so far as I can recollect, Count Pourtalès never made any such report.

That Austria-Hungary wished to intervene against the repeated provocations fomented by Russia (Herr von Hartwig), which reached their climax in the Serajevo assault, we had to recognize as justified. In spite of all former compromises and adjustments of threatened conflicts, Russia did not abandon her policy, which aimed at the complete exclusion of the Austrian influence (and naturally of ours also) from the Balkans. The Russian agents inspired by St. Petersburg, continued their incitement. It was a question of the prestige and the existence of the Danube monarchy. It must either submit to the Russo-Serbian machinations, or command a *quos ego*, even at the risk of war. We could not leave our ally in the lurch. Had it been intended to exclude altogether the *ultima ratio* of war, the alliance should not have been concluded. Besides, it was plain that the Russian military preparations (for instance, the extension of railroads and reconstruction of forts in Poland), for which a France lusting for revenge had lent the money and which would have been completed in a few years, were directed principally against us. But despite all this, despite the fact that the aggressive tendency of the Russian policy was becoming constantly more evident, the idea of a preventive war was far removed from us. We did not decide to declare war on Russia until we had to face the Russian mobilization and to defend ourselves against a Russian invasion.

I have not at hand the letters exchanged with the Prince—it was a matter of private letters. Lich-

nowsky pleaded for an abandonment of Austria. I replied, so far as I remember, that we, aside from our treaty obligation, could not sacrifice our ally for the uncertain friendship of England. If we abandoned our only trustworthy ally, we should stand later entirely isolated, face to face with the Entente. It is probable that I also wrote that "Russia was becoming more and more anti-German" and that we must "just risk it." Furthermore, it is possible that in order to steel Lichnowsky's nerves a little and to prevent him from exposing his views in London also, I wrote that there would probably be some "blustering," and that "the more firmly we stood by Austria the more certainly would Russia give way." I have said already that our policy was not based upon alleged reports excluding war. At that time, it is true, I still thought war could be avoided, but, like all of us, I was fully aware of the very serious danger.

We could not agree to the English proposal of a conference of ambassadors, for it would undoubtedly have led to a serious diplomatic defeat. For Italy, too, was Serbophil and, with its Balkan interests, stood rather opposed to Austria. The "intimacy of the relations between Italy and Russia" is admitted by Prince Lichnowsky himself. The best and only feasible way of escape was a localization of the conflict and an understanding between Vienna and St. Petersburg. We worked toward that end with all our energy. That we "insisted upon" the war is an unheard-of assertion, which is sufficiently invalidated by the telegrams of His Majesty the Emperor to the Czar and to King George, published in the White Books—Prince Lichnowsky chooses to speak only of "the Czar's positively humble telegram"—as well as by the instructions

[141]

we sent to Vienna. The worst distortion of facts is contained in the following sentence:

"When Count Berchtold at last decided to change his course, and after Russia had negotiated and waited a whole week in vain, we answered the Russian mobilization with the ultimatum and the declaration of war."

Should we, perhaps, have waited until the mobilized Russian army was streaming over our borders? The reading of the Sukhomlinof trial has probably given even Prince Lichnowsky a feeling of *"O si tacuisses!"* On July 5th, I was absent from Berlin. The statement that I was "soon afterwards in Vienna to talk everything over with Count Berchtold" is false. I returned to Berlin on July 6th, from my wedding journey, and I did not stir from there until August 15th, on the occasion of the shifting of the Great Headquarters. As secretary of state I was only once in Vienna before the war, in the spring of 1913.

Prince Lichnowsky slides over the matter of the confusing dispatch that he sent us on August 1st— I have not the exact wording at hand—as a "misunderstanding" and even seems to intend to reproach us because "without waiting for the interview," we "made the news the basis for far-reaching activity." The question of war with England was a matter of minutes, and immediately after the arrival of the dispatch it was decided to make an eleventh-hour attempt to avert the war with France and England. His Majesty sent the well-known telegram to King George. The content of the Lichnowsky dispatch could not have been understood in any other way than we understood it.

In matters of fact, Prince Lichnowsky's narrative presents such an abundance of inaccuracies and distortions that it is scarcely surprising that his conclusions are also entirely wrong. A really grotesque effect is produced when he reproaches us for sending an ultimatum to St. Petersburg on July 30th, merely because of the mobilization of Russia, and for declaring war upon the Russians, on July 31st, although the Czar had pledged his word that not a man should march so long as negotiations were under way, thus willfully destroying the possibility of a peaceful adjustment. At the close, his point of view seems to become almost identical with that of our enemies.

When the ambassador makes the accusation that our policy identified itself "with Turks and Austro-Magyars" and subordinated itself to the "viewpoints of Vienna and Budapest," he may be suitably answered by saying that he saw things only through London spectacles and exclusively from the point of view of his desired *rapprochement* with England *à tout prix*. He also appears to have forgotten completely that the Entente was formed much more against us than against Austria.

I, too, pursued a policy which aimed at an understanding with England, because I was of the opinion that this was the only way for us to escape from the unfavorable position in which we were placed by the unequal division of strength and the weakness of the Triple Alliance. But Russia and France pressed towards war. We were under obligations resulting from our treaty with Austria, and we too were menaced in our position as a Great Power—*hic Rhodus, hic salta*. But England, that was not tied up in the same way with Russia and that had received far-reaching

[143]

assurances from us regarding the sparing of France and of Belgium, seized the sword.

In saying this, I by no means accept the view that is widely held among us today, that England laid all the mines for the outbreak of the war; on the contrary, I believe in Sir Edward Grey's love of peace and in his earnest wish to arrive at an understanding with us. But he had allowed himself to become entangled too far in the net of the Franco-Russian policy; he no longer found the way out, and he did not prevent the World War—a thing that he could have done. Neither was the war popular with the English people; Belgium had to serve as battle field.*

"Political marriages until death do us part" are, as Prince Lichnowsky says, not possible in international unions. But neither is isolation, under the present condition of affairs in Europe. The history of Europe consists of coalitions, which sometimes have led to the avoidance of warlike outbreaks and sometimes to violent clashes. A loosening and dissolving of old alliances that no longer answer all conditions is only in order when new constellations are attainable. This was the object of the policy of a *rapprochement* with England. So long as this policy did not offer reliable guarantees we could not sacrifice the old guarantees—even with their obligations.

The Morocco policy had led to a political defeat. In the Bosnian crisis this had been luckily avoided, as was the case also at the London Conference. A fresh diminution of our prestige was not endurable for our position in Europe and in the world. The

* *"Schlachtfeld."* This may possibly be a misprint for *Schlachtruf* (battle-cry).

prosperity of states, their political and economic successes, are based upon the prestige that they enjoy in the world.

The personal attacks contained in the article, the unheard-of aspersions and slanders of others, condemn themselves. The ever-recurring suspicion that everything happened only because it was not desired to allow him, Lichnowsky, any successes speaks of wounded self-love, of disappointed hopes for personal successes, and has a painful effect.

In closing, let me recall the memorandum of Prince Bismarck, which Hermann Oncken also has quoted in his work, *The Old and The New Middle Europe*—the memorandum which was written in the year 1879, and in which the idea is developed that the German Empire can never permit a situation to arise in which it would remain isolated on the European Continent between Russia and France, side by side with a defeated Austria-Hungary that Germany had left in the lurch.

APPENDIX TO PRINCE LICHNOWSKY'S MEMORANDUM

Personal and Historical Notes

By Munroe Smith and Henry F. Munro

I

The Berlin Foreign Office

During Prince Lichnowsky's term of service in the Foreign Office (1899–1904), Count (later Prince) von Bülow was chancellor, Baron von Richthofen was foreign secretary, and Herr von Mühlberg was undersecretary. The foreign secretary was director of the section of politics and personnel, in which Lichnowsky was employed, and it is he, presumably, who is described as laboring under insane delusions. The senior counselor in the same section was Herr von Holstein. His long service, which began in 1879, and the fact that he represented the traditions of the Bismarckian period naturally gave him a certain authority. His retirement from office, in April, 1906, was ascribed to "differences" with Prince von Bülow. It gave rise to much comment, since he had been regarded, in many circles, as the virtual director of German foreign policy since 1890. [*Schultess, Europäischer Geschichtskalender*, 1906, p. 97, citing *Zukunft*, July, 1906, and *Preussische Jahrbücher*, vol. 125, 3.]

In 1912, when Lichnowsky was sent to London, Herr von Bethmann-Hollweg was chancellor, Herr von Kiderlen-Wächter was foreign secretary, and Herr von Stumm was director of the political section. Von

Stumm had previously been connected with the German embassies in London, Washington, Paris, Vienna, St. Petersburg and Madrid, and then, a second time, with the London embassy. It is he, apparently, who is described by Lichnowsky as endeavoring to play the rôle of Herr von Holstein.

In January, 1913, Herr von Jagow was appointed foreign secretary.

II

Austro-Prussian and Austro-German Relations

The long struggle between the Hapsburgs and the Hohenzollerns for a controlling influence in German affairs was brought to an end by the Prussian victory of Sadowa in 1866. Germany was reorganized under a Prussian hegemony.

In the 18th century, Count (later Prince) Kaunitz (1711–1794) was one of Prussia's most dangerous enemies. In retaliation for the conquest of a large part of Silesia by Frederick the Great, Kaunitz succeeded in forming an Austrian-French alliance against Prussia, to which Russia became a party. In the Seven Years' War which followed (1756–1763) Prussia was brought to the verge of destruction. It was saved only by Russia's abandonment of the Austrian cause.

After the dissolution of the Holy Roman Empire of the German nation in 1804 and the reconstruction of Germany as a confederation in 1814, Austria remained the dominant power in Germany. On account of the large proportion of non-German elements in the Austro-Hungarian Empire, many Germans began to desire a closer union of the rest of Germany under Prussian leadership. These were called "Little Germans" (*Kleindeutsche*). A more numerous party advo-

cated the retention of all Germans within a single federal union. These were the "Great Germans" (*Grossdeutsche*). Inasmuch as neither of the two leading states could be expected to submit to a superior authority exercised by the other, it was clear that any such wider union must remain decentralized. "Great German" and "particularist" thus became practically interchangeable terms. The looser union recommended itself to 'most of the smaller states of Germany, as preserving their independence. In order that these states might be more effectively protected against both Austria and Prussia, a closer union among them and the organization of Germany as a "triad" found many advocates. The "old Bavarian" policy, to which Prince Lichnowsky alludes, aimed at the establishment of such a union of the smaller states under the leadership of Bavaria.

The question of a greater or smaller Germany became one of the chief issues in the revolutionary Frankfort Parliament of 1848. The refusal of Austria to come into the new German Empire with its German territories only, Hungary and the Slav provinces remaining outside, gave the Little Germans the victory; and the imperial crown was offered to King Friedrich Wilhelm IV of Prussia. He rejected the offer; but his ministers took steps for a narrower union of North Germany through the coöperation of the kings of Prussia, Saxony and Hanover. This plan was not really welcome either to Saxony or to Hanover, and was bitterly resisted by Austria. A conflict was averted by a complete Prussian surrender at Olmütz, in 1850, and the old confederation, as it had existed since 1814, was reëstablished.

In this period the Austrian policy was directed by

Prince Felix Schwarzenberg (1800–1852). It was under his leadership that Austria forced Prussia to submit at Olmütz. His program was, first to humiliate Prussia, then to destroy it—*"avilir puis démolir."*

Count Moritz Esterhazy (1807–1890) was a member of the Austrian ministry from 1861 to 1866. He was of the clerical party and was bitterly hostile to Prussia. He is said to have been one of the strongest advocates of war with Prussia.

By the victory of Prussia in 1866, Austria was excluded from the new Germany. It was, of course, not reconciled to the new order of things, and its continued hostility to Prussia is shown in the selection of Friedrich Ferdinand von Beust (1809–1886) as Austro-Hungarian minister of foreign affairs. From 1867–1871 he held the post of Austrian premier. He had been minister of foreign affairs in Saxony since 1849 and Saxon prime minister since 1853, and had been a persistent opponent of Prussia. After 1866 he was, of course, impossible as a Saxon minister. From 1866 to 1870 there were negotiations between France and Austria for an alliance against Prussia, but these came to nothing. At the outbreak of the Franco-Prussian war, von Beust found it inadvisable to take sides with France in a war which was regarded, even in South Germany, as a national German war. Before the end of 1870 he established fairly friendly relations between Austria and Prussia.

Baron (later Count) Aloys von Ährenthal (1854–1912), whom Lichnowsky describes as more independent in his attitude than his immediate predecessors, was Austro-Hungarian foreign minister from 1907 to his death in February, 1912. In this office he was succeeded by Count Berchtold.

III

The Berlin Congress (1878)

The war of 1877–1878 between Russia and Turkey was terminated by the treaty of San Stefano. The provisions of this treaty were unsatisfactory to other Great Powers, notably to Great Britain and to Austria, and Russia agreed that the arrangements made at San Stefano should be revised by a European Congress. This met at Berlin, in July, under the presidency of Prince Bismarck, who declared that his rôle was that of an "honest broker." The Congress restored to Turkey much of the territory ceded at San Stefano and changed the status and limits assigned to the Christian Balkan states. In giving to Austria the right to occupy and administer Bosnia and Herzegovina, the Congress, as we now know, simply put into execution a secret agreement made between Russia and Austria at Reichstadt before the outbreak of the war—an agreement by which Russia secured Austrian neutrality in that war (Bismarck, speech in the Reichstag, February 6, 1888; see also Hofmann, *Fürst Bismarck*, vol. ii, p. 5). This concession to Austria, however, as well as other provisions of the Berlin Treaty, aroused resentment in Russia, and this resentment was directed largely against Germany. In return for the friendly neutrality of Russia in the Franco-Prussian war of 1870–1871, the Russians had expected that Germany would support their interests in the Near East. Bismarck subsequently claimed that he had given them all possible support, that he had acted almost as "the fourth Russian plenipotentiary" in the Congress; but the Russians held him largely responsible for their diplomatic defeat. Rela-

tions between the two countries became so strained that, much against the wishes of Emperor William I, who regarded friendship with Russia as the first of German political interests, Bismarck formed, in 1879, a defensive alliance with Austria.

IV

German-Russian Relations (1884–1908)

The relations between Germany and Russia, strained by the revision of the Peace of San Stefano at the Congress of Berlin, were greatly improved in 1884, when Bismarck negotiated a treaty by which Germany and Russia each agreed to remain neutral in case the other should be attacked by a third Power. This is generally known as the "reinsurance treaty"; because by the treaty of 1879 with Austria Germany was assured of Austrian support in case it should be attacked by Russia, and by this new treaty it was assured of Russian neutrality in case it should be attacked by France. This treaty was renewed in 1887; but in 1890, when Bismarck was removed from office, his successor, General von Caprivi, declined to renew it, because he found the relations of Germany to Austria and to Russia "too complicated." The real reason, apparently, why it was not renewed was because William II wished to be free to support Austria against Russia in the Near East, even if it should be found advisable that Austria should attack Russia. The existence of this German-Russian treaty from 1884 to 1890 was first made known to the general public by Bismarck, after his retirement from office, in an article published in the *Hamburger Nachrichten*, October 24, 1896.

It was Bismarck's desire to lessen the chance of war between Austria and Russia by inducing them to recognize that each had its special sphere of influence in the Balkans, Austria in the West, Russia in the East. Bulgaria, accordingly, was in the Russian sphere of influence.

Alexander of Battenberg, Prince of Bulgaria, succeeded in 1885 in uniting East Rumelia with Bulgaria, thus establishing for his principality the boundaries which Russia had sought to give it in the Peace of San Stefano. Attacked by Serbia, "to maintain the balance of power in the Balkans," the Bulgarian army, under Prince Alexander's leadership, was completely victorious. Serbia was protected against loss of territory only by the diplomatic intervention of Austria. Prince Alexander, however, had accomplished all these results without the consent of Russia. He had shown himself independent of Russian influence; and in August, 1886, Russian agents stirred up a revolution, kidnapped the Prince, and carried him out of the country. Reinstated by a counter-revolution, he resigned his throne, in order, as he said, to save Bulgaria from occupation by Russian troops.

In Germany there was general sympathy with Alexander, as a German prince. Great admiration was aroused by his achievements, and extreme indignation was felt on account of the treatment he had received at the hands of Russia. Bismarck, however, supported Russia, insisting that Germany had no interests in the Balkans.

After Bismarck's retirement from office, Germany not only supported Austrian interests in the Balkans, but also sought to acquire a dominant influence in Constantinople. This was regarded in Russia as an

invasion of its special sphere of influence, justifying a counter-invasion of the Austrian sphere. When, in 1908, Austria converted its occupation and administration of Bosnia and Herzegovina into a formal annexation of these provinces, the protest of the Serbs was supported by Russia. The German Emperor, however, "took his stand in shining armor at the side of his ally," and Russia, weakened by its recent conflict with Japan, was forced to acquiesce.

V

The Krüger Telegram (1896)

One of the aspirations of Germany has been the creation of a great colonial empire in Africa. To that end she began, in the nineties, to cultivate intimate relations with President Krüger of the Transvaal, in the hope of controlling and, possibly, of ultimately absorbing the Boer republic. German support of Krüger, it was clearly realized, would make trouble for Great Britain, between which and the Transvaal there were serious controversies over suzerainty and over the political grievances of the Uitlanders. Early in 1895 President Krüger stated, at a celebration in honor of the Kaiser's birthday, that "the time had arrived for the establishment of the closest friendly relations between the Transvaal and Germany."

On December 29, 1895, in response to an invitation from the Uitlanders, Dr. Jameson, with 400 or 500 troopers of the British South African Company, crossed the Transvaal frontier and marched towards Johannesburg. The Reform Committee (Uitlanders) failed to coöperate, and Jameson was forced to surrender. The situation, already serious, was intensified

by the action of the Kaiser, who, on January 3, 1896, after consultation with his chancellor and other ministers, sent the following telegram to President Krüger:

I express to you my sincere congratulations that, without appealing to the help of friendly powers, you and your people have succeeded in repelling with your own forces the armed bands which had broken into your country and in maintaining the independence of your country against foreign aggression.

In Great Britain this telegram caused profound indignation. It was felt to be directed against Great Britain, and it was regarded as a deliberate attempt to challenge the British position in South Africa. The incident marked the beginning of, and in large part contributed to, that settled antagonism between Great Britain and Germany which is being fought out in the present war. By holding out specious hopes to President Krüger, it helped to bring on the South African War and the defeat of the Boers. In this instance, as in others, Germany, as Lichnowsky points out, "backed the wrong horse."

The English journalist, Mr. Valentine Chirol, has recently given the substance of a conversation which he, as correspondent of the London *Times*, had with Baron Marschall at the German Foreign Office concerning the Krüger telegram. See the London *Times* of May 14, 1918.

VI

The British-French Colonial Agreements (1898-1904)

The chief cause of friction between France and Great Britain during the later decades of the 19th century had been their colliding interests in Egypt, which Britain occupied in 1882. When in 1898 the control of the upper Nile was wrested from the Mahdi by the

British-Egyptian forces under Kitchener, a conflict arose over the French occupation of Fashoda. This was adjusted March 21, 1899, by a joint declaration, supplementing an earlier convention, which had been signed June 14, 1898. The convention of 1898 delimited French and British possessions and spheres of influence east and west of the Niger; the supplementary agreement of 1899 drew a boundary between the British Egyptian Soudan and the French possessions and spheres of influence in Central Africa.

A general settlement of all outstanding differences between the two countries was attained by a convention and two declarations signed at London, April 8, 1904. In this general settlement, France recognized the existing British control of Egypt, and Great Britain recognized that France was entitled to a dominant interest in Morocco (see note vii, below). France undertook to come to an understanding with Spain regarding their respective interests on the Moorish coast, and a treaty embodying such an understanding was concluded in the same year (1904). The British-French agreement contained five secret articles; and, although it was officially announced in October, 1904, that Spain had accepted the British-French arrangements and had itself signed a convention with France, this convention was not published. The only reason, apparently, why these further arrangements were kept secret was that the contingency that the Sultan of Morocco might "cease to exercise authority" was envisaged, in which event there was to be a division of his realm between France and Spain.

On the west coast of Africa minor cessions of territory were made to France by Great Britain, and in Central Africa the line drawn in 1898 was modified

to the advantage of the French. British objections to the tariff introduced by France in Madagascar were withdrawn.

In Siam the British and French spheres of influence were delimited.

Privileges in the Newfoundland fishing industry secured to France by the Treaty of Utrecht were relinquished, French citizens engaged in that industry being indemnified by Great Britain. The respective rights of British and French fishermen in the Newfoundland waters were accurately defined.

All the British-French conventions above summarized were published in *British and Foreign State Papers*. The Egypt-Morocco convention of 1904 was republished in 1911, with the secret articles, as number 24 of the *Treaty Series*. According to Bertrand Russell (*Justice in War Time*, 1916, page 144) the French-Spanish Morocco treaty was published in *Le Matin* (Paris), in November, 1911.

VII

The Moroccan Question (1905–1906)

Morocco, at the beginning of the present century, was one of the few desirable fields still open for colonial enterprise on the part of the Powers. In consequence, it was for a decade or so one of the storm centers of European diplomacy. By reason of geographical proximity (in Algeria) France had a special interest in suppressing the chronic disorder in Morocco, particularly on the Algerian border. This French interest was recognized by Great Britain in the following article of the convention of April 8, 1904:

His Britannic Majesty's Government, for their part, recognize that it appertains to France, more particularly as a Power whose dominions are coterminous for a great distance with those of Morocco, to preserve order in that country, and to provide assistance for the purpose of all administrative, economic, financial and military reforms which it may require.

Apparently this was satisfactory to Germany; for on April 2, 1904, von Bülow, the German chancellor, stated in the Reichstag that "from the point of view of German interests we have nothing to complain of."

But Germany was not satisfied, because the convention indicated that England and France were ready to compose their quarrels, which had long been a source of diplomatic profit to Germany. Nothing was done, however, until the defeat of Russia in the battle of Mukden revealed the weakness of France's ally. Suddenly, on March 31, 1905, the German Emperor appeared at Tangier, Morocco, and proceeded to pay a visit to the Sultan, Abdul-Aziz, in the course of which he spoke as follows:

It is to the Sultan in his position of an independent sovereign that I am paying my visit today. I hope that under the Sovereignty of the Sultan a free Morocco will remain open to the peaceful rivalry of all nations, without monopoly or annexation, on the basis of absolute equality. The object of my visit to Tangier is to make it known that I am determined to do all that is in my power to safeguard efficaciously the interests of Germany in Morocco, for I look upon the Sultan as an absolutely independent sovereign.

This demonstrative intervention created a diplomatic crisis in Europe and was generally regarded as a challenge to the recently formed Entente. The demand of Germany that France bring the Moroccan

question before an international conference was accepted, in spite of the opposition of M. Delcassé, the French foreign minister, who was thus virtually compelled to resign at German dictation.

The Conference met at Algeciras, in Spain, in January, 1906. The participants were the twelve Powers (including the United States) who were parties to the Convention of Madrid of 1880, and Morocco. The outcome was a diplomatic defeat for Germany, which was supported by Austria-Hungary alone, even Italy, the ally of Germany, ranging itself on the side of France. The Act of Algeciras provided for the settlement of the Moroccan question upon "the triple principle of the sovereignty and independence of His Majesty the Sultan, the integrity of his domains, and economic liberty without any inequality." However, while accepting in theory the German demand for internationalization of control, the Act accorded to France and Spain a privileged position with respect to financial and police measures in Morocco.

VIII

Agadir (*1911*)

Germany's last card in Moroccan diplomacy was played in 1911. On July 1 of that year the German gunboat *Panther* appeared at Agadir, on the southern coast of Morocco, ostensibly to protect German interests, but in reality to test the strength of the Triple Entente. This action of Germany was the more surprising because, by the treaty of February, 1909, it had recognized the paramount position of France in Morocco. For some time Germany ignored the repeated requests of Great Britain for explanation as to

German intentions, but the positive intimation by Lloyd George, in his speech at the Mansion House, July 21, that Great Britain intended to back up France, led Germany to compromise, by withdrawing completely from Morocco in consideration of territorial concessions by France in West Africa (Franco-German treaty of November 4, 1911). With this adjustment the Moroccan question disappeared from European diplomacy.

IX

The British-Russian Convention (1907)

On August 31, 1907, a convention was signed by Great Britain and Russia, similar in its nature to that concluded by Great Britain and France in 1904. The purpose of the British-Russian agreement was to settle all outstanding differences between the two Powers with respect to their interests in Asia. It comprises three separate arrangements, as follows:

1. The two parties mutually engage to respect the integrity and independence of Persia; but, having regard to each other's special geographical or economic interests, they agree to recognize certain spheres of influence in that country: a Russian sphere in the north and a British sphere in the south, with Central Persia not directly included in either.

2. Afghanistan is recognized as lying outside of Russian influence. All Russian relations with Afghanistan are to be carried on through the British government, which declares that it has no intention of changing the political status of Afghanistan. The principle of equality of commercial opportunity in Afghanistan is maintained.

3. Thibet is recognized as under the suzerainty of China. All negotiations with Thibet are to be conducted through the

Chinese government. Its territorial integrity is to be respected; neither party is to send representatives to Lhassa; and no concessions or other rights in Thibet are to be sought or obtained.

X

The Grey-Cambon Correspondence (1912)

Sir Edward Grey to M. Cambon, French Ambassador in London

Foreign Office, November 22, 1912

My dear Ambassador:

From time to time in recent years the French and British naval and military experts have consulted together. It has always been understood that such consultation does not restrict the freedom of either Government to decide at any future time whether or not to assist the other by armed force. We have agreed that consultation between experts is not, and ought not to be regarded as, an engagement that commits either Government to action in a contingency that has not arisen and may never arise. The disposition, for instance, of the French and British fleets respectively at the present moment is not based upon an engagement to coöperate in war.

You have, however, pointed out that, if either Government had grave reason to expect an unprovoked attack by a third Power, it might become essential to know whether it could in that event depend upon the armed assistance of the other.

I agree that, if either Government had grave reason to expect an unprovoked attack by a third Power, or something that threatened the general peace, it should immediately discuss with the other whether both Governments should act together to prevent aggression and to preserve peace, and, if so, what measures they would be prepared to take in common. If these measures involved action, the plans of the General Staffs would at once be taken into consideration, and the Governments would then decide what effect should be given to them.

M. Cambon, French Ambassador in London, to Sir Edward Grey

French Embassy, London
November 23, 1912

Dear Sir Edward:

You reminded me in your letter of yesterday, 22nd November, that during the last few years the military and naval authorities of France and Great Britain had consulted with each other from time to time; that it had always been understood that these consultations should not restrict the liberty of either Government to decide in the future whether they should lend each other the support of their armed forces; that, on either side, these consultations between experts were not and should not be considered as engagements binding our Governments to take action in certain eventualities; that, however, I had remarked to you that, if one or other of the two Governments had grave reasons to fear an unprovoked attack on the part of a third Power, it would become essential to know whether it could count on the armed support of the other.

Your letter answers that point, and I am authorized to state that, in the event of one of our two Governments having grave reasons to fear either an act of aggression from a third Power, or some event threatening the general peace, that Government would immediately examine with the other the question whether both Governments should act together in order to prevent the act of aggression or preserve peace. If so, the two Governments would deliberate as to the measures which they would be prepared to take in common; if those measures involved action, the two Governments would take into immediate consideration the plans of their General Staffs and would then decide as to the effect to be given to those plans.

[*British Diplomatic Correspondence, relating to the outbreak of the War*, No. 105, enclosures 1 and 2.]

XI

The First Balkan War (1912–1913)

In 1912 Turkey was at war with Italy over Tripoli. In addition, Albania was in revolt, Crete was clamoring for annexation to Greece, and Macedonia, for years in a state of anarchy, became the scene of frightful massacres of Bulgarians and Serbians at the hands of the Mohammedan Turks. All this at a time when German influence was paramount at Constantinople. Early in the year, the Balkan states achieved what had been deemed impossible—a league against the common enemy. This was brought about by a series of treaties between Bulgaria, Serbia, Greece, and Montenegro, supplemented by military conventions, all of which contemplated not only relief for the subject Christian populations of Turkey but also the extension of territory at Turkey's expense.

In spite of efforts by the Great Powers to preserve peace, the Balkan League mobilized in the early autumn of 1912. Montenegro declared war against Turkey on October 8, and its allies issued similar declarations ten days later. Then followed a remarkable series of campaigns, in which the Balkan Allies were uniformly successful. By the first of December, Adrianople was invested; Macedonia and, in part, Albania were occupied; Serbia had reached the Adriatic; Greeks and Bulgarians were at Saloniki, and the Montenegrins were laying siege to Skutari. An armistice was signed on December 3, and a peace conference between Turkey and the Allies was opened at London on December 16.

By this time, however, the Balkan War had raised several questions affecting the general peace of Europe

and necessitating action on the part of the European Powers to prevent a general war. Consequently, parallel with the peace conference, an ambassadorial conference sat in London under the presidency of Sir Edward Grey for the purpose of advising the belligerent parties and of taking necessary decisions on matters of European concern. The demand of Serbia for territory on the Adriatic conflicted with the foreign policies of Austria and Italy. So, also, did the desire of Montenegro to capture and retain Skutari. This town, in the opinion of Austria and Italy as well as of the other Powers, should form part of an autonomous Albania, "the independence and neutrality" of which had already been proclaimed by an Albanian assembly at Avlona on November 28. The ambassadorial conference promptly agreed that Albania should be autonomous and that Serbia should have commercial access to Adriatic ports.

The peace conference, however, found it impossible to reconcile the demands of the respective belligerents and, the armistice having expired, the war was renewed. Again Turkey was defeated and again, after much diplomatic discussion with the Great Powers, an armistice was signed by all the belligerents save Montenegro. The Balkan Allies accepted the mediation of the Powers, and the peace conference opened for a second time in London on May 20. On this occasion a treaty of peace was successfully negotiated. It was signed on May 30. By its terms the frontier of Turkey in Europe was established by a line running from Enos on the Ægean to Midia on the Black Sea. All territory west of this line was ceded to the Allies, who were left to divide it among themselves in accordance with their respective treaties of alliance.

Turkey gave up Crete, which was later apportioned to Greece; the autonomy of Albania was recognized; and the disposal of the Ægean islands was left in the hands of the Great Powers.

Meanwhile Montenegro, in defiance of the Powers, had persisted in the siege of Skutari. On April 10 a blockade of the Montenegrin coast was put in force by an international squadron. On April 22 Skutari fell, but this made the Powers only the more insistent that Montenegro should evacuate the captured fortress. Finally, faced by an intervention which would probably be entrusted to Austria-Hungary, Montenegro yielded. For its compliance, it received assurance of a loan.

At the London ambassadorial conference in 1912, it was agreed that a European prince should be nominated as ruler of Albania. Early in 1914 the new throne was offered to William of Wied. He arrived at Durazzo March 7, 1914. Early in the summer of the same year he was driven out of Albania by a successful insurrection.

XII

The Second Balkan War (1913)

The Second Balkan War arose out of disputes over the spoils of the war against Turkey. The peace conference had failed to reach agreement on this matter, and the treaty left it to the Balkan Allies to apportion the ceded territory among themselves by supplementary conventions. But there was slight prospect of settlement. Bulgaria disputed the claim of Greece to possess Saloniki and the territory to the north and east of it. Serbia challenged the arrangement made in the Bulgar-Serbian treaty of 1912, maintaining that

the creation of Albania had essentially modified the equity of that arrangement. A military convention was promptly concluded between Greece, Serbia and Montenegro. An attempt was made to avert conflict through Russian mediation, but difficulties were raised over demobilization and all parties refused to recede. Suddenly, on June 30, 1913, the Bulgarians attacked the Greek and Serbian armies, hoping to crush them separately before they could unite. In the campaign that followed the Greeks and Serbians were more than a match for the Bulgarians, but the issue was decided by the intervention of the Rumanian army. Meanwhile Turkey took advantage of Bulgaria's extremity to recover Adrianople. As a result Bulgaria was compelled to ask for an armistice. Peace was restored in the Balkans by the Treaty of Bucharest (August 10, 1913). Bulgaria, recognizing defeat, had to yield most of its new acquisitions to Greece and Serbia and a considerable portion of its former territory to Rumania. A treaty of peace with Turkey on September 29 involved further cessions on the part of Bulgaria.

XIII

Rumanian Intervention (1913)

In the negotiations following the First Balkan War, Rumania had demanded a "rectified" frontier in the Dobrudja, in return for its neutrality, which was alleged to have been maintained on the understanding that Austria-Hungary and Russia would support the Rumanian claims when the war was over. In consequence, Bulgaria ceded to Rumania the town of Silistria with some adjoining territory. This did not

satisfy Rumania; and, as already stated, it intervened in the Second Balkan War. Its reasons for intervening were set forth in its declaration of July 9:

The Rumanian Government gave due warning to the Bulgarian Government that, if the Balkan allies were to find themselves in a state of war, Rumania would not be able to maintain the reserve which it has hitherto observed in the interests of peace and would be compelled to take action. The Bulgarian Government did not consider it necessary to reply to this communication. On the contrary, war unhappily began by a series of sudden attacks by the Bulgarians against the Serbian troops, without any observance by the Bulgarians of even the elementary rules of preliminary notification, which would at least have testified to a respect for the conventions of international usage. In presence of this situation the Rumanian Government has ordered the Rumanian army to enter Bulgaria.

[*Annual Register*, 1913, p. 351.]

XIV

San Giuliano's Warning to Austria (1913)

In a speech delivered in the Italian Parliament, December 5, 1914, Signor Giolitti declared that on August 9, 1913, Austria communicated to Italy and to Germany its intention of taking action against Serbia. It described such action as defensive and stated that it hoped to receive Italian as well as German support. Signor Giolitti was at that time prime minister and, on receiving the report of the Italian minister of foreign affairs, Marquis di San Giuliano, he directed the latter to reply in the following sense:

If Austria intervenes against Serbia, it is clear that a *casus foederis* cannot be established. It is a step which she is taking on her own account. There is no question of defense, inas-

[166]

much as no one is thinking of attacking her. It is necessary that a declaration to this effect should be made to Austria in the most formal manner, and we must hope for action on the part of Germany to dissuade Austria from this most perilous adventure.

XV

Liman von Sanders

After its crushing defeat at the hands of the Balkan Allies, Turkey applied to Germany for a military commission to reorganize its army. In October, 1913, it was announced that General Liman von Sanders had been chosen head of such a commission, which was to include some thirty other German officers. Russia at once began to protest, and protested the more strongly when it was stated that Liman von Sanders, in addition to his advisory duties, was to command the First Army Corps at Constantinople. This created a delicate situation. According to the Russian contention, this German military command would control the capital and the Straits and would thus be in a position to affect Russian interests adversely. Besides, the German ambassador at Constantinople would, in effect, be backed up by military power to the prejudice of the other (and especially of the Entente) ambassadors. The Russian press was intensely excited over the appointment, but the Russian government worked for a compromise, suggesting that Liman's headquarters be transferred to Adrianople and that Germany support Armenian reforms. On December 14, the Russian, French and British ambassadors asked the grand vizier for information as to the scope of the powers conferred on Liman von Sanders. No official answer was given, but it was

announced in the course of a day or two that Turkey was not actuated by political motives but had merely applied for the services of an expert whose duties were to be chiefly educational. It was further stated that Liman would not command the garrisons at the Bosporus and the Dardanelles.

According to Mr. Henry Morgenthau, former American ambassador to Turkey, it was asserted by the German *chargé d'affaires*, in the matter of precedence at a diplomatic dinner given by Mr. Morgenthau, that von Sanders was "the personal representative of the Kaiser and as such . . . entitled to equal rank with the ambassadors. He should have been placed ahead of the cabinet ministers and the foreign ministers" [*The World's Work*, May, 1918, p. 66]. Fortunately for Morgenthau, the order of precedence at the dinner had been arranged by Pallavicini, the Austrian ambassador, who was at the time doyen of the diplomatic corps.

It may be added that after the outbreak of the war in August, 1914 (but before Turkey had become a belligerent), Liman von Sanders was appointed commander-in-chief of the Turkish army.

XVI

British-German Negotiations (1912–1914)

The rapid development of German naval power had, as Prince Lichnowsky indicates, aroused anxiety in Great Britain; and the necessity, arising from Britain's insular position, of keeping its fleet equal to the combined fleets of any two other Powers was throwing a heavy burden on the British taxpayers. Lord Haldane was sent to Berlin early in 1912, to see whether

the German plan for the creation of a third squadron could not be modified. This suggestion being negatived, he inquired whether it would not be possible to delay construction, to "spread the tempo." It was indicated, on the German side, that no concessions could be made in the matter of naval construction unless Germany could be assured that, in case it should be involved in war, Great Britain would remain neutral. It was proposed that such assurance should be given by a formal treaty. After Haldane's return to London, negotiations on this matter were continued between Sir Edward Grey and the German ambassador, Count Metternich. Various formulas were suggested, but no agreement was attained, because the German diplomats found the British proposals inadequate, while the British regarded the German proposals as ambiguous. The Germans wished for an agreement that, if either nation should become involved in a war "in which it cannot be said to be the aggressor," the other nation should remain neutral; but they proposed to add:

The duty of neutrality which arises out of the preceding article has no application in so far as it may not be reconcilable with existing agreements which the high contracting parties have already made.

This, as Lord Haldane puts it, meant that while Germany, in the case of a European conflict, would have remained free to support her friends, this country would have been forbidden to raise a finger in defense of hers. Germany could arrange without difficulty that the formal inception of hostilities should rest with Austria.

Another clause in the German draft forbade "the making of new agreements which render it impossible for either of the parties to observe neutrality towards

the other." This, of course, meant that while the Triple Alliance treaties were to remain binding and Great Britain was to be pledged to neutrality if Germany should make war to support Austria, Great Britain was to make no similar treaty arrangements with Russia or with France. "In a word," as Lord Haldane observes, "there was to be a guaranty of absolute neutrality on one side, but not on the other."

In response to a request for counter-proposals, Sir Edward Grey, on March 14, 1912, gave Count Metternich the following draft formula, which had been approved by the Cabinet:

England will make no unprovoked attack upon Germany, and pursue no aggressive policy towards her.

Aggression upon Germany is not the subject, and forms no part of any treaty, understanding or combination to which England is now a party, nor will she become a party to anything that has such an object.

Count Metternich thought this formula inadequate, and suggested two alternative additional clauses:

England will therefore observe at least a benevolent neutrality should war be forced upon Germany, or: England will therefore, as a matter of course, remain neutral if a war is forced upon Germany.

Sir Edward Grey considered that the British proposals were sufficient. He explained that if Germany desired to crush France, England might not be able to sit still, though if France were aggressive or attacked Germany, no support would be given by His Majesty's government or approved by England. He eventually proposed the following formula:

The two powers being mutually desirous of securing peace and friendship between them, England declares that she will neither make nor join in any unprovoked attack upon Ger-

many. Aggression upon Germany is not the subject, and forms no part of any treaty, understanding or combination to which England is now a party, nor will she become a party to anything that has such an object.

· Count Metternich, in accordance with instructions received from Berlin, stated that the project for a further increase of the German navy could not be abandoned except on the basis of a neutrality treaty of a far-reaching character and leaving no doubt as to its interpretation. "He admitted," Lord Haldane writes, "that the chancellor's wish amounted to a guaranty of absolute neutrality."

At this point the negotiations for a reduction of naval armaments and for a neutrality agreement were dropped.

Sir Edward Grey, however, expressed the hope that this result would not put an end to negotiations or form an insurmountable obstacle to better relations. The British government hoped that the formula which it had suggested might be considered in connection with the discussion of territorial arrangements, even if it did not prove effective in preventing the increase of naval expenditure. Sir Edward Grey added that, if some arrangement could be made between the two governments, it would have a favorable though indirect effect upon naval expenditure as time went on; it would have, moreover, a favorable and direct effect upon public opinion in both countries.

This suggestion was taken up; and at this point the British-German negotiations entered upon their third phase, that of the adjustment of conflicting interests in Africa and in Asia. These, as Prince Lichnowsky indicates, were under way when he came to London.

Brief statements regarding the negotiations for a

neutrality agreement were made by Prime Minister Asquith, in a speech at Cardiff, October 2, 1914, and by Sir Edward Grey, in a speech at London, March 22, 1915. These statements were substantially confirmed by extracts from the correspondence of 1912, published by the German Foreign Office in July, 1915. Further documentary material was published by the British Foreign Office, August 31, 1915. The fullest account of the negotiations—an account in which the question of naval armaments is brought into connection with the question of British neutrality—is given in Lord Haldane's report, made in 1912, a large part of which was published by the British government late in May, 1918.

See *New York Times*, June 2, 1918.

XVII

The Portuguese Colonies in Africa

The African treaty negotiated by Prince Lichnowsky dealt, as he states, with German and British spheres of influence in the Portuguese colonies. The following are the Portuguese dependencies in Africa (excluding the Cape Verde Islands), with statistical data, as given in the *Statesman's Year Book* for 1915:

1. Portuguese Guinea, on the west coast of Africa, south of Cape Verde; area, 13,940 square miles; population, 820,000.

2. Islands of Principe and St. Thomas, in the Gulf of Guinea; area, 360 square miles; population, 42,103.

3. Angola, between German South-West Africa on the south and the Belgian and French Congo on the north; area, 484,800 square miles; population, 4,119,000.

4. Portuguese East Africa, bounded by British Central and South Africa and German East Africa; area, 293,400 square miles; population, 3,120,000.

XVIII

Anglo-Portuguese Treaties

According to the *British and Foreign State Papers*
(vol. i, page 462) there were still subsisting in 1814
(and presumably still subsist) several ancient treaties
of friendship and alliance between England and Portugal, the earliest dating back to 1373, in the reign of
Edward III. The treaty of Charles II's time, referred
to by Lichnowsky, was made in 1661 and constituted
the marriage contract between Charles II and Cathe-
rine, Infanta of Portugal. Article 16 promised that

if the King of Portugal shall be pressed in any extraordinary
manner by the power of the enemies, all the King of Great
Britain's ships which shall at any time be in the Mediterranean
Sea or at Tangier shall have instructions in such cases to obey
any orders they shall receive from the King of Portugal and
shall betake themselves to his succour and relief.

Also, under Article 17, the King of Great Britain
was to

afford timely assistance of men and shipping according to
the exigency of the circumstances, and proportionable to the
necessity of the King of Portugal.

XIX

The British-German Bagdad Agreement

In his book entitled *Obstacles to Peace* (Boston, 1917,
pp. 41–42), Mr. S. S. McClure states that in 1916
he obtained from Dr. Jaeckh, who had been private
secretary to von Kiderlen-Wächter, the terms of the
Bagdad Treaty which was to have been signed in 1914.
He took this statement, he tells us, to the German
Foreign Office in Berlin, where certain slight corrections were made; and he publishes the document

"exactly as I got it from Dr. Zimmermann, the foreign minister of the imperial German government."

1. The Bagdad Railway from Constantinople to Basra is definitely left to German capital in coöperation with Turkey. In the territory of the Bagdad Railway German economical working will not be hindered by England.

2. Basra becomes a sea harbor in the building of which German capital is concerned with sixty per cent. and English capital with forty per cent. For the navigation from Basra to the Persian Gulf the independence of the open sea is agreed to.

3. Kuweit is excluded from the agreement between Germany and England.

4. In the navigation of the Tigris, English capital is interested with fifty per cent., German capital with twenty-five per cent., and Turkish with twenty-five per cent.

5. The oil-wells of the whole of Mesopotamia shall be developed by a British company, the capital of which shall be given at fifty per cent. by England, at twenty-five per cent. by the German Bank, at twenty-five per cent. by the "Royal Dutch Company" (a company which is Dutch, but closely connected with England). For the irrigation works there had been intended a similar understanding. The rights of the Anglo-Persian Oil Company, in which, as is known, the English Government is concerned, remained unaffected. This society exercises south of Basra, on the Shatt-el-Arab as well as in all south and central Persia, a monopoly on the production and transport of oil.

6. A simultaneous German-French agreement leaves free hand to French capital for the construction of railways in southern Syria and Palestine.

Besides this, there is an agreement, already made before, between Germany and England, concerning Africa, with a repartition of their spheres of influence in Angola and Mozambique.

Finally there is to be mentioned the Morocco agreement, which established the political predominance of France in

Morocco, but, on the other hand, stated the principle of "open door" to the trade of all nations.

An analysis of the German-French agreement alluded to above, under point 6, is to be found in a dispatch dated February 20, 1914, from the Belgian minister at Berlin to the Belgian foreign minister. This dispatch is to be found in the collection of Belgian documents seized by the Germans at Brussels and published by the German imperial government. [See *American Journal of International Law*, April, 1918, page 392; or this volume, page 238.]

XX

The Potsdam Conference of July 5, 1914

In "Ambassador Morgenthau's Story," of which the first two instalments have appeared in *The World's Work*, May and June, 1918, Mr. Morgenthau, our ambassador at Constantinople during the earlier part of the World War, tells what he learned from the German ambassador, Baron von Wangenheim.

On July 4, 1914, Mr. Morgenthau was surprised to note the absence of the German ambassador from the requiem mass for the Archduke Ferdinand and his wife, and also from the celebration of Independence Day at the American embassy. Afterwards Mr. Morgenthau had the explanation from Wangenheim's own lips. He had left some days before for Berlin. The Kaiser had summoned him to an imperial council, which met on July 5th at Potsdam (page 73).

The Kaiser presided; nearly all the ambassadors attended; Wangenheim came to tell of Turkey and enlighten his associates on the situation in Constantinople. Moltke, then chief of staff, was there, representing the army, and Admiral von Tirpitz spoke for the navy. The great bankers, railroad direc-

tors, and the captains of German industry, all of whom were as necessary to German war preparations as the army itself, also attended.

Wangenheim now told me that the Kaiser solemnly put the question to each man in turn: Was he ready for war? All replied "Yes" except the financiers. They said that they must have two weeks to sell their foreign securities and to make loans. At that time few people had looked upon the Serajevo tragedy as something that was likely to cause war. This conference took all precautions that no such suspicion should be aroused. It decided to give the bankers time to readjust their finances for the coming war, and then the several members went quietly back to their work or started on vacations. The Kaiser went to Norway on his yacht, von Bethmann Hollweg left for a rest, and Wangenheim returned to Constantinople.

In telling me about this conference, Wangenheim, of course, admitted that Germany had precipitated the war. I think that he was rather proud of the whole performance; proud that Germany had gone about the matter in so methodical and far-seeing a way; especially proud that he himself had been invited to participate in so momentous a gathering.
. . . Whenever I hear people arguing about the responsibility for this war or read the clumsy and lying excuses put forth by Germany, I simply recall the burly figure of Wangenheim as he appeared that August afternoon, puffing away at a huge black cigar, and giving me his account of this historic meeting. Why waste any time discussing the matter after that? . . .

This imperial conference took place July 5; the Serbian ultimatum was sent on July 22. That is just about the two weeks interval which the financiers had demanded to complete their plans. All the great stock exchanges of the world show that the German bankers profitably used this interval. Their records disclose that stocks were being sold in large quantities and that prices declined rapidly. At that time the markets were somewhat puzzled at this movement; Wangenheim's explanation clears up any doubts that may still remain. Ger-

many was changing her securities into cash, for war purposes. . . .

Wangenheim not only gave me the details of this Potsdam conference, but he disclosed the same secret to the Marquis Garroni, the Italian ambassador at Constantinople. Italy was at that time technically Germany's ally (pages 170, 171).

XXI

Sir Edward Grey's Warning of July 29, 1914

Sir Edward Grey to Sir E. Goschen,
British Ambassador at Berlin

Foreign Office, July 29, 1914

Sir:

After speaking to the German ambassador this afternoon about the European situation, I said that I wished to say to him, in a quite private and friendly way, something that was on my mind. The situation was very grave. While it was restricted to the issues at present actually involved we had no thought of interfering in it. But if Germany became involved in it, and then France, the issue might be so great that it would involve all European interests; and I did not wish him to be misled by the friendly tone of our conversation—which I hoped would continue—into thinking that we should stand aside.

He said that he quite understood this, but he asked whether I meant that we should, under certain circumstances, intervene?

I replied that I did not wish to say that, or to use anything that was like a threat or an attempt to apply pressure by saying that, if things became worse, we should intervene. There would be no question of our intervening if Germany was not involved, or even if France was not involved. But we knew very well, that if the issue did become such that we thought British interests required us to intervene, we must intervene at once, and the decision would have to be very rapid, just as the decisions of other Powers had to be. I hoped

[177]

that the friendly tone of our conversations would continue as at present, and that I should be able to keep as closely in touch with the German Government in working for peace. But if we failed in our efforts to keep the peace, and if the issue spread so that it involved practically every European interest, I did not wish to be open to any reproach from him that the friendly tone of all our conversations had misled him or his Government into supposing that we should not take action, and to the reproach that, if they had not been so misled, the course of things might have been different.

The German ambassador took no exception to what I had said; indeed, he told me that it accorded with what he had already given in Berlin as his view of the situation.

That this warning was promptly transmitted to Berlin is shown by the following extract from a dispatch sent to Sir Edward Grey by Sir Edward Goschen, British ambassador at Berlin, on July 30, reporting a conversation with Foreign Secretary von Jagow:

His Excellency added that [the] telegram received from Prince Lichnowsky last night contains matter which he had heard with regret, but not exactly with surprise, and at all events he thoroughly appreciated [the] frankness and loyalty with which you had spoken.

[*British Diplomatic Correspondence*, *relating to the outbreak of the War*, Nos. 89, 98.]

XXII

Correspondence between the President of the French Republic and King George

The President of the French Republic to His Majesty King George

Paris, July 31, 1914

Dear and Great Friend:

In the grave events through which Europe is passing, I feel bound to convey to your Majesty the information which the

Government of the Republic have received from Germany. The military preparations which are being undertaken by the Imperial Government, especially in the immediate neighbourhood of the French frontier, are being pushed forward every day with fresh vigour and speed. France, resolved to continue to the very end to do all that lies within her power to maintain peace, has, up to the present, confined herself solely to the most indispensable precautionary measures. But it does not appear that her prudence and moderation serve to check Germany's action; indeed, quite the reverse. We are, perhaps, then, in spite of the moderation of the Government of the Republic and the calm of public opinion, on the eve of the most terrible events.

From all the information which reaches us it would seem that war would be inevitable if Germany were convinced that the British Government would not intervene in a conflict in which France might be engaged: if, on the other hand, Germany were convinced that the *entente cordiale* would be affirmed, in case of need, even to the extent of taking the field side by side, there would be the greatest chance that peace would remain unbroken.

It is true that our military and naval arrangements leave complete liberty to your Majesty's Government, and that, in the letters exchanged in 1912 between Sir Edward Grey and M. Paul Cambon, Great Britain and France entered into nothing more than a mutual agreement to consult one another in the event of European tension, and to examine in concert whether common action were advisable.

But the character of close friendship which public feeling has given in both countries to the *entente* between Great Britain and France, the confidence with which our two Governments have never ceased to work for the maintenance of peace, and the signs of sympathy which your Majesty has ever shown to France, justify me in informing you quite frankly of my impressions, which are those of the Government of the Republic and of all France.

[179]

It is, I consider, on the language and the action of the British Government that henceforward the last chances of a peaceful settlement depend.

We, ourselves, from the initial stages of the crisis, have enjoined upon our Ally an attitude of moderation from which they have not swerved. In concert with your Majesty's Government, and in conformity with Sir E. Grey's latest suggestions, we will continue to act on the same lines.

But if all efforts at conciliation emanate from one side, and if Germany and Austria can speculate on the abstention of Great Britain, Austria's demands will remain inflexible, and an agreement between her and Russia will become impossible. I am profoundly convinced that, at the present moment, the more Great Britain, France, and Russia can give a deep impression that they are united in their diplomatic action, the more possible will it be to count upon the preservation of peace.

I beg that your Majesty will excuse a step which is only inspired by the hope of seeing the European balance of power definitely reaffirmed.

His Majesty King George to the President
of the French Republic

Buckingham Palace, August 1, 1914

Dear and Great Friend:

I most highly appreciate the sentiments which moved you to write to me in so cordial and friendly a spirit, and I am grateful to you for having stated your views so fully and frankly.

You may be assured that the present situation in Europe has been the cause of much anxiety and preoccupation to me, and I am glad to think that our two Governments have worked so amicably together in endeavouring to find a peaceful solution of the questions at issue.

It would be a source of real satisfaction to me if our united efforts were to meet with success, and I am still not without hope that the terrible events which seem so near may be averted.

I admire the restraint which you and your Government are exercising in refraining from taking undue military measures on the frontier and not adopting an attitude which could in any wise be interpreted as a provocative one.

I am personally using my best endeavours with the Emperors of Russia and of Germany towards finding some solution by which actual military operations may at any rate be postponed, and time be thus given for calm discussion between the Powers. I intend to prosecute these efforts without intermission so long as any hope remains of an amicable settlement.

As to the attitude of my country, events are changing so rapidly that it is difficult to forecast future developments; but you may be assured that my Government will continue to discuss freely and frankly any point which might arise of interest to our two nations with M. Cambon.

[*Collected Diplomatic Documents*, part ix, sec. v, pp. 542–544.]

XXIII

Bonar Law's Letter of August 2, 1914

The letter to which Lichnowsky alludes is undoubtedly that in which the Conservative leader tendered to the prime minister the support of his party.

2d August, 1914

Dear Mr. Asquith:

Lord Lansdowne and I feel it our duty to inform you that in our opinion, as well as in that of all the colleagues whom we have been able to consult, it would be fatal to the honour and security of the United Kingdom to hesitate in supporting France and Russia at the present juncture; and we offer our unhesitating support to the Government in any measures they may consider necessary for that object.

Yours very truly,

A. BONAR LAW

[First published in the London *Times*, December 15, 1914.]

XXIV

King Albert's Telegram

Sir Edward Grey to Sir E. Goschen,
British Ambassador at Berlin

Foreign Office, August 4, 1914

The King of the Belgians has made an appeal to His Majesty the King for diplomatic intervention on behalf of Belgium in the following terms:

"Remembering the numerous proofs of your Majesty's friendship and that of your predecessor, and the friendly attitude of England in 1870 and the proof of friendship you have just given us again, I make a supreme appeal to the diplomatic intervention of your Majesty's Government to safeguard the integrity of Belgium."

His Majesty's Government are also informed that the German Government have delivered to the Belgian Government a note proposing friendly neutrality entailing free passage through Belgian territory, and promising to maintain the independence and integrity of the kingdom and its possessions at the conclusion of peace, threatening in case of refusal to treat Belgium as an enemy. An answer was requested within twelve hours.

We also understand that Belgium has categorically refused this as a flagrant violation of the law of nations.

His Majesty's Government are bound to protest against this violation of a treaty to which Germany is a party in common with themselves, and must request an assurance that the demand made upon Belgium will not be proceeded with and that her neutrality will be respected by Germany. You should ask for an immediate reply.

[*British Diplomatic Correspondence*, No. 153.]

II

Memoranda and Letters of Dr. Muehlon

Reprint of INTERNATIONAL CONCILIATION No. 130, September, 1918

INTRODUCTION

At the outbreak of the World War, Dr. Muehlon was a member of the Krupp board of directors at Essen. As his letters show, he was in touch with persons well informed of the real course of events. He was, therefore, one of the relatively few Germans who knew, from the outset, that the Central Empires had forced an unnecessary and unjustifiable war upon Europe; and he was one of the far smaller number of Germans whom the conduct of their government stirred to indignation and moral revolt. He was unwilling to further Germany's military activities by continued service in the munitions business, and he accordingly severed his connection with the Krupp Company and betook himself to Switzerland. He was willing, at first, to serve his country in other and peaceful ways, and he conducted negotiations on behalf of the German government to obtain wheat from Rumania, at a time when Rumania was still neutral. In 1917, however, he notified Chancellor von Bethmann-Hollweg that he had lost all confidence in the persons who were directing Germany's policies and saw no hope for the world or for Germany itself except in the transfer of power to men of a different stamp. In the spring and early summer of 1918 he published the memoranda and letters reproduced in the following pages, and also a collection of extracts from his war diary, extending from the early part of August to the middle of November, 1914.

In several important matters, Muehlon's revelations supplement the evidence previously at our disposal and confirm our earlier inferences. As regards the Austrian dispute with Serbia, he shows that, before the middle of July, 1914, full agreement had been reached between Berlin and Vienna as to the substance of the ultimatum to be sent to Belgrade. That the framing of this document was left to the Austrian Foreign Office seemed to Muehlon and to Krupp von Bohlen, as it seemed to the French ambassador at Berlin, almost incredible. There is no good reason, however, to doubt von Jagow's statement that the text of the ultimatum was not communicated to the German Foreign Office. Since 1890 the German Emperor had been, not only his own chancellor, but also his own foreign secretary; and the titular incumbents of these offices had been virtually vice-chancellors and under-secretaries.[1]

As regards the attitude of the German government towards an eventual Russian mobilization, Muehlon shows that the German Emperor had fully accepted, in advance, the fatal military theory that mobilization is not to be regarded as a precautionary measure but as an act of war.[2]

Of especial interest is Muehlon's report of the interview between the Emperor and von Bohlen. This confirms the impression, derived from other sources, that the unfavorable outcome of the Emperor's Moroccan enterprise (1905–1911) had left him in a warlike frame of mind. The failure of German diplomacy, directed by the monarch himself, had convinced him that in the next crisis he must unsheathe the German sword.

[1] Munroe Smith, *Militarism and Statecraft* (Putnam, 1918), p. 84.
[2] *Ibid.*, pp. 46, 77–78, 93–95, 101–103, 137–139.

He was stung by the knowledge that his conduct had been regarded as irresolute; and he repeatedly assured von Bohlen that, this time, he would not "fall down." His insistence struck von Bohlen as "comic." Sooner or later, all Germans will realize that it was tragic.

Of interest, also, is Helfferich's statement that the Emperor had gone on his Norwegian cruise in July, 1914, only for the sake of appearances. It will be remembered that in the summer of 1870, when the trap of the Hohenzollern candidacy for the throne of Spain was sprung on France, Bismarck was at his country home and King William was taking a cure at Ems. To equal the substantial achievements of a man of genius is not easy, but it is very easy to imitate his tricks.

Muehlon's evidence on these matters is, of course, hearsay evidence. He tells us what Helfferich heard from persons who are not named, but are described as men in a position to know the facts, and he repeats what von Bohlen heard from the Emperor and from von Jagow. Hearsay evidence, however, may be of great value. If the historian excluded all evidence that is barred by the technical rules of English judicial procedure, history would lose much of its clarity and completeness. The value of hearsay evidence depends upon the position and character of the immediate and ultimate witnesses. Its credibility is enhanced when the statements cited fit in with fully established facts and help to explain the course of events. Muehlon's revelations satisfy all these tests.

In one important matter Muehlon's evidence is direct. The dealings of the Belgian government with the Krupp Company were matters of which he had immediate personal knowledge. The German assertion that the Belgian government had arranged to

coöperate with Great Britain in aggressive war against Germany has never been substantiated; it has, indeed, been disproved; but Muehlon's testimony that, for years before the war, Belgium had made itself dependent on Germany for military supplies and that, at the outbreak of war, fortress artillery, ordered and fully paid for by the Belgian government and long ready for shipment, was, at the request of the Belgians themselves, still held in storage in the Krupp works at Essen—this testimony reduces the German assertion to an absurdity. It leaves the Belgians at fault in one respect only: they had misplaced their confidence. They believed that the German government would observe its treaty obligations and keep its repeatedly plighted faith.

Muehlon's recent pamphlet, made up of extracts from his war diary and entitled *The Devastation of Europe* (*Die Verheerung Europas*, Füssli, Zürich, 1918, 149 pp.), brings no revelations comparable in importance to those contained in his earlier memoranda and letters. The diary is nevertheless of interest and value as a contemporary picture of German sentiments and beliefs in the early months of the war. It is of interest, also, because it depicts, more fully than the letters, the reaction of at least one German conscience against the conduct of the German government—not only against the way in which that government precipitated the war, but also against the manner in which the war was waged. In this respect the pamphlet is a valuable addition to the scanty but growing German literature of protest.

MUNROE SMITH

DENKSCHRIFTEN UND BRIEFE VON DR. W. MUEHLON

Bis zum Kriegsausbruch Mitglied des Direktoriums der
Kruppwerke in Essen

I

DAS WIENER ULTIMATUM AN SERBIEN [1]

Mitte Juli 1914 hatte ich, wie des öfteren, eine
Besprechung mit Dr. *Helfferich*, dem damaligen
Direktor der Deutschen Bank in Berlin und heutigen
Stellvertreter des Reichskanzlers. Die Deutsche
Bank hatte eine ablehnende Haltung gegenüber
einigen grossen Transaktionen eingenommen (Bul-
garien und Türkei) an denen die Firma Krupp aus
geschäftlichen Gründen (Lieferung von Kriegsmaterial) ein lebhaftes Interesse hatte. Als einen der
Gründe zur Rechtfertigung der Haltung der Deutschen
Bank nannte mir Dr. Helfferich schliesslich den
folgenden: *Die politische Lage ist sehr bedrohlich
geworden*. Die Deutsche Bank muss auf jeden Fall
abwarten, ehe sie sich in Ausland weiter engagiert.
Die Österreicher sind dieser Tage beim Kaiser gewesen. Wien wird in acht Tagen ein sehr scharfes,
ganz kurz befristetes *Ultimatum* an Serbien stellen,
in dem Forderungen enthalten sind, wie Bestrafung

[1] Published in the *Berliner Tageblatt*, March 21, 1918. Reprinted
in *Die Freie Zeitung* (Bern), March 27, 1918. Also in *Meine Londoner
Mission*, von Fürst Lichnowsky (Füssli, Zürich, 1918), Anhang,
pp. 50–53.

MEMORANDA AND LETTERS OF DR. W. MUEHLON

Until the outbreak of the war a member of the Board of Directors of the Krupp Works at Essen

I

THE VIENNESE ULTIMATUM TO SERBIA

In the middle of July, 1914, I had, as I frequently had, a conversation with Dr. Helfferich, at that time director of the Deutsche Bank in Berlin, and now vice-chancellor of the Empire. The Deutsche Bank had indicated unwillingness to take part in several large transactions (in Bulgaria and Turkey) in which the Krupp Company, for business reasons (delivery of war material) had a lively interest. One of the reasons ultimately given me by Dr. Helfferich to justify the attitude of the Deutsche Bank was as follows: The political situation had become very menacing. The Deutsche Bank must in any case wait before entering into any further engagements in foreign countries. The Austrians had recently been with the Emperor. Within a week Vienna would send to Serbia a very sharply worded ultimatum with a very short term for reply. In it would be contained such demands as punishment of a number of officers, dissolution of political associations, criminal investigations in Serbia

einer Reihe von Offizieren, Auflösung politischer Vereine, Strafuntersuchungen in Serbien durch Beamte der Doppelmonarchie, überhaupt eine Reihe bestimmter, sofortiger Genugtuungen verlangt wird, andernfalls Österreich-Ungarn an Serbien den Krieg erklärt.

Dr. Helfferich fügte noch hinzu, dass *der Kaiser mit Entschiedenheit für dieses Vorgehen Österreich-Ungarns ausgesprochen habe*. Er habe gesagt, dass er einen österreichisch-ungarischen Konflikt mit Serbien als eine interne Angelegenheit zwischen diesen beiden Ländern betrachte, in die er keinem andern Staat eine Einmischung erlauben werde. Wenn Russland mobil mache, dann mache er auch mobil. Bei ihm aber bedeute Mobilmachung den sofortigen Krieg. *Diesmal gäbe es kein Schwanken*. Die Österreicher seien über diese entschlossene Haltung des Kaisers sehr befriedigt gewesen.

Als ich Dr. Helfferich daraufhin sagte, diese unheimliche Mitteilung mache meine ohnehin starken Befürchtungen eines Weltkrieges zur völligen Gewissheit, erwiderte er, es sehe jedenfalls so aus. Vielleicht überlegten sich aber Russland und Frankreich die Sache doch noch anders. Den Serben gehöre entschieden eine bleibende Lektion. Dies war die erste Mitteilung, die ich erhielt über die Besprechung des Kaisers mit den Bundesgenossen. Ich kannte Dr. Helfferichs besonders vertrauensvolle Beziehungen zu den Persönlichkeiten, die eingeweiht sein mussten, und die Verlässlichkeit seiner Mitteilung. Deshalb unterrichtete ich nach meiner Rückkehr von Berlin unverzüglich Herrn *Krupp von Bohlen und Halbach*, dessen Direktorium in Essen ich damals als Mitglied angehörte. Dr. Helfferich hatte mir dies übrigens ausdrücklich erlaubt. (Es bestand damals die Absicht,

by officials of the Dual Monarchy, and, in general, a series of definite and immediate satisfactions; otherwise Austria-Hungary would declare war on Serbia.

Dr. Helfferich added that the Emperor had expressed decided approval of this procedure on the part of Austria-Hungary. He had said that he regarded an Austro-Hungarian conflict with Serbia as an internal affair between these two countries, in which he would permit no other state to interfere. If Russia mobilized, he would then mobilize also. To him, however, mobilization meant immediate war. This time there would be no wavering. The Austrians were very well satisfied by this resolute attitude on the part of the Emperor.

When I thereupon said to Dr. Helfferich that this gruesome communication converted my fears of a world war, which were already strong, into absolute certainty, he replied that it certainly looked like that. Perhaps, however, France and Russia would think twice on the matter and reach a different decision. The Serbs certainly deserved a lasting lesson. This was the first information I received about the Emperor's conversations with our allies. I knew Dr. Helfferich's particularly confidential relations with the personages who were sure to have inside information and the trustworthiness of his communication. Accordingly, after my return from Berlin, I promptly communicated my information to Herr Krupp von Bohlen und Halbach, of whose board of directors at Essen I was at that time a member. Dr. Helfferich, I may add, had expressly given me permission to do

ihn in den Aufsichtsrat der Firma Krupp aufzunehmen.)
Von Bohlen schien betroffen, dass Dr. Helfferich im
Besitz solcher Kenntnisse war, machte eine abfällige
Bemerkung, dass die Leute von der Regierung doch
nie ganz den Mund halten könnten, und eröffnete mir
alsdann folgendes: Er sei selbst beim Kaiser dieser
Tage gewesen. Der Kaiser habe auch zu ihm von der
Besprechung mit den Österreichern und deren Ergebnis gesprochen, jedoch die Sache als so geheim be-
zeichnet, dass er nicht einmal gewagt haben würde,
seinem Direktorium davon Mitteilung zu machen.
Da ich aber einmal Bescheid wisse, könne er mir
sagen, die Angaben Helfferichs seien richtig. Dieser
scheine freilich noch mehr Details zu wissen, als er,
Bohlen, selbst. Die Lage sei in der Tat sehr ernst.
Der Kaiser habe ihm persönlich erklärt, er werde
sofort den Krieg erklären, wenn Russland mobil
mache. *Diesmal werde man sehen, dass er nicht
umfalle.* Die wiederholte kaiserliche Betonung, in
diesem Falle werde ihm kein Mensch wieder Unschlüs-
sigkeit vorwerfen können, habe sogar fast komisch
gewirkt.

Genau an dem mir von Helfferich bezeichneten Tage
erschien denn auch das Ultimatum Wiens an Serbien.
Ich war zu dieser Zeit wieder in Berlin und äusserte
mich gegenüber Helfferich, dass ich Ton und Inhalt
des Ultimatums geradezu ungeheuerlich fände. Dr.
Helfferich aber meinte, das klinge nur in der deutschen
Übersetzung so. Er habe das Ultimatum in französischer Sprache zu sehen bekommen und da könne man
es keineswegs als übertrieben empfinden. Bei dieser
Gelegenheit sagte mir Helfferich auch, dass der
Kaiser nur des Scheins wegen auf die *Nordlandreise*

this. (At that time there was an intention to appoint him to membership in the supervisory council of the Krupp Company.) Von Bohlen seemed disturbed that Dr. Helfferich was in possession of such information, and he made a censorious remark to the effect that the government people could never quite hold their tongues. He then disclosed to me the following facts. He had himself been with the Emperor recently. The Emperor had spoken to him also of the conversation with the Austrians and of its outcome, but had characterized the affair as so secret that he would not have ventured to communicate it even to his board of directors. Since, however, I was already posted, he could tell me that Helfferich's statements were correct. Indeed, the latter appeared to know more details than he, Bohlen, himself. The situation was really very serious. The Emperor had told him personally that he would declare war immediately if Russia mobilized. People would see this time that he would not weaken.[1] The Emperor's repeated insistence that in this matter no one would be able to reproach him again with want of resolution had produced an almost comic effect.

On the very day indicated to me by Helfferich the ultimatum from Vienna to Serbia appeared. At this time I was again in Berlin, and I told Helfferich that I regarded the tone and contents of the ultimatum as absolutely monstrous. Dr. Helfferich, however, thought that the note had that ring only in the German translation. He had had opportunity to see the ultimatum in French, and in that text it could not give any impression of over-statement. On this occasion Helfferich also said to me that it was only for the

[1] More literally: "would not fall down."

gegangen sei, ihr keineswegs die übliche Ausdehnung gegeben habe, sondern sich in jederzeit erreichbarer Nähe und in ständiger Verbindung halte. Nun müsse man eben sehen, was komme. Hoffentlich handelten die Österreicher, die auf eine Annahme des Ultimatums natürlich nicht rechneten, rasch, bevor die anderen Mächte Zeit fänden, sich hineinzumischen. Die Deutsche Bank habe ihre Vorkehrungen schon so getroffen, dass sie auf alle Eventualitäten gerüstet sei. So habe sie das einlaufende Gold nicht mehr in den Verkehr zurückgegeben. Das lasse sich ganz unauffällig einrichten und mache Tag für Tag schon sehr bedeutende Beträge aus.

Alsbald nach dem Wiener Ultimatum an Serbien gab die deutsche Regierung Erklärungen dahin ab, dass Österreich-Ungarn auf eigene Faust gehandelt habe ohne Vorwissen Deutschlands. Bei dem Versuch, diese Erklärungen mit den oben genannten Vorgängen überhaupt vereinigen zu wollen, blieb nur etwa die Lösung, dass der Kaiser sich schon festgelegt hatte, ohne seine Regierung mitwirken zu lassen, und dass bei der Besprechung mit den Österreichern deutscherseits davon abgesehen wurde, den Wortlaut des Ultimatums zu vereinbaren. Denn dass der Inhalt des Ultimatums in Deutschland ziemlich genau bekannt war, habe ich oben gezeigt.

Herr Krupp von Bohlen, mit dem ich über diese wenigstens der Wirkung nach lügnerischen deutschen Erklärungen sprach, war davon gleichfalls wenig erbaut, weil in einer so schwerwiegenden Angelegenheit Deutschland doch keine Blankovollmacht an einen Staat wie Österreich hätte ausstellen dürfen, und es

sake of appearances that the Emperor had gone on his northern cruise; that he was not going anything like so far as usual, but was keeping himself near enough to be reached at any time and in constant [telegraphic] connection. Now one must wait and see what would happen. It was to be hoped that the Austrians, who, of course, did not expect the ultimatum to be accepted, would act rapidly before the other Powers would have time to interfere. The Deutsche Bank had already made such arrangements as to be prepared for all eventualities. For instance, it was no longer putting back into circulation the gold that came in. This could be done without attracting any notice, and the amounts thus secured day by day were already very considerable.

Immediately after the [publication of the] Viennese ultimatum to Serbia, the German government issued declarations to the effect that Austria-Hungary had acted on its own hand, without Germany's prior knowledge. When one attempted to bring these declarations into any sort of harmony with the proceedings mentioned above, the only possible explanation was that the Emperor had already committed himself without arranging that his government should coöperate, and that, in the conversation with the Austrians, no provision was made on the German side for agreement upon the wording of the ultimatum. For, as I have already shown, the contents of the ultimatum were pretty accurately known in Germany.

Herr Krupp von Bohlen, with whom I spoke about these German declarations—which, in effect at least, were lies—was also far from edified by them, because in so weighty an affair Germany ought not to have given unlimited power of attorney to a state like Aus-

Pflicht der leitenden Staatsmänner gewesen wäre, so-
wohl vom Kaiser wie von den Bundesgenossen zu verlangen, dass die österreichischen Forderungen und
das Ultimatum an Serbien auf das eingehendste diskutiert und festgelegt werden und gleichzeitig das
genaue Programm des weiteren Vorgehens überhaupt.
Gleichviel auf welchem Standpunkt man stehe, man
dürfe sich doch nicht den Österreichern in die Hände
geben, sich nicht Eventualitäten aussetzen, die man
nicht vorher berechnet habe, sondern hätte an seine
Verpflichtungen entsprechende Bedingungen knüpfen
müssen. Kurz, Herr von Bohlen hielt die deutsche
Ableugnung eines Vorwissens, falls in ihr eine Spur
von Wahrheit stecke, für einen Verstoss gegen die
Anfangsgründe diplomatischer Staatskunst und stellte
mir in Aussicht, er werde mit Herrn von Jagow, dem
damaligen Staatssekretär des auswärtigen Amtes, der
ein besonderer Freund von ihm war, in diesem Sinne
reden. Als Ergebnis dieser Besprechung teilte mir
Herr von Bohlen folgendes mit: Herr von Jagow sei
ihm gegenüber fest dabei geblieben, dass er an dem
Wortlaut des österreichisch-ungarischen Ultimatums
nicht mitgewirkt habe, und dass eine solche Forderung
von Deutschland überhaupt nicht erhoben worden sei.
Auf den Einwand, das sei doch unbegreiflich, habe
Herr von Jagow erwidert, dass er als Diplomat natürlich auch daran gedacht habe, ein solches Verlangen zu
stellen. Der Kaiser habe sich aber in dem Zeitpunkt,
in dem Herr von Jagow mit der Angelegenheit befasst
und hinzugezogen wurde, schon so festgelegt gehabt,
dass es für ein Vorgehen nach diplomatischem Brauch
schon zu spät und nichts mehr zu machen gewesen sei.
Die Situation sei so gewesen, dass man mit Verklausulierungen gar nicht mehr habe kommen können.

tria. It was the duty of our leading statesmen to demand, as well of the Emperor as of our allies, that the Austrian demands and the ultimatum to Serbia should be discussed and settled in minute detail and that at the same time the exact program of all further proceedings should be determined. No matter what point of view one took, we ought not to have put ourselves into the hands of the Austrians and exposed ourselves to eventualities that had not been reckoned out in advance. On the contrary, we ought to have attached suitable conditions to our engagements. In short, Herr von Bohlen regarded the German denial of previous knowledge, if there was any trace of truth in it, as an offense against the elementary principles of diplomatic statecraft; and he told me that he intended to speak in this sense to Herr von Jagow, then secretary of state in the Foreign Office, who was a special friend of his. The outcome of this conversation, as communicated to me by Herr von Bohlen, was as follows: Herr von Jagow remained firm in assuring von Bohlen that he had not collaborated in formulating the text of the Austro-Hungarian ultimatum, and that no demand whatever for such collaboration had been advanced by Germany. In reply to the objection that this was incomprehensible, Herr von Jagow said that he, as a diplomatist, had naturally thought of making such a demand. At the time, however, when Herr von Jagow was consulted and drawn into the affair, the Emperor had so committed himself that it was too late for any action on customary diplomatic lines, and there was nothing more to be done. The situation was such that it was no longer possible to suggest modifying clauses. In the end, he, Jagow, had thought that the failure to

Schliesslich habe er, Jagow, sich gedacht, die Unterlassung werde auch ein Gutes haben, nämlich den guten Eindruck, den man in Petersburg und Paris deutscherseits mit der Erklärung machen könne, dass man an dem Wiener Ultimatum nicht mitgearbeitet habe.

True translation filed with the Postmaster at New York, N. Y., on August 28, 1918, as required by the Act of October 6, 1917.

II

ULTIMATUM AN SERBIEN
RUSSLANDS MOBILMACHUNG

Eine Antwort an die *Norddeutsche Allgemeine Zeitung* [2]

An meiner Darstellung ist wohl die Hauptsache längst bekannt und von der deutschen Regierung nicht geleugnet, nämlich:

1. Dass nach deutscher Auffassung Österreich-Ungarn Serbien züchtigen solle, ohne dass eine dritte Macht darein zu reden habe;
2. Dass die russische Mobilmachung die sofortige Kriegserklärung Deutschlands bedeute.

Beide Standpunkte waren schwere politische Fehler. Das Verhältnis Russlands zu Serbien war näher als das zwischen blossen Verbündeten. Deutschland, das seine Hilfsstellung gegenüber Österreich-Ungarn mit seinen Bündnispflichten erklärte, hätte Russland mindestens als in der gleichen Lage gegenüber Serbien befindlich anerkennen müssen. Wie verhängnisvoll der starre Standpunkt hinsichtlich der russischen Mobilmachung war, ergibt sich schon daraus, dass Deutschland seine Kriegserklärungen in dem Augen-

[2] *Die Freie Zeitung* (Bern), May 15, 1918.

take such precautions would have its advantages—
namely, the good impression which could be made on
the German side in St. Petersburg and in Paris by
the declaration that Germany had not coöperated in
the preparation of the Viennese ultimatum.[2]

II

THE ULTIMATUM TO SERBIA AND
RUSSIA'S MOBILIZATION

A Reply to the *Norddeutsche Allgemeine Zeitung*

Long known and not denied by the German government are, I take it, the chief points in my statement,
namely:

1. That, as the Germans conceived, Austria-Hungary was to chastise Serbia and no other Power was
to interfere in the affair.

2. That Russian mobilization meant immediate
declaration of war by Germany.

Both these positions were grave political mistakes.
The relation of Russia to Serbia was closer than that
between ordinary allies. Germany, which explained
its attitude of support as regarded Austria-Hungary
by pleading its duties as an ally, was bound to recognize that Russia was, at the very least, in the same
position as regarded Serbia. The peril involved in
Germany's rigid attitude toward Russian mobilization
was shown when it sprang upon the world its declarations of war at the moment when Vienna and St.

[2] See Appendix, note i.

blicke in die Welt rief, an dem Wien und St. Petersburg eine gemeinsame Basis zu friedlichen Verhandlungen gefunden hatten.

Neu an meiner Darstellung ist etwa, dass die Haltung des Kaisers in Person entschieden im Sinne der genannten beiden Standpunkte war. Wer die Zustände in Deutschland kannte, dürfte ohnehin an der starken persönlichen Stellungnahme des Kaisers nicht gezweifelt haben.

Dass die sogenannte Unkenntnis des Ultimatums an Serbien und das angebliche Unbeteiligtsein an den österreichisch-ungarischen Plänen gegen Serbien nur ein deutsches sophistisches Spiel mit Worten waren, ergab sich unter anderm längst aus der Einleitung des deutschen Weissbuches selbst.

Ich antworte zugleich auf ein Dementi meiner Niederschrift, das unlängst die *Norddeutsche Allgemeine Zeitung* brachte, wenn ich weiter sage, aus meinen Aufzeichnungen gehe nicht hervor, dass der Kaiser unter allen Umständen den Weltkrieg *gewollt* habe. Aber er hat ihn verschuldet in engerem Sinne. Gewollt hat er eine blutige Züchtigung Serbiens. Warum hätte er statt eines Weltkrieges, dessen Lorbeeren nicht billig zu erringen waren, nicht lieber den Zaren, seinen Freund, überreden wollen, um auf diese Weise die Macht Deutschlands zu vermehren?

Aber dieses Mal war sein Spiel zu verwegen. Er musste es in Ernst verwandeln, als er die russische Mobilmachung nicht verhindern konnte. Es ist wohl glaubwürdig, dass Berlin sogar einen gewissen Druck in jenen kritischen Tagen auf Wien ausübte, die Fäden

Petersburg had discovered a common basis for peaceful negotiations.

What is perhaps new in my statement is that the personal attitude of the Emperor was decidedly in line with these two points of view. No one, however, who knew the conditions obtaining in Germany could have doubted, even in default of positive evidence, the strong stand personally taken by the Emperor.

That the alleged ignorance of the ultimatum to Serbia and the claim to have played no part in the shaping of the Austro-Hungarian plans against Serbia were, on Germany's part, only sophistical juggling with words, was proved long ago, apart from other evidence, by the introduction to the German White Book.

In reply, at the same time, to an article recently published in the *Norddeutsche Allgemeine Zeitung*, which disputes my assertions, I make the further statement that my memoranda do not indicate that the Emperor had decided, no matter what happened, to bring on the World War. In a narrower sense, however, he was responsible for its outbreak. He had decided on a sanguinary chastisement of Serbia. Why, instead of risking a World War, in which the laurels of victory were not to be bought cheap, should he not rather have decided to win over his friend, the Czar, by argument, in order thus to increase Germany's power?

This time, however, his play was over rash. He was obliged to follow it up in earnest when he failed to prevent Russian mobilization. We may well believe that, in those critical days, Berlin went so far as to put a degree of pressure on Vienna, urging that

mit St. Petersburg nicht ganz zu zerreissen, um die russische Mobilmachung hintan zu halten. Als sie aber da war, war es nicht Wien, das Russland den Krieg erklärte; Wien war vielmehr gerade auf dem besten Weg zur Einigung, sondern der Kaiser in Berlin, gemäss dem feierlichen, aber trotzdem wahnwitzigen Standpunkt, den er von Anfang an rücksichtslos einzunehmen für gut befunden hatte.

Wenn die *Norddeutsche Allgemeine Zeitung* ausdrücklich sagt, dass die russische Mobilmachung den Krieg bedeute, habe Berlin stets ausdrücklich betont, so gibt sie die Hauptsache zu: Durch Drohung mit einem grösseren Unrecht und Unglück sollte die Welt eingeschüchtert werden in ihren Versuchen, ein kleineres Unrecht und Unglück (gegen Serbien) abzuwenden, und dadurch sollte nicht nur Serbien, sondern der ganzen Welt eine brutale, für Deutschlands künftige Geltung ausschlaggebende Vergewaltigung, wenn auch eventuell eine unblutige, zugefügt werden.

Auf die übrigen Behauptungen der *Norddeutschen Allgemeinen Zeitung*, die nur ablenken sollen, verlohnt es sich kaum einzugehen. Ich habe nichts von einem Potsdamer Kronrat am 5. Juli gesagt, sondern nur, dass der Kaiser in einer Besprechung mit den Österreichern sich in der und der Weise festgelegt habe. Ich habe auch keinen Anlass zu bestreiten, dass die zuständigen Organe die Verhandlungen über die durch den Mord in Serajewo geschaffene schwierige Lage geführt haben, aber wohlverstanden gemäss der allerhöchst ausgegebenen Direktive: Niemand hat in den Streit zwischen Österreich-Ungarn und Serbien hinein zu reden, russische Mobilmachung bedeutet sofortigen Krieg.

connections with St. Petersburg be not wholly cut off, but that efforts be made to delay the Russian mobilization. Nevertheless, when the mobilization came, it was not Vienna that declared war against Russia. On the contrary, Vienna was on the direct road to an understanding. It was the Emperor in Berlin, maintaining the solemnly assumed but nevertheless insane attitude which, regardless of consequences, he had seen fit to take from the outset.

When the *Norddeutsche Allgemeine Zeitung* expressly declares that Berlin expressly and uniformly emphasized the view that Russian mobilization meant war, it concedes the main point: by the threat of a greater wrong and calamity the world was to be frightened out of its effort to avert from Serbia a lesser wrong and calamity, and so not only Serbia but all the world was to be subjected to a brutal, although possibly bloodless duress, which was decisively to establish Germany's future position.

The other assertions of the *Norddeutsche Allgemeine Zeitung*, which are meant only to throw its readers off the track, are scarcely worth discussing. I said nothing about a Potsdam crown council on July 5; I said only that in a conversation with the Austrians the Emperor had committed himself in such and such a manner. I have, moreover, no occasion to deny that the negotiations concerning the difficult situation created by the murder in Serajevo were conducted by the agencies in whose competence the matter lay. I maintain, however, that they were conducted on the lines laid down by the Emperor: no one has any right to interfere in the conflict between Austria-Hungary and Serbia; Russian mobilization means instant war.

Nicht einmal die Bemühungen um Erhaltung des Friedens bestreite ich, wie schon eben gesagt, aber Bemühungen nicht im Sinne einer Verständigung, sondern im Sinne der restlosen Kapitulation vor dem deutschen Standpunkt, mit andern Worten Friedensbemühungen mittels Kriegsdrohungen.

Zu verwahren hat man sich nur noch gegen die Behauptung der *Norddeutschen Allgemeinen Zeitung*, der Suchomlinowprozess habe erwiesen, dass die wahren Schuldigen am Weltbrand in St. Petersburg sitzen. Dieser Prozess hat nichts neues erwiesen, als einige interne Vorgänge anlässlich der russischen Mobilmachung. Diese sind nicht erheblicher als etwa die Feststellung wäre, dass auch der deutsche Kaiser geschwankt habe, bevor er sich zum äussersten entschloss.

Auf die Taten kommt es an. Mobilmachung musste nicht Krieg bedeuten, das wussten die Österreicher am besten, die an lange Mobilmachungen ohne Krieg gewohnt waren.

Schuldige im weiteren Sinne am Weltkriege mag es genug und seit langer Zeit geben, Schuldige im engeren Sinne nur wenige und hinsichtlich der hier behandelten Vorgänge sitzen sie in Berlin und Wien.

True translation filed with the Postmaster at New York, N. Y., on August 28, 1918, as required by the Act of October 6, 1917.

III

DEUTSCHLAND UND BELGIEN [3]

Die Vergewaltigung Belgiens war ebenso wie die Hollands zwar oft vor dem Kriege als Eventualität erörtert worden, jedoch war es ein militärisches Ge-

[3] *Die Freie Zeitung* (Bern), May 4, 1918.

I do not for a moment dispute, I have indeed already reaffirmed, that efforts were made to preserve the peace. These efforts, however, were not directed towards an understanding; their purpose was to secure an unconditional surrender to the German point of view. In a word, they were efforts to preserve peace by threats of war.

Further protest needs to be made only against the assertion of the *Norddeutsche Allgemeine Zeitung* that the Sukhomlinof trial has conclusively shown that the real culprits who set the world on fire are to be found in St. Petersburg. This trial has brought out nothing new, except certain internal occurrences connected with the Russian mobilization. These are of no greater importance than would be, let us say, decisive evidence that the German Emperor also wavered before he decided to proceed to extremes.

It is the facts that are of importance. Mobilization did not necessarily mean war. No people knew this better than the Austrians, who were accustomed to long mobilizations without war.

Of those who are to blame in the broader sense for the World War there may be a plenty, and their guilt may date far back. Of those to blame in the narrower sense there are but few; and, as regards the occurrences here under discussion, they are to be found in Berlin and in Vienna.

III

GERMANY AND BELGIUM

The forcible occupation of Belgium, as well as that of Holland, was, it is true, often discussed before the war as a possibility; but it remained a military secret

heimnis geblieben, dass für den Fall eines gleichzeitigen Krieges gegen Russland und Frankreich der deutsche Plan definitiv feststand, Frankreich auf die schnellste Weise und mit allen Kräften niederzuwerfen, bevor das langsame Russland schlagbereit sei, und deshalb *unter allen Umständen* den Durchmarsch durch Belgien zu fordern.

Nachdem der Reichskanzler die dem militärischen Gebot entsprechenden Schritte getan hatte und nachdem er schon wusste, dass Belgien sich zur Wehr setze, trat er vor den Reichstag und entschuldigte sich: Not kenne kein Gebot. Belgien werde wiederhergestellt und entschädigt werden. Seine Rede zeigte klar, dass *Belgien ohne eigenes Verschulden,* lediglich aus deutschen strategischen Erwägungen misshandelt werde. Wenn seine Rechtfertigung auch nicht die Notwendigkeit, gerade diesen Feldzugsplan zu wählen, enthüllte, sondern vielmehr die schrankenlose Brutalität der Pläneschmiede, so war doch sein Eingeständnis der Schuldlosigkeit Belgiens sein grösster Augenblick im Kriege. Das will im heutigen Deutschland etwa so viel heissen, als dass dieses Eingeständnis seine grösste und unverzeihlichste Ungeschicklichkeit war, die gutgemacht werden musste. Es dauerte auch nicht lange, so fingen die bekannten Verdächtigungen der belgischen Neutralität an, die für denkende Menschen zur Genüge widerlegt sind. Belgien sollte eben—besten Falles für dieses Land—ein Handelsobjekt beim Friedensschlusse werden. Inzwischen hat der Krieg so lange gedauert und die Deutschen haben ihre Fänge so tief in das unglückliche Land eingeschlagen, dass man nur mit Schauder daran denken kann, was sie einmal davon zurücklassen.

that in the event of a simultaneous war against Russia and France, the German authorities had definitively adopted the plan of overthrowing France in the quickest possible way and with all available forces, before slow-moving Russia was ready to strike, and had therefore decided, whatever might be the situation, to demand passage through Belgium.

After the imperial chancellor had taken action in conformity with the military mandate, and after he was aware that Belgium was preparing to defend itself, he appeared before the Reichstag and gave his excuse: "Necessity knows no law." Belgium, he said, would be restored and indemnified. His speech showed plainly that Belgium was being maltreated without any fault of its own, solely because of German strategic considerations. Although his plea in justification did not reveal the necessity of choosing precisely this plan of campaign, but rather the boundless brutality of those who framed the plan, his admission of Belgium's innocence was, nevertheless, his greatest moment in the war. In the Germany of today that amounts to saying that this admission was his greatest and most unpardonable blunder. It was a blunder that had to be rectified. It was not long before the now familiar aspersions against Belgian neutrality were started—aspersions which have been sufficiently refuted to satisfy all those who are capable of thinking. Belgium—in the outcome least unfortunate for that country—was to be simply an object of barter at the conclusion of peace. In the meantime the war has lasted so long and the Germans have sunk their fangs so deep in the unhappy country, that one shudders to think how little of it they will leave.

Immerhin kein Reichskanzler hat das Wort vom 4. August 1914 zurückgenommen, nur vor einer klaren Wiederholung hat man sich gescheut.

Ich habe selbst in Deutschland zwar manchen kompetenten Mann gesprochen, aber niemals einen, der mir gegenüber auch nur versucht hätte, mit irgend einem Wort eine Schuld Belgiens anzudeuten. Trotzdem liess man und lässt man Tausende von Handlangern immer neue Anschuldigungen verbreiten, die jene Erklärung des Reichskanzlers vergessen machen und *das deutsche Volk* gegenüber Belgien hart machen sollen. Das deutsche Volk, das ohnehin seine Führer wenig mit Fragen nach Wahrheit und Gerechtigkeit im Kriege beunruhigt, *das vor allem das unvermeidliche Elend auf andere abwälzen möchte* und von seinen Führern in der Hauptsache *nur verlangt,* dass sie *keinen materiellen Misserfolg* haben! Das deutsche Volk, das ohnehin—mag der Reichskanzler gesagt haben was nur immer—gewissermassen glauben will, die Belgier hätten den Überfall verdient und keine Bereicherung seines alten Märchenschatzes über Belgien (die Franzosen waren zuerst in Belgien—die Engländer wären doch nach Belgien gekommen—die Belgier hätten sich anständigerweise nicht wehren dürfen, etc.) braucht.

Da mag es denn nicht unnütz sein, wenn ich an meinem bescheidenen Teile etwas zur Steuer der Wahrheit beitrage. Was ich jedem Bekannten mündlich gesagt habe, wirkt vielleicht mehr, wenn ich es den Unbekannten öffentlich unterbreite. Und wenn es nichts nützt, so sei es wenigstens ein Trost für

Up to the present time, indeed, no imperial chancellor has retracted the promise of August 4th; there has only been reluctance to repeat it clearly.

I have myself talked, in Germany, with many men qualified to form an opinion on the subject, but never with one who so much as attempted, with a single word, to hint at any fault on the part of Belgium. Nevertheless, thousands of hirelings were and are still permitted to circulate a constantly growing series of accusations, which are intended to cause that declaration of the imperial chancellor to be forgotten and to harden the hearts of the German people against Belgium. The German people, who, as it is, trouble their leaders with few questions about truth and justice in the war, who above all things desire to roll off upon others the inevitable burden of misery and, in the main, demand from their leaders one thing only—that they encounter no material reverse of fortune! The German people, who, as it is—no matter what the imperial chancellor may have said —are to a certain degree determined to believe that the Belgians got only their deserts when their country was raided, and who do not need any addition to their old stock of fairy tales about Belgium: that the French were in Belgium first; that the English would have come to Belgium anyway; that the Belgians should have behaved themselves and offered no resistance, etc.

It may therefore be not altogether useless, if I contribute my modest share towards the establishment of the truth. What I have told every acquaintance of mine orally, may perhaps be more effective if I submit it publicly to those with whom I am unacquainted. And if it does not help, may it at least be

die Freunde der Wahrheit und für die Belgier im besonderen. Jedenfalls haben meine Angaben den Vorteil, dass sie bei einigem guten Willen nachgeprüft werden können und dass man in Deutschland Tausende von Zeugen und reichliche schriftliche Belege finden kann.

Belgien hatte vor dem Kriege bei der Firma Krupp in Essen vier grosse, moderne Geschütze (28 Centimeter) für die Befestigung von Antwerpen bestellt. Die Geschütze waren Anfang 1914 fertig, abgenommen und völlig bezahlt und versandbereit, aber *die Arbeiten an der Befestigung von Antwerpen waren noch nicht soweit fortgeschritten, dass die Geschütze aufgestellt werden konnten.* Man erinnert sich vielleicht der belgischen Kammerdebatten über diesen Gegenstand. Nun richtete die belgische Regierung an Krupp das Ersuchen, die Geschütze einstweilen selbst noch aufzubewahren. Krupp willfahrte, aber ungern. Eine solche Aufbewahrung kommt selten vor und hat mancherlei Unannehmlichkeiten. Krupp tat wiederholte mündliche und schriftliche Schritte, um die Geschütze loszubekommen, die belgische Regierung erneuerte stets ihr Ersuchen um die Gefälligkeit der Aufbewahrung und war sogar bereit, eine Entschädigung dafür zu zahlen. Es wurde immer wieder ein *modus vivendi* gefunden, der beiderseitige Standpunkt blieb unverändert, bis der Krieg ausbrach und das preussische Kriegsministerium diese Geschütze sofort als Beute (Wert vier Millionen) in Essen beschlagnahmte.

. Daraus folgere ich: Hätte die belgische Regierung irgendwelche bösen Absichten gegen Deutschland gehabt, oder sich eines deutschen Überfalls versehen, so würde sie, spätestens als der Krieg drohte, ihre

a consolation to the friends of truth and, especially, to the Belgians. In any case, my testimony has the advantage that, with a little good will, it may be substantiated and that thousands of witnesses and ample written evidence may be found in Germany.

Before the war Belgium had ordered from the Krupp Company in Essen four large modern guns (twenty-eight centimeters) [3] for the fortifications of Antwerp. At the beginning of 1914 the guns were completed, accepted, paid in full, and ready for shipment; but the work on the fortifications of Antwerp had not yet been carried so far that the guns could be set up. The debates on this subject in the Belgian Chamber of Deputies will perhaps be recalled. At this point the Belgian government requested Krupp to keep the guns in storage for the time being. Krupp agreed, but not willingly. Such storage is unusual, and it entails many inconveniences. Krupp repeatedly took steps, both by word of mouth and in writing, to get rid of the guns; the Belgian government continually repeated its request that Krupp be kind enough to keep them, and was even ready to pay for the accommodation. A *modus vivendi* was repeatedly found, but the attitude of both parties remained unchanged until the war broke out, when the Prussian Ministry of War at once seized these guns in Essen as booty (value four million marks).

From this I draw the following conclusion: Had the Belgian government had any evil intentions whatsoever against Germany, or had it expected a

[3] A little more than eleven inches.

kostbaren Geschütze an sich genommen haben, statt darauf zu beharren, dass sie Krupp anvertraut blieben.

Aber ich bin nicht auf dieses eine Beispiel angewiesen. Belgien unterhielt seit langem rege Verbindungen mit Deutschland hinsichtlich seines Kriegsmaterials. Soweit Krupp nicht selbst an die belgische Regierung lieferte, arbeitete die belgische Firma Cockerill in Seraing und viele Staatswerkstätten in enger Fühlung mit Krupp (nach seinen Konstruktionen, Patenten, etc.; Kruppsche Teillieferungen, etc.). Diese Beziehungen sind in allen Ländern ein ziemlich zuverlässiges Barometer politischer Natur, was ich hier nicht weiter ausführen will. Es liegt auf der Hand, dass ein Land umso mehr abhängig wird (nicht nur im Kriegsfall, aber besonders in diesem) und umso schwerer sich umschalten lässt, je mehr es sich auf eine bestimmte ausländische Lieferungsquelle für Kriegsmaterial eingerichtet hat. Es lag für Belgien auch keinerlei technische Notwendigkeit vor, sich an Krupp zu wenden, der z. B. Frankreich gegenüber in seinen Konstruktionen von jeher weit unterlegen war und nur mühsam nachhinkte, wie jeder Fachmann, auch in Deutschland, weiss. Krupps Qualitäten liegen auf einem ganz anderen Gebiet als dem der besseren Konstruktionen und Erfindungen. Kurz, Belgiens Beziehungen zu Krupp waren der Ausdruck eines freundschaftlichen Bestrebens gegenüber Deutschland. Ich habe immer den Eindruck gehabt, dass Belgien das geschäftsgierige, empfindliche, scharf nachdrängende Deutschland durch reichliche Aufträge bei guter Laune erhalten zu können glaubte, während es von Frankreich, dessen Industrie wenig

German attack, it would, at the very latest when war threatened, have secured possession of its expensive guns, instead of insisting that they should remain in Krupp's care.

My evidence, however, is not confined to this single instance. For many years Belgium kept up active connections with Germany in the matter of its war materials. In those instances in which the Krupp Company did not itself fill the orders of the Belgian government, the Belgian firm of Cockerill in Seraing and many government shops worked in close touch with the Krupp Company (using its designs, patents, etc.; receiving part-shipments from Krupp, etc.). These relations are in all countries a pretty trustworthy sort of political barometer. This is a point on which I shall not at present enlarge. It is obvious that a country becomes increasingly dependent (not solely in case of war, but especially in that event) and finds it increasingly difficult to wheel round, in proportion to the extent to which it has arranged to obtain its war materials from a definite foreign source.[4] For Belgium, moreover, there was no sort of technical necessity to turn to the Krupp Company, which has always been far inferior to France, for example, in its designs and has only with difficulty limped along after that country, as every expert, even in Germany, is well aware. Krupp's advantages are found in quite another field than that of better designs and inventions. In short, Belgium's relations with Krupp were the expression of an effort to keep on a friendly footing with Germany. I have always had the impression that by giving large orders to Germany, which is greedy for business, keen in its pursuit, and quick to

[4] See Appendix, note ii.

[215]

Regierungsunterstützung genoss und zudem sorgloser
war, Verständnis für die Gründe der Bevorzugung
Deutschlands und Begnügung mit den menschlichen
Sympathien erwartete.

Wenige Monate nun vor dem Kriege knüpfte Belgien ein weiteres und besonders wichtiges Band
zwischen sich und Krupp. Es überliess sich hinsichtlich einer neuen (kaum erprobten) Munition für
Feldartillerie ganz dieser Firma. Krupp, der sich
bedeutende direkte Bestellungen zusicherte, übertrug
die Berechtigung zur Fabrikation dieser Munition an
Cockerill unter Mitwirkung, natürlich, der zuständigen
Behörden, die sich für ihre eigenen Werkstätten das
gleiche sicherten. Das hiess für Cockerill und das
belgische Kriegsministerium rege und andauernde
Zusammenarbeit mit Kruppschen Vertretern, In-
genieuren, etc., und entsprechende Abhängigkeit vom
Lizenzgeber. Ich hatte damals häufig den Besuch
eines Cockerillschen Direktors und halte es nicht für
überflüssig zu bemerken, dass mir noch bei Kriegsausbruch ein Schreiben von Cockerill vorlag, dass er
eine Lizenzanzahlung von einer Million Franken
soeben überweise.

Man bedenke, die enge Abhängigkeit des Kriegs-
materialgeschäfts von Regierungsintentionen und
beurteile dann auf Grund der hier erwähnten und
offenkundigen Vorgänge die *mala fides* der belgischen
Regierung gegenüber Deutschland.

take offense, Belgium believed that it could keep that country in good humor, whereas she expected France, whose industry enjoyed little support from the government and was, moreover, less keen as regarded its own development, to understand her reasons for favoring Germany and to be content with general indications of sympathy.

A few months before the war Belgium established another and particularly important connection between itself and Krupp. For its supply of a new (scarcely tested) ammunition for field artillery it placed itself entirely in the hands of this company. After securing large direct orders, Krupp conceded the privilege of manufacturing this ammunition to Cockerill, with the coöperation, of course, of the competent [Belgian] authorities, who saw to it that their own works also secured the same privilege. For Cockerill and the Belgian Ministry of War this arrangement meant active and sustained coöperation with Krupp's representatives, engineers, etc., and a corresponding dependence on the grantor of the licenses. At that time one of Cockerill's directors paid me frequent visits; and I do not consider it superfluous to note that, at the moment of the outbreak of the war, a letter from Cockerill lay before me, informing me that he was just sending a payment on the license amounting to one million francs.

Consider the close dependency of the war-material business on governmental intentions, and then, on the basis of the occurrences I have here recounted, which are matters of public knowledge, pass judgment on the alleged *mala fides* of the Belgian government towards Germany.

IV

BRIEF AN BETHMANN-HOLLWEG [4]

Bern, den 7. Mai 1917

Seiner Exzellenz dem Herrn Reichskanzler von Bethmann-Hollweg, Berlin.

Euer Exzellenz!

So zahlreich und schwer auch die Irrtümer und
Verfehlungen auf deutscher Seite von Kriegsbeginn an
waren, so glaubte ich doch lange Zeit hoffen zu können,
dass eine bessere Einsicht und Gesinnung bei unsern
massgebenden Persönlichkeiten allmählich durchdringen werde. In dieser Hoffnung hatte ich während
des Krieges meine Arbeit in Rumänien in gewissem
Masse zur Verfügung gestellt, und war ich bereit,
auch in meinem jetzigen Aufenthaltslande, der
Schweiz, mitzuhelfen, soweit das Ziel der Bemühungen
Annäherung der feindlichen Parteien sein sollte. Dass
ich jeder andern Tätigkeit, die nicht auf Versöhnung
und Wiederherstellung unmittelbar sich richtete,
abgeneigt war, habe ich schon kurz nach Kriegsausbruch dadurch gezeigt, dass ich meine Stellung als
Mitglied des Kruppschen Direktoriums niedergelegt
habe.

Seit Anfang dieses Jahres ist mir nun jede Hoffnung
hinsichtlich der heutigen Leiter Deutschlands ge-
schwunden. Das Friedensangebot *ohne Angabe der
Kriegsziele*, der verschärfte Unterseebootskrieg, die
Deportationen der Belgier, die Verwüstungen in

[4] *Die Freie Zeitung* (Bern), May 4, 1918.

LETTER TO BETHMANN-HOLLWEG

To His Excellency the German Imperial Chancellor von Bethmann-Hollweg, Berlin.

Your Excellency:

Many and grave as were the mistakes and failures on the German side from the beginning of the war, I still believed for a long time that there was room for the hope that a clearer view and a better frame of mind would gradually come to prevail among the personages in control of our affairs. It was in this hope that, during the war, I placed my services in Rumania to a certain extent at the disposal of the government,[5] and was ready to coöperate also in my present country of residence, Switzerland, in so far as the object of my efforts was to be a *rapprochement* of the hostile parties. That I was averse to any activity of a different character, not immediately directed toward reconciliation and restoration, I showed shortly after the outbreak of the war, by resigning my position as a member of the Krupp Board of Directors.

Since the beginning of this year [1917] all my hopes have disappeared as regards the present leaders of Germany. The offer of peace without any statement of our war aims, the more trenchant conduct of submarine warfare, the deportations of Belgians, the de-

[5] Before Rumania entered the war, Dr. Muehlon, acting for Germany, had concluded agreements with Minister Bratiano concerning the delivery of wheat. *L'Humanité*, March 31, 1918.

Frankreich, die Versenkung englischer Hospital-
schiffe sind Beispiele der Handlungen, die immer
wieder von neuem unsere verantwortlichen Persönlichkeiten derartig disqualifiziert haben, dass sie nach
meiner Überzeugung für eine gutwillige, gerechte
Verständigung überhaupt nicht mehr in Betracht
kommen dürfen. Sie mögen für ihre Person sich noch
ändern, aber sie können nicht Repräsentanten der
deutschen Sache bleiben. Als solche verdienen sie
weder Langmut noch Nachsicht mehr. Das deutsche
Volk kann die geschehenen schweren Versündigungen
an seiner, Europas und der Menschheit Gegenwart
und Zukunft erst dann wieder gutzumachen beginnen,
wenn es sich durch andere Männer von anderer Art
vertreten lässt. Es ist keine Ungerechtigkeit, dass es
heute dem Odium der ganzen Welt verfallen ist, so
fehlerhaft und unvollkommen diese auch sein und
bleiben möge: Der Triumph unserer bisherigen militärischen und politischen Kriegführung würde eine
Niederlage der höchsten Gedanken und Hoffnungen
der Menschheit sein. Man braucht nur den Fall zu
setzen, ein erschöpftes, demoralisiertes oder die
Gewalt verabscheuendes Volk werde den Frieden aus
der Hand dieser selben Regierung annehmen, die den
Krieg geführt hat, um zu erkennen, wie trügerisch und
trüb es um das Niveau und die Aussichten des
Völkerlebens bestellt bliebe.

Als Mensch und als Deutscher, der es gut meint mit
dem irregeführten und gequälten deutschen Volke,
wende ich mich endgiltig von den Männern des
heutigen deutschen Regimes ab. Möge jeder, der
dazu in der Lage ist, ebenso handeln. Mögen bald
viele Deutsche so weit sein.

vastations in France, the sinking of English hospital ships—these are samples of the constantly recurring acts which have so disqualified our responsible authorities that, in my judgment, they can no longer be taken into account in any effort to attain an honestly meant and just understanding. They may change their personal attitude, but they cannot remain representatives of the German cause. As such they no longer deserve either patience or indulgence. The German nation cannot begin to repair the grievous offenses committed against its own as well as Europe's present and future until it gets itself represented by other men of a different stamp. It suffers no injustice in being exposed today to odium throughout the world. However faulty and imperfect this world may be and may remain, the triumph of our military and political warfare, as it has thus far been conducted, would be a defeat of the highest ideals and hopes of mankind. We need only imagine that a nation that is exhausted or demoralized, or that abhors violence, should accept a peace granted by this same government that has conducted the war, and we shall recognize how deceptive and dark the situation would be as regards the level of international life and the prospects of national existence.[6]

As a human being and as a German who desires the welfare of the misled and maltreated German people, I turn away, once for all, from the men of the present German régime. May everyone, who is in a position to do so, act in the same way. May many Germans soon reach such a position.

[6] The character of the peace which Germany imposed upon Russia at Brest-Litovsk, in February, 1918, shows how clearsighted a prophet Dr. Muehlon was in May, 1917. *L'Humanité*, March 31, 1918.

Da mir eine Kundgebung in der deutschen Öffentlichkeit nicht möglich ist, habe ich es für den gegebenen Weg gehalten, Euer Exzellenz von diesem meinem Standpunkt zu unterrichten.

Dr. W. Muehlon

Since it is not possible for me to make a statement in the German press, I have regarded it as the suitable course to inform your Excellency of the position I occupy.

DR. W. MUEHLON

APPENDIX

I. THE AUSTRIAN ULTIMATUM TO SERBIA

The documents published by the French government shortly after the outbreak of the war show that the text of the ultimatum was known at Munich before it was delivered to the Serbian government; also that the French ambassador at Berlin found it difficult to believe that it was not known to the German Foreign Office.

M. Allizé, French Minister at Munich, to M. Bienvenu-Martin Acting Minister for Foreign Affairs, Paris.

Munich, July 23, 1914

The Bavarian press seems to believe that a peaceful solution of the Austro-Serbian incident is not only possible but even probable; on the other hand, official circles have for some time been assuming with more or less sincerity an air of real pessimism.

In particular the President of the Council said to me today that the Austrian note, the contents of which were known to him (*dont il avait connaissance*), was in his opinion drawn up in terms which could be accepted by Serbia, but that none the less the existing situation appeared to him to be very serious.[1]

M. Jules Cambon, French Ambassador at Berlin, to M. Bienvenu-Martin, Acting Minister for Foreign Affairs.

Berlin, July 24, 1914

I asked the Secretary of State today, in the interview which I had with him, if it was correct, as announced in the newspapers, that Austria had presented a note to the Powers on her dispute

[1] French Yellow Book, No. 21; *Collected Diplomatic Documents*, p. 153.

with Serbia; if he had received it; and what view he took of it.

Herr von Jagow answered me in the affirmative, adding that the note was forcible, and that he approved it, the Serbian government having for a long time past wearied the patience of Austria. Moreover, he considers this question to be a domestic one for Austria, and he hopes that it will be localized.

I then said to him that, not having as yet received any instructions, the views which I wished to exchange with him were strictly personal. Thereupon I asked him if the Berlin Cabinet had really been entirely ignorant of Austria's requirements before they were communicated to Belgrade, and as he told me that that was so, I showed him my surprise at seeing him thus undertake to support claims, of whose limit and scope he was ignorant.

Herr von Jagow interrupted me, and said: "It is only because we are having a personal conversation that I allow you to say that to me."

"Certainly," I replied, "but if Peter I. humiliates himself, domestic trouble will probably break out in Serbia; that will open the door to fresh possibilities, and do you know where you will be led by Vienna?" I added that the language of the German newspapers was not the language of persons who were indifferent to, and unacquainted with, the question, but betokened an active support. Finally, I remarked that the shortness of the time limit given to Serbia for submission would make an unpleasant impression in Europe. . .

All the evidence shows that Germany is ready to support Austria's attitude with unusual energy. . .

It is not less striking to notice the pains with which Herr von Jagow, and all the officials placed under his orders, pretend to every one that they were ignorant of the scope of the note sent by Austria to Serbia.[2]

II. RELATIONS BETWEEN THE BELGIAN GOVERNMENT AND THE KRUPP COMPANY

Dr. Muehlon corroborates the assertions previously made by M. Emile Waxweiler, director of the Solvay Institute of Sociology, University of Brussels. M.

[2] French Yellow Book, No. 30; *Collected Diplomatic Documents*, pp. 161, 162.

Waxweiler's statements, however, are somewhat fuller.

There is one typical fact which may be set against the imputations that aim at representing Belgium as having been in military accord with France before the present war. Why has the German press never indicated that all Belgium's supply of cannons and artillery ammunition, as well as part of her other war material, comes from Germany? At the most, the Krupp Company permitted some Belgian factories to coöperate in the manufacture of certain guns and projectiles. At the moment of the outbreak of war, a considerable part of the following orders, which had been entrusted to the Krupp Company with the coöperation of Belgian firms, was not yet delivered:

> 30,000 universal shells (7.5 cm.)
> 18,000 fuses with detonators
> 70,000 double-acting fuses
> 4 eclipse guns (28 cm.)
> 4 embrasure guns (28 cm.)

In addition, various orders had been placed with other German firms, such as Werner, Siemens and Halske, Siemens and Schückert, Erhardt, etc.

If Belgium had contemplated military coöperation with France, would she not have placed her orders in French factories? Moreover, during the course of the war, a highly critical situation arose for the Belgian army. Not having received from Germany all the expected deliveries, and, on the other hand, having been obliged to transfer into France its base of operations together with all its elements of production, it found itself dependent on material and supplies of quite a different type from its own. And it was only after serious study of the matter by Belgian and French engineers that a way was found of solving the complicated problem of supplying the Belgian army, equipped with German material, with munitions of a slightly modified French type.

A similar difficulty presented itself as regards rifle equipment. Taken by surprise, in the midst of a complete army reorganization, Belgium did not possess at the moment of the outbreak of hostilities a sufficient number of rifles. This shortage led her, after the war had begun, to ask France, in particular, for 10,000 Lebel rifles and 1,000 rounds of ammunition per rifle. These rifles were distributed among the soldiers of the fortress of Antwerp. This

circumstance affords a very simple explanation of a fact that has been construed against Belgium by the *Tägliche Rundschau* of October 15. The Germans had found a French rifle in the hands of a Belgian soldier; they alleged, moreover, that the "Belgian cartridges," carried by the soldier, corresponded with the caliber of the "French rifle," and from all this they drew the conclusion that an arrangement existed between Belgium and France. The Belgian Government issued in November, in a communication made by their Minister at The Hague, a formal denial: all the cartridges with which the Belgian troops were armed at the time of the outbreak of the war were of Belgian manufacture, and none of them corresponded with the caliber of the French Lebel rifle, which they obviously did not fit.[3]

[3] Waxweiler, *La Belgique neutrale et loyale* (Paris, Payot, 1915), pp. 155–157; *Belgium Neutral and Loyal* (New York, Putnam, 1915), pp. 161–164.

III

The Dawn in Germany?

The Lichnowsky and Other Disclosures
by James Brown Scott

Reprint of INTERNATIONAL CONCILIATION, Special Bulletin, November, 1918

THE DAWN IN GERMANY?

The Lichnowsky and Other Disclosures

By James Brown Scott

(Reprinted from *The American Journal of International Law*, April, 1918)

In the earlier part of March extracts appeared in the German press of a Memorandum written by Prince Lichnowsky, Imperial German Ambassador to Great Britain at the outbreak of the war of 1914, and more of this Memorandum is said to have been published in the Stockholm *Politiken*. In the account given in the London *Times* for March 15, 1918, it is said that:

> The Memorandum was written by Prince Lichnowsky about eighteen months ago, for the purpose of explaining and justifying his position to his personal friends, and only half-a-dozen typewritten copies were made. One of these copies, through a betrayal, reached the Wilhelmstrasse, and caused a great scandal, and another was communicated to some members of the Minority Socialist Party; but how it happened that a copy got across the German frontier forms a mystery to which *Politiken* declines to give any clue. Internal evidence, however, leaves no doubt in regard to the authenticity of the document. It is entitled "My London Mission, 1912–1914," and is dated Kuchelna (Prince Lichnowsky's country seat), August, 1916.

The most casual reading of the Memorandum will disclose why the Prince's Memorandum has created a sensation in Germany, where the views expressed by the former Ambassador to Great Britain have not been avowed by the authorities. Naturally, they have been discussed in the Reichstag, and statements have

appeared from time to time in the press that the Prince would be tried and punished for treason, or sedition, or for some other heinous offense.

As regards the Reichstag, the London *Times*, in its issue of March 21, 1918, says in a dispatch from Amsterdam, dated the 19th:

> In the Main Committee of the Reichstag the subject of Prince Lichnowsky's Memorandum was discussed. Herr von Payer, the Vice-Chancellor, read a letter from the Prince, in which he stated that the Memorandum had been written with a view to his future justification. These notes were intended for the family archives. They have found their way into wider circles by an "unprecedented breach of confidence." The Prince expressed regret for the incident.
>
> Herr von Payer stated that the Prince had tendered his resignation, which had been accepted, but as he had been simply guilty of imprudence, no further steps would be taken against him.

A few of the more significant passages of the Memorandum are quoted, with summaries of omitted portions.

The Prince arrived in London in November, 1912, and found that "people had quieted down about Morocco," as an agreement had been reached concerning this question between France and Germany. The Haldane Mission had, he said, failed because Germany insisted upon a promise of neutrality, instead of contenting itself with a treaty with Great Britain insuring it against attacks from that country. However, Sir Edward Grey, then British Secretary of State for Foreign Affairs, had, to quote the Prince's exact language, "not given up the idea of reaching an understanding with us and he tried it first in colonial and economic matters." The purpose of Sir Edward Grey as stated by the German Ambassador was to settle outstanding controversies with France and

Great Britain, and thereafter reach similar agreements with Germany, "not to isolate us," to quote the Prince, "but as far as possible to make us partners in the existing union. As British-French and British-Russian differences had been bridged over, he wished also the British-German differences to be settled as far as possible and to insure world peace by means of a network of treaties," which the Prince said would probably have included an agreement on the naval question after an understanding had been reached obviating the dangers of war. Such was Grey's program in his own words, the Prince says, apparently quoting Sir Edward Grey, upon which the Prince comments that it had "'no aggressive aims, and involved . . . for England no binding obligations, to reach a friendly *rapprochement* and understanding with Germany'. In short, to bring the two groups nearer together."

Prince Lichnowsky's disclosures concerning the attitude on the Balkan situation of Austria-Hungary and Germany, on the one hand, and Great Britain, on the other, are of the utmost importance, as they show an agreement of the Central European Powers to exclude Russia from Balkan affairs, to substitute their own influence for that of Russia, and to make of those states dependencies instead of making them independent, inasmuch as the Prince shows that Russian influence had really ceased in each instance with the independence of each of the Balkan States.

It will be recalled that Bulgaria, Greece, Montenegro and Serbia, after having beaten Turkey in what is known as the First Balkan war, fell out about the distribution of the spoils of victory, and that in a conference by their plenipotentiaries held in London they failed to agree. The consequence was the

Second Balkan war, of Greece, Montenegro and Serbia, in which Rumania joined, against Bulgaria, which had insisted upon the lion's share of the common victory. In this second war Bulgaria was badly beaten, and the Treaty of Bucharest was concluded in 1913. In these various negotiations, Austria was an interested party, insisting that the principality of Albania should be created out of the spoils claimed by Greece, Serbia and Montenegro, and that Serbia be denied an outlet to the seas. The attitude of the Central German Powers and of Great Britain is thus stated by Prince Lichnowsky, who was then German Ambassador to London:

Soon after my arrival in London, at the end of 1912, Sir Edward Grey suggested an informal conversation in order to prevent a European war developing out of the Balkan war. The British statesman from the beginning took the stand that England had no interest in Albania on account of this question and was therefore not willing to let it come to a war. He wished simply as an honest broker to mediate between the two groups and settle difficulties. He therefore by no means placed himself on the side of the members of the alliance, and during the negotiations, which lasted about eight months, he contributed not a little by his good will and effectual influence toward bringing about concord and agreement. Instead of assuming an attitude similar to that of the English, we without exception took the position prescribed to us from Vienna. Count Mensdorff represented the Triple Alliance in London. I was his second. My mission consisted in supporting his propositions.

So much for the attitude of the different Powers. Next as to the conduct of Sir Edward Grey and the consequences of the Balkan settlement conducted by Austria-Hungary and Germany. On these points the Prince said in his Memorandum:

Grey conducted the negotiations with circumspection, calmness, and tact. Whenever a question threatened to become com-

plicated, he would draft a form of agreement which hit the matter right and always met approval. His personality enjoyed equal confidence from all members of the conference. We really again successfully stood one of the many tests of strength which characterize our politics. Russia had had to yield to us everywhere, so that she was never in a position to insure success of the Serbian wishes. Albania was created as an Austrian vassal state and Serbia was driven from the sea. The result of the conference was therefore a fresh humiliation for the Russian self-consciousness. As in 1878 and 1908, we had taken a stand against the Russian program without German interests being at stake. Bismarck knew how to mitigate the error of the Congress by secret treaty and by his attitude in the Battenberg question. The downward path again taken in the Bosnian question was continued in London, and when it led into the abyss it was not opportunely abandoned.

It is common knowledge that Austria-Hungary had picked Bulgaria as the winner in the Second Balkan war, and that its defeat was a blow to what it considered its prestige. The Prince calls attention to this in the following passage, and the absence of a specious pretext evidently was the reason in the Prince's mind, although he does not say so, for the outbreak of the war a year earlier than it actually occurred:

The idea of wiping it out by a campaign against Serbia seems soon to have gained ground in Vienna. The Italian revelations prove this and it is to be supposed that the Marquis San Giuliano, who very appropriately characterized the plan as a most dangerous adventure, preserved us from becoming involved in a world war as early as the summer of 1913.

But however interesting these passages may be, they are merely episodes in a memoir whose great value consists in the disclosure that before the outbreak of the war of 1914, Great Britain had not only, as is well known, settled its differences with France and Russia, but also that Sir Edward Grey, representing Great Britain, had peaceably settled its controversies with

Germany; that the terms of the treaty adjusting their conflicting claims to the satisfaction of Germany had not only been substantially agreed upon, but that the treaty itself had been drafted and initialed by Sir Edward Grey on behalf of Great Britain, and by Prince Lichnowsky on behalf of Germany.

It appears that the agreement between the two countries extended to colonial matters in Africa, as well as economic questions in Asia. In regard to the former, the Prince says, speaking of the treaty of 1898:

Thanks to the obliging attitude of the British Government, I succeeded in giving the new treaty a form which fully coincided with our wishes and interests. All of Angola up to the 20th degree of longitude was assigned to us, so that we reached the Congo region from the south; besides this there were the valuable islands of San Thomé and Principe. . . . Furthermore, we received the northern part of Mozambique. . . .

"The British Government," the Prince says again, "showed the greatest obligingness in behalf of our interests. Grey purposed proving to us his good will and also furthering our colonial development in general, as England hoped to divert German development of strength from the North Sea and from Europe to the ocean. 'We do not begrudge Germany her colonial development', said a member of the Cabinet to me."

Of the Asiatic situation, and especially of the Bagdad Railway, the Prince has much to say, and the purpose of the two governments appears to have been to divide Asia Minor into two spheres of influence. The economic enterprises were adjusted essentially in accordance with the wishes of the German Bank, and the railroad itself was prolonged to Basra, so that Bagdad was no longer constituted the terminal point of the road. An international commission was to

attend to the navigation on the Shatt-el-Arab. Germany was to have a part in the construction of the harbor at Basra, and obtain rights in the navigation of the Tigris.

The success of these negotiations and their consequences not merely to the contracting Powers, but to the world at large, are thus stated by the German negotiator:

Under this treaty the whole of Mesopotamia as far as Basra became our interest zone, without prejudice to more ancient British rights in the Tigris navigation and the Wilcox irrigation establishments. Furthermore, we received the whole territory of the Bagdad and Anatolian railroad.

The coasts of the Persian Gulf and the Smyrna-Aidin railroad were considered as British economic territory, Syria as French, and Armenia as Russian. If both treaties had been concluded and published, an understanding would thereby have been reached with England which would forever have dispelled all doubts as to the possibility of an Anglo-German coöperation.

In connection with Prince Lichnowsky's Memorandum, the following three documents are to be considered.

The first is entitled "Terms of the Anglo-German Agreement of 1914," as corrected by Dr. Zimmermann, Under-Secretary at the outbreak of the war, and later Imperial German Secretary of State, and handed in 1916 to Mr. S. S. McClure.[1] It is thus worded:

1. The Bagdad Railway from Constantinople to Basra is definitely left to German capital in coöperation with Turkey. In the territory of the Bagdad Railway German economical working will not be hindered by England.

2. Basra becomes a sea harbor in the building of which German capital is concerned with 60 per cent. and English capital with 40 per cent. For the navigation from Basra to the Persian Gulf the independence of the open sea is agreed to.

[1] Mr. S. S. McClure's *Obstacles to Peace*, 1917, pages 40–42.

3. Kuweit is excluded from the agreement between Germany and England.

4. In the navigation of the Tigris, English capital is interested with 50 per cent., German capital with 25 per cent., and Turkish with 25 per cent.

5. The oil-wells of the whole of Mesopotamia shall be developed by a British company, the capital of which shall be given at 50 per cent. by England, at 25 per cent. by the German Bank, at 25 per cent. by the "Royal Dutch Company" (a company which is Dutch, but closely connected with England). For the irrigation works there had been intended a similar understanding. The rights of the Anglo-Persian Oil Company, in which, as is known, the English Government is concerned, remained unaffected. This society exercises south of Basra, on the Schatel-Arabia, as well as in all south and central Persia, a monopoly on the production and transport of oil.

6. A simultaneous German-French agreement leaves free hand to French capital for the construction of railways in southern Syria and Palestine.

Besides this, there is an agreement, already made before, between Germany and England, concerning Africa, with a repartition of their spheres of influence in Angola and Mozambique.

Finally there is to be mentioned the Morocco agreement, which established the political predominance of France in Morocco, but, on the other hand, stated the principle of "open door" to the trade of all nations.

The second is the dispatch of the Belgian Minister at Berlin to the Belgian Minister for Foreign Affairs dated February 20, 1914, as officially published by the German Government in its collection of Belgian documents found in the Foreign Office at Brussels, upon the occupation of that city by German troops.[2]

---

[2] Baron Beyens, Belgian Minister at Berlin, to M. Davignon, Minister for Foreign Affairs, February 20, 1914. (Reports of the Belgian Representatives in Berlin, London and Paris to the Minister for Foreign Affairs in Brussels, 1905–1914.) Issued by the Imperial German Foreign Office, 1915, under the title "Belgian Diplomatists". No. 111, pages 131–132.

The material portion of this document, confirming Prince Lichnowsky's statements regarding the French agreement, is as follows:

The Franco-German agreement concerning Asia Minor, concluded very recently at Berlin after difficult negotiations and thanks to the personal intervention of the Chancellor, assures to France a large sphere of action and influence in Syria. She will be able to build a railway line starting from Beirut along the valley of the Orontes, back of the Antilebanon as far as Aleppo, the point of junction with the German lines. Another French line, also starting from Beirut, passing through Homs, will reach the Euphrates in the direction of the 35th parallel. M. Cambon showed me on the map these lines which are not yet known to the public. The coast of the Mediterranean between Alexandretta and Beirut will be neutralized; no railway can be built there either by Germany, or by France, be it along the coast or across the Antilebanon. A line of this sort was not considered necessary. It would arouse the hostility of the fanatic tribes of the Antilebanon, who close their country to Europeans and carry the products of the soil, the chief one of which is tobacco, to the harbor of Latakia themselves. The difficulty of the negotiations consisted principally in the exact delimitation of the French and German zones of influence (60 kilometers on each side of the railway), so as to prevent them from overlapping. In addition to this, France retains the railway concessions which she obtained from Turkey in the rich mineral district of ancient Cappadocia, along the Black Sea, and the very profitable railway of Smyrna and Casaba.

The third document is entitled "The Bagdad Railway. Complete Anglo-German Agreement," and, as contained in the London *Times* for June 16, 1914, is as follows:

Berlin, June 15 (Through Reuter's Agency)

The Anglo-German Agreement regarding the Bagdad Railway and Mesopotamia has been initialed in London by Sir Edward Grey and Prince Lichnowsky, the German Ambassador. A complete understanding has been reached on all questions at issue.

The agreement will not come into force until after the conclusion of the negotiations with Turkey, as on some material

points the assent of the Porte will be necessary. The contents of the agreement can therefore not be divulged at present.

In another portion of the Memorandum the German Ambassador writes of the Serbian crisis that led to the war of 1914, and this section of his revelations is a damaging indictment of the policy which his country pursued. "On board the *Meteor* [the Kaiser's yacht], we heard," he says, "of the death of the Archduke, the heir to the Austrian Throne. His Majesty expressed regret that his efforts to win the Archduke over to his ideas had thus been rendered vain." What these views were, the Ambassador evidently did not know.

Going to Berlin, he found von Bethmann-Hollweg, then Imperial Chancellor, much troubled at the outlook, and he complained of Russian armaments. The distrust and dislike of Russia appeared to pervade the Foreign Office. Dr. Zimmermann, the Under-Secretary for Foreign Affairs, stated that Russia was about to raise nine hundred thousand fresh troops, and "his words showed an unmistakable animosity against Russia, who, he said, was everywhere in our way."

The Prince refers to the Potsdam council on July 5, 1914, of which he was not informed at the time, and about which he contents himself with saying: "Subsequently I learned that at the decisive conversation at Potsdam on July 5 the inquiry addressed to us by Vienna found absolute assent among all the personages in authority; indeed, they added that there would be no harm if a war with Russia were to result." Apparently the die had been cast; Austria-Hungary was to take action against Serbia, and the attempt was to be made to localize the trouble. That is to say, the whole affair was to be looked upon as a bout between

[240]

Austria-Hungary and Serbia, to which the European Powers might be spectators, but not participants. This is indicated by the Prince, who says: "I then received instructions that I was to induce the English press to take up a friendly attitude if Austria gave the 'death-blow' to the Great Serbian movement, and as far as possible I was by my influence to prevent public opinion from opposing Austria."

The Prince believed that England could not be counted upon and he warned his government against the projected punitive expedition against the little country; indeed, he says that he gave a warning against the whole project, which he described as "adventurous and dangerous," and he advised that moderation be recommended to the Austrians because he did not believe in the localization of the conflict. To this warning Herr von Jagow is reported to have answered that Russia was not "ready," that there would doubtless be a certain amount of "bluster," but that the firmer Germany stood by Austria, "the more would Russia draw back." The Prince states that the then German Ambassador, Count Pourtalès, had informed his government "that Russia would not move in any circumstance," and that these reports caused Germany to "stimulate" Austria-Hungary "to the greatest possible energy." Sir Edward Grey's influence with Russia was the only hope of maintaining peace, and the Prince therefore begged him to urge moderation in Russia if Austria should demand satisfaction from Serbia. The Prince was not successful with the English press, which felt that exploitation of the assassination of the Austrian heir for political purposes could not be justified, and the English press urged moderation on Austria's part.

Upon the appearance of the ultimatum on July 24, giving Serbia twenty-four hours in which to accept the conditions, "the whole world," the Prince says, "except in Berlin and Vienna, understood that it meant war, and indeed world-war. The British fleet, which chanced to be assembled for a review, was not demobilized."

In order to prevent this catastrophe, the Prince apparently urged Sir Edward Grey to press for a conciliatory reply from Serbia, as the attitude of the Russian Government showed that the situation was very serious. Sir Edward Grey complied, and to quote the Prince's language, on the attitude of the British Government at this time, "the Serbian reply was in accordance with British efforts; M. Pashitch [the Serbian Premier] had actually accepted everything except two points, about which he declared his readiness to negotiate." The action of Sir Edward Grey and of Russia, which had already suggested modification, was indeed very important, so important that the Prince felt himself justified in saying: "If Russia and England wanted war, in order to fall upon us, a hint to Belgrade would have been sufficient, and the unheard-of note would have remained unanswered."

Sir Edward went over the Serbian reply with the German Ambassador, and they discussed Sir Edward's mediation proposal, "to arrange an interpretation of the two points acceptable to both parties." The French, the Italian, and the German Ambassadors were to have met under Sir Edward's presidency, and the whole difficulty could have been adjusted, the Prince saying, "It would have been easy to find an acceptable form for the disputed points which in the main concerned the participation of the Austrian

officials in the investigation at Belgrade. Given good will, everything could have been settled in one or two sittings, and the mere acceptance of the British proposal would have relieved the tension and would have improved our relations to England." The Prince was so convinced of this that he urged it upon his government, saying that "otherwise a world-war was imminent, in which we had everything to lose and nothing to gain." The advice, however, was rejected, as it was against the dignity of Austria, and Germany did not want to interfere in the Serbian affair which was the affair of its ally, and the Prince was directed to work for "localization of the conflict."

The Prince had no illusions as to the attitude of his government, or misgivings as to the result of Sir Edward's policy, for he says: "Of course it would only have needed a hint from Berlin to make Count Berchtold [Austrian Minister for Foreign Affairs] satisfy himself with a diplomatic success and put up with the Serbian reply. But this hint was not given. On the contrary, we pressed for war."

Germany not only refused Sir Edward's proposal, but had none of its own to make. The impression, the Prince said, became stronger that his country desired war, and after calling attention to the Russian appeals and declarations of the Russian Minister for Foreign Affairs, the Czar's humble telegrams, Sir Edward's repeated proposals, the warning of the Italian Foreign Minister, of the Italian Ambassador in Berlin, and his own urgent advice, the Prince concludes, "It was all of no use, for Berlin went on insisting that Serbia must be massacred."

"After that," the Prince says, "events moved rapidly. When Count Berchtold, who hitherto had played the

[243]

strong man on instructions from Berlin, at last decided to change his course, we answered the Russian mobilization—after Russia had for a whole week negotiated and waited in vain—with our ultimatum and declaration of war."

With England's entry into the conflict the Prince's mission was at an end. "It was wrecked," he says, "not by the perfidy of the British, but by the perfidy of our policy."

Under the next section of the Memorandum the Prince has some reflections under the title of "Retrospect," written two years later, in which he ruefully comments that there was no place for him in a system which "tolerates only representatives who report what one wants to read," and he might have added in this connection what he says elsewhere, under a system which keeps an Ambassador uninformed of negotiations taking place elsewhere, and even has the counselor of the Embassy spy upon the Ambassador, report his conduct to the Foreign Office, and conduct negotiations behind his back.

After some observations that might be considered of a personal character, he says:

In spite of former aberrations, everything was still possible in July, 1914. Agreement with England had been reached. We should have had to send to Petersburg a representative who at any rate reached the average standard of political ability, and we should have had to give Russia the certainty that we desired neither to dominate the Straits nor to throttle the Serbs.

Germany, he insists, "needed neither alliances nor wars, but merely treaties which would protect us and others, and which would guarantee us an economic development for which there had been no precedent in history." The Prince even believes that his country

could have taken up the question of the limitation of armaments, without needing to think of Austria, much less to follow whithersoever it cared to go, but, "I had to support in London a policy which I knew to be fallacious. I was punished for it, for it was a sin against the Holy Ghost."

There are passages from two sections which should be quoted in the Prince's own words, as the intervention of a third hand might convey the impression that they had been tampered with. They are the "Question of Guilt," and "The Enemy Point of View."

Under the first caption the Prince writes:

As appears from all official publications, without the facts being controverted by our own White Book, which, owing to its poverty and gaps, constitutes a grave self-accusation;

1. We encouraged Count Berchtold to attack Serbia, although no German interest was involved, and the danger of a world-war must have been known to us—whether we knew the text of the ultimatum is a question of complete indifference;

2. In the days between July 23 and July 30, 1914, when M. Sazonoff emphatically declared that Russia could not tolerate an attack upon Serbia, we rejected the British proposals of mediation, although Serbia, under Russian and British pressure, had accepted almost the whole ultimatum, and although an agreement about the two points in question could easily have been reached, and Count Berchtold was even ready to satisfy himself with the Serbian reply;

3. On July 30, when Count Berchtold wanted to give way, we, without Austria having been attacked, replied to Russia's mere mobilization by sending an ultimatum to Petersburg, and on July 31 we declared war on the Russians, although the Tsar had pledged his word that as long as negotiations continued not a man should march—so that we deliberately destroyed the possibility of a peaceful settlement.

In view of these indisputable facts, it is not surprising that the whole civilized world outside Germany attributes to us the sole guilt for the world-war.

Under the second caption he says:

Is it not intelligible that our enemies declare that they will not rest until a system is destroyed which constitutes a permanent threatening of our neighbors? Must they not otherwise fear that in a few years they will again have to take up arms, and again see their provinces overrun and their towns and villages destroyed? Were those people not right who declared that it was the spirit of Treitschke and Bernhardi which dominated the German people—the spirit which glorifies war as an aim in itself and does not abhor it as an evil? Were those people not right who said that among us it is still the feudal knights and Junkers and the caste of warriors who rule and who fix our ideals and our values —not the civilian gentlemen? Were they not right who said that the love of duelling, which inspires our youth at the universities, lives on in those who guide the fortunes of the people? Had not the events at Zabern and the parliamentary debates on that case shown foreign countries how civil rights and freedoms are valued among us, when questions of military power are on the other side? . . .

That is what our enemies think, and that is what they are bound to think, when they see that, in spite of capitalistic industrialization, and in spite of socialistic organization, the living, as Friedrich Nietzsche says, are still governed by the dead. The principal war aim of our enemies, the democratization of Germany, will be achieved.

In the same issue of the London *Times* of March 28, 1918, from which this account of Lichnowsky's revelations have been summarized, there is a translation of a very interesting, and what the *Times* calls "astonishing memorandum" by one Dr. Wilhelm Muehlon, a Director of the Krupp Works at Essen at the time of the outbreak of the war, and for some time thereafter. Muehlon's memorandum figured in the debate in the Reichstag committee on March 16, and it is stated by the *Times* to have appeared in the *Berliner Tageblatt*, from which it is reproduced in translated form. It should be stated, before proceeding to the analysis of

[246]

the memorandum, that Dr. Muehlon is now a resident of Switzerland.

It is natural that this memorandum should be considered in connection with that of the late German Ambassador to Great Britain, as it confirms some of his statements and furnishes precious information hitherto withheld from the public, as it apparently was from the Imperial Ambassador at London. Dr. Muehlon records conversations which he had about the middle of July, 1914, with Dr. Helfferich, then Director of the Deutsche Bank in Berlin, and later Vice-Chancellor of the Empire, and with Herr Krupp von Bohlen and Halbach, head of the Krupp firm, of which Dr. Muehlon was a Director.

The Krupp people were interested in some large transactions in Bulgaria and Turkey, and apparently Dr. Muehlon saw Helfferich in regard to them. The Deutsche Bank was evidently unwilling to meet Dr. Muehlon's advances. Dr. Helfferich stated the reasons in a peculiarly frank and interesting manner:

The political situation has become very menacing. The Deutsche Bank must in any case wait before entering into any further engagements abroad. The Austrians have just been with the Kaiser. In a week's time Vienna will send a very severe ultimatum to Serbia, with a very short interval for the answer. The ultimatum will contain demands such as punishment of a number of officers, dissolution of political associations, criminal investigations in Serbia by Austrian officials, and, in fact, a whole series of definite satisfactions will be demanded at once; otherwise Austria-Hungary will declare war on Serbia.

This implied a very considerable familiarity with the future as well as with the past, and it is not surprising, as German finance and German diplomacy are so interrelated, that one involves the other.

The future Vice-Chancellor had evidently and prop-

erly enough been taken into the secret, for Dr. Muehlon continues that Dr. Helfferich added:

The Kaiser had expressed his decided approval of this procedure on the part of Austria-Hungary. He had said that he regarded a conflict with Serbia as an internal affair between these two countries, in which he would permit no other state to interfere. If Russia mobilized, he would mobilize also. But in his case mobilization meant immediate war. This time there would be no oscillation.

This was probably a reference to the Moroccan question, in which war trembled in the balance, but peace eventually tipped the scales.

According to Helfferich, "the Austrians were extremely well satisfied at this determined attitude on the part of the Kaiser."

This disclosure made a very great impression upon Dr. Muehlon, who had feared a world-war, and apparently felt that it could not be avoided unless France and Russia reconsidered their attitude. Upon his return from Berlin to Essen it was natural that Dr. Muehlon should communicate this bit of news to Herr Krupp von Bohlen, and Dr. Helfferich had given him permission to do so, but it was not news to Herr von Bohlen, who had recently been with the Kaiser and who, according to Dr. Muehlon, "had spoken to him also of his conversation with the Austrians, and of its result, but he [evidently meaning the Kaiser] had described the matter as so secret that he [Krupp] would not even have dared to inform his own directors." Krupp confirmed Helfferich's statements, saying that the situation was very serious, and that "the Kaiser had told him that he would declare war immediately if Russia mobilized, and that this time people would see that he did not turn about." The

subsequent events have shown that these two gentlemen were only too well informed, as on the very day indicated by Helfferich, the Austrian ultimatum appeared.

Meeting Dr. Helfferich after the ultimatum had been sent, that gentleman is reported by Dr. Muehlon to have said "that the Kaiser had gone on his northern cruise only as a 'blind'; he had not arranged the cruise on the usual extensive scale but was remaining close at hand and keeping in constant touch;" there was nothing to do but to wait and to see what would happen, and according to Dr. Helfferich, as recorded by Dr. Muehlon, the Austrians did not expect the ultimatum to be accepted, and they were "acting rapidly, before the other Powers could find time to interfere."

In a subsequent conversation had with Herr Krupp von Bohlen, the statement of the German Government that Austria-Hungary had acted alone, without Germany's previous knowledge, was the subject of discussion, and such conduct on the part of Germany appeared to them inexplicable, as it has to many others, inasmuch as by so doing Germany apparently gave Austria a free hand, without informing itself as to what that hand would do. Herr von Bohlen, therefore, asked his friend, von Jagow, then Imperial Secretary of State for Foreign Affairs, with whom he was very intimate, who informed him that "he had nothing to do with the text of the Austro-Hungarian ultimatum, and that Germany had never made any such demands." Herr von Bohlen remarked that such action was inconceivable, and Herr von Jagow is stated to have replied that he, as a diplomatist, had naturally thought of inquiring as to the extent to which Austria

had intended to go, but when called in "the Kaiser had," to quote Dr. Muehlon's memorandum, "so committed himself that it was too late for any procedure according to diplomatic custom, and there was nothing more to be done."

It was not to be expected that Lichnowsky's Memorandum would be allowed to pass without notice on the part of the Imperial officials whom the Prince had implicated in the misconduct of German affairs. On March 20, 1918, Herr von Jagow made some observations on the Memorandum in the *North German Gazette*. Certain minor matters are questioned, and some errors of detail corrected, but the former Imperial Secretary of State proceeds with the care and caution becoming one who was apparently writing from memory. Certain statements which von Jagow advances on his own account are of more than ordinary interest, and seem to be admissions of the general correctness of Lichnowsky's Memorandum, and in any event are to be considered as evidence coming from German sources that Great Britain had by negotiation removed great and outstanding differences which, but for other reasons, would and should have prevented the two nations from falling out. Thus Herr von Jagow says:

When, in January, 1913, I was appointed Secretary of State I regarded an Anglo-German *rapprochement* as desirable, and an agreement about the points at which our interests touched or crossed as obtainable. In any case, I wanted to try to work in this sense. A main point for us was the Mesopotamia-Asia Minor question—the so-called Bagdad policy—because it had become for us a question of prestige. If England wanted to push us out there, a conflict seemed, indeed, to me to be hardly avoidable. As soon as possible I took up in Berlin the settlement about the Bagdad Railway. We found the English Government ready to

meet us, and the result was the agreement which had almost been completed when the world-war broke out.

At the same time the negotiations about the Portuguese colonies, which had been begun by Count Metternich and continued by Baron Marschall, were resumed by Prince Lichnowsky. I intended to begin later on—when the Bagdad Railway question, in my opinion the most important question, had been settled—further agreements about other questions, in the Far East, for example.[2]

This would seem to be an admission that agreement was reached with Great Britain concerning the Bagdad policy and the Portuguese colonies, and of the correctness of Lichnowsky's account of these transactions. The reason for the refusal to complete and to publish these treaties at that time is thus stated by the former Imperial Secretary:

With well-justified prudence we intended to postpone publication until an appropriate moment, when the danger of adverse criticism was no longer so acute—if possible simultaneously with the publication of the Bagdad Treaty, which also was on the eve of conclusion. The fact that *two* great agreements had been concluded between England and us would have made the reception considerably more favorable, and would have helped us over the defects of the Portuguese agreement. Our hesitation was due to respect for the effect of the agreement, with which we desired to achieve an improvement of our relations to England and not a fresh disturbance of them. It is true—although this was a secondary consideration—that we were also influenced by the aims which we were then making to secure economic interests in the Portuguese colonies; these interests would, of course, have been more difficult to secure if the agreement had been published.

Herr von Jagow, like Prince Lichnowsky, pays his tribute to Sir Edward Grey, but reproaches him with not preventing the war. This would indeed be a serious charge, if Sir Edward could have prevented it,

[2] Reproduced in part, in English translation, in the London *Times*, April 1, 1918.

but it is at any rate less serious than that he had begun it. On this point and the apparent disinclination of the English people to go to war, Herr von Jagow remarks:

I am by no means willing to adopt the opinion, which is at present widely held in Germany, that England laid all the mines which caused the war; on the contrary, I believe in Sir Edward Grey's love of peace and in his serious wish to reach an agreement with us. But he had involved himself too deeply in the net of Franco-Russian policy. He could no longer find the way out, and he did not prevent the world-war—as he could have done. Among the English people also the war was not popular, and Belgium had to serve as a battlefield.

It is with difficulty that the undersigned has resisted the temptation of an observation here and there of his own, but as a citizen of a belligerent country, he has endeavored to refrain from comment, and to allow the views of the various personages quoted or summarized to speak for themselves. But what would seem prejudice on the part of a citizen of a country at war with the Imperial German Government may not seem to be so on the part of a German subject. Therefore, a portion of a letter is quoted in conclusion, written from Bern, to the then Imperial Chancellor, Herr von Bethmann-Hollweg, under date of May 7, 1917, by Dr. Wilhelm Muehlon, who, after the outbreak of the war, had, in 1916, negotiated treaties on behalf of Germany with Rumania before its entry into the war. This letter is printed in the London *Times* of April 4, 1918, and is said to have been given to the correspondent of the Parisian Socialist journal *L'Humanité* and published by him with the writer's consent:

However great the number and weight of the mistakes accumulated on the German side since the beginning of the war, I never-

theless persisted for a long time in the belief that a belated foresight would at last dawn upon the minds of our directors. . . .

But since the first days of 1917 I have abandoned all hope as regards the present directors of Germany. Our offer of peace without indication of our war aims, the accentuation of the submarine war, the deportation of Belgians, the systematic destruction in France, and the torpedoing of English hospital ships have so degraded the governors of the German Empire that I am profoundly convinced that they are disqualified forever from the elaboration and conclusion of a sincere and just agreement. The personalities may change, but they cannot remain the representatives of the German cause.

The German people will not be able to repair the grievous crimes committed against its own present and future, and against that of Europe and the whole human race until it is represented by different men with a different mentality. To tell the truth, it is mere justice that its reputation throughout the whole world is as bad as it is. The triumph of its methods—the methods by which it has hitherto conducted the war both militarily and politically—would constitute a defeat for the ideas and the supreme hopes of mankind. One has only to imagine that a people exhausted, demoralized, or hating violence, should consent to a peace with a government which has conducted such a war, in order to understand how the general level and the changes of life of the peoples would remain black and deceptive.

As a man and as a German who desires nothing but the welfare of the deceived and tortured German people, I turn away definitely from the present representatives of the German *régime.* And I have only one wish—that all independent men may do the same, and that many Germans may understand and act.

That the soul of Germany, as its friends in other days have seen it or felt it to be, may regain the ascendancy, and that the ideals of Kant may prevail over the practices of Clausewitz and his successors, is the hope and prayer of the undersigned.

JAMES BROWN SCOTT

LIST OF PUBLICATIONS

1. Program of the Association, Baron d'Estournelles de Constant. April, 1907.

2. Results of the National Arbitration and Peace Congress, by Andrew Carnegie. April, 1907.*

3. A League of Peace, by Andrew Carnegie. November, 1907.*

4. The results of the Second Hague Conference, by Baron d'Estournelles de Constant and Hon. David Jayne Hill. December, 1907.*

5. The Work of the Second Hague Conference, by James Brown Scott. January, 1908.*

6. Possibilities of Intellectual Coöperation Between North and South America, by L. S. Rowe. April, 1908.*

7. America and Japan, by George Trumbull Ladd. June, 1908.*

8. The Sanction of International Law, by Elihu Root. July, 1908.*

9. The United States and France, by Barrett Wendell. August, 1908.

10. The Approach of the Two Americas, by Joaquim Nabuco. September, 1908.*

11. The United States and Canada, by J. S. Willison. October, 1908.*

12. The Policy of the United States and Japan in the Far East. November, 1908.*

13. European Sobriety in the Presence of the Balkan Crisis, by Charles Austin Beard. December, 1908.*

14. The Logic of International Coöperation, by F. W. Hirst. January, 1909.*

15. American Ignorance of Oriental Languages, by J. H. DeForest. February, 1909.*

16. America and the New Diplomacy, by James Brown Scott. March, 1909.*

17. The Delusion of Militarism, by Charles E. Jefferson. April, 1909.

18. The Causes of War, by Elihu Root. May, 1909.*

19. The United States and China, by Wei-ching Yen. June, 1909.*

20. Opening Address at the Lake Mohonk Conference on International Arbitration, by Nicholas Murray Butler. July, 1909.*

44. The United States and Latin America at the Hague, by William I. Hull. July, 1911.*

45. The Emotional Price of Peace, by Professor Edward L. Thorndike. August, 1911.*

46. Letter to the Apostolic Delegate to the United States of America, by His Holiness Pope Pius X. September, 1911.*

47. The Existing Elements of a Constitution of the United States of the World, by H. La Fontaine. October, 1911.*

48. The General Arbitration Treaties of 1911. November, 1911.*

49. The Anglo-American Arbitration Treaty, by Heinrich Lammasch; and Forces Making for International Conciliation and Peace, by Jackson H. Ralston. December, 1911.*

50. Finance and Commerce: Their Relation to International Good Will; A Collection of Papers by Sereno S. Pratt, Isaac N. Seligman, E. H. Outerbridge, Thomas F. Woodlock, and George Paish. January, 1912.*

51. Do the Arts Make for Peace? by Frank Jewett Mather, Jr. February, 1912.*

52. An Anthropologist's View of War, by Franz Boas. March, 1912.*

53. The Mirage of the Map, by Norman Angell. April, 1912.*

54. Philosophy of the Third American Peace Congress, by Theodore Marburg. May, 1912.*

55. The International Mind, by Nicholas Murray Butler. June, 1912.*

56. Science as an Element in the Developing of International Good Will, by Sir Oliver Lodge. July, 1912.*

57. The Interest of the Wage-earner in the Present Status of the Peace Movement, by Charles Patrick Neill. August, 1912.*

58. The Relation of Social Theory to Public Policy, by Franklin H. Giddings. September, 1912.*

59. The Double Standard in Regard to Fighting, by George M. Stratton. October, 1912.*

60. As to Two Battleships. Debate upon the Naval Appropriation Bill, House of Representatives. November, 1912.*

61. The Cosmopolitan Club Movement, by Louis P. Lochner. December, 1912.*

62. The Spirit of Self-Government, by Elihu Root. January, 1913.*

63. The Panama Canal Tolls, by William Howard Taft and Amos S. Hershey. February, 1913.*

64. Internationalism; A Selected List of Books, Pamphlets and Periodicals, by Frederick C. Hicks. March, 1913.*

65. The Interparliamentary Union, by Christian L. Lange. April, 1913.*

85. Documents Regarding the European War. Series No. III.
    I. The Neutrality of Belgium and Luxemburg.
    II. Address of the President of the Council to the French Senate, August 4, 1914.
    III. Official Japanese Documents.
    IV. Address to the People by the German Emperor, December, 1914.

86. Documents Regarding the European War. Series No. IV.
    I. Turkish Official Documents. November, 1914.
    II. Speech of the Imperial Chancellor to the Reichstag. December 2, 1914.
    III. The Belgian Gray Book. (July 24, August 29, 1914.) January, 1915.

87. Documents Regarding the European War. Series No. V.
    The French Yellow Book, Translated and Prepared for Parliament by the British Government. February, 1915.

88. Documents Regarding the European War. Series No. V.
    The French Yellow Book, Translated and Prepared for Parliament by the British Government. March, 1915.

89. Documents Regarding the European War. Series No. VI.*
    The Austrian Red Book, Official Translation Prepared by the Austrian Government. April, 1915.

90. Documents Regarding the European War. Series No. VII.
    The Serbian Blue Book. May, 1915.

91. The Fundamental Causes of the World War, by Alfred H. Fried. June, 1915.

92. To the Citizens of the Belligerent States, by G. Heymans. July, 1915.

93. Documents Regarding the European War. Series No. VIII.
    Italy's Green Book. Translation approved by Royal Italian Embassy, Washington, D. C. August, 1915.

94. Documents Regarding the European War. Series No. IX.
    Official Correspondence Between the United States and Germany.
    I. Declaration of London, August 6, 1914—October 24, 1914.
    II. Contraband of War, September 4, 1914—April 26, 1915.
    III. Restraints of Commerce, February 6, 1915—September 7, 1915.
    IV. Case of the William P. Frye, March 31, 1915—July 30, 1915. September, 1915.

95. Documents Regarding the European War. Series No. X.
    Official Correspondence Between the United States and Great Britain.
    I. Declaration of London, August 6, 1914—October 22, 1914.
    II. Contraband of War, August 5, 1914—April 10, 1915.
    III. Restraints of Commerce, December 26, 1914—July 31, 1915.
    IV. Case of the Wilhelmina, February 15, 1915—April 8, 1915. October, 1915.

96. Documents Regarding the European War. Series No. XI.
    I. Secretary Bryan's Letter to Senator Stone Regarding Charges of Partiality Shown to Great Britain, January 20, 1915.

II. The Austro-Hungarian Minister for Foreign Affairs to Ambassador Penfield, June 29, 1915.

III. The Secretary of State to Ambassador Penfield, August 12, 1915. November, 1915.

97. Referendum on the Report of the Special Committee on Economic Results of the War and American Business. Reprinted by permission of the Chamber of Commerce of the United States. December, 1915.*

98. The Land Where Hatred Expires, by Albert Léon Guérard. January, 1916.

99. America's Opinion of the World War, by Eduard Bernstein. Translated by John Mez. February, 1916.

100. International Coöperation, by John Bassett Moore. The Outlook for International Law, by Elihu Root. March, 1916.

101. Documents Regarding the European War. Series No. XII.
Statement of Measures Adopted to Intercept the Sea-Borne Commerce of Germany. Presented to Both Houses of Parliament by Command of His Majesty. January, 1916.
Great Britain's Measures Against German Trade. A Speech Delivered by the Rt. Hon. Sir E. Grey, Secretary of State for Foreign Affairs, in the House of Commons, on the 26th of January, 1916. April, 1916.

102. Super-Resistance, by Harold C. Goddard. May, 1916.

103. Official Documents Regarding the European War. Series No. XIII.
German White Book on Armed Merchantmen. June, 1916.

104. Official Documents Regarding the European War. Series No. XIV.
Speech of Imperial German Chancellor before the Reichstag, on April 5, 1916. July, 1916.

105. Inter Arma Veritas, by William Allan Neilson. August, 1916.

106. The Proposal for a League to Enforce Peace. Affirmative—William Howard Taft; Negative—William Jennings Bryan. September, 1916.

107. Nationality and Beyond, by Nicholas Murray Butler. Do We Want Half the Hemisphere? by Brander Matthews. October, 1916.

108. War and Human Progress, by James Bryce. November, 1916.

109. The Principle of Nationality, by Theodore Ruyssen. Translated by John Mez. December, 1916.

110. Official Documents Looking Toward Peace. Series I. January, 1917.

111. Official Documents Looking Toward Peace. Series II. February, 1917.

112. What is a Nationality? Part II of The Principle of Nationality, by Theodore Ruyssen. March, 1917.

113. The Bases of an Enduring Peace, by Franklin H. Giddings. April, 1917.

114. Documents Regarding the European War. Series No. XV.
The Entry of the United States. May, 1917.

115. The War and the Colleges, from an Address to Representatives of Colleges and Universities, delivered by the Hon. Newton D. Baker, May 5, 1917. June, 1917.

116. The Treaty Rights of Aliens, by William Howard Taft. July, 1917.

117. The Effect of Democracy on International Law, by Elihu Root. August, 1917.

118. The Problem of Nationality. Part III of The Principle of Nationality, by Theodore Ruyssen. September, 1917.

119. Official Documents Looking Toward Peace, Series III. October, 1917.

120. The United States and Great Britain, by Walter H. Page. The British Commonwealth of Nations, by Lieutenant-General J. C. Smuts. America and Freedom, by Viscount Grey. November, 1917.

121. The Conference on the Foreign Relations of the United States, held at Long Beach, N. Y., May 28–June 1, 1917. An Experiment in Education, by Stephen Pierce Duggan. December, 1917.

122. The Aims of the War: Letter of Lord Lansdowne to the London *Daily Telegraph*, November 29, 1917. Reply by Cosmos printed in the New York *Times*, December 1, 1917. The President's Address to the Congress, December 4, 1917. January, 1918.

123. Victory or Defeat: No Half-way House, speech delivered by the Rt. Hon. David Lloyd George, December 14, 1917; British Labor's War Aims, statement adopted at the Special National Labor Conference at Central Hall, Westminster, December 28, 1917; Great Britain's War Aims, speech delivered by the Rt. Hon. David Lloyd George at the Trade Union Conference on Man Power, January 5, 1918; Labor's After-War Economic Policy, by Rt. Hon. Arthur Henderson, M.P.; America's Terms of Settlement, address by President Wilson to the Congress, January 8, 1918. British Labor Party's Address to the Russian People, January 15, 1918. February, 1918.

124. The United States and Japan: text of the Root-Takahira Understanding of November 30, 1908, and of the Lansing-Ishii Agreement of November 3, 1917; Japan and the United States, address by the Hon. Elihu Root, October 1, 1917; The Lansing-Ishii Agreement, address by the Hon. James L. Slayden, November 15, 1917; What of Our Fears of Japan? by Kenneth S. Latourette. March, 1918.

125. The Awakening of the German People, by Otfried Nippold. April, 1918.

126. The Anniversary of America's Entry into the War: An address delivered by President Wilson at Baltimore, Maryland, April 6, 1918; an article written for *The Daily Chronicle* of London by Professor Gilbert Murray. May, 1918.

127. The Lichnowsky Memorandum: Introduction and translation by Munroe Smith, German text from the *Berliner Börsen-Courier*, Appendix by Munroe Smith and Henry F. Munro; Reply of Herr von Jagow. June, 1918.

128. America and the Russian Dilemma, by Jerome Landfield. The German Peace Treaties with the Ukraine, Russia, Finland and Rumania. The Constitution of Middle Europe, by Friedrich Naumann. July, 1918.

129. A Voice from Germany: Why German Peace Declarations Fail to Convince, by Professor F. W. Foerster. Austria's Peace Proposals: The Letter to Prince Sixtus. August, 1918.

130. Memoranda and Letters of Dr. Muehlon: Introduction and translation by Munroe Smith, German text and Appendix. September, 1918.

131. The League of Nations, by Viscount Grey of Falloden and Nicholas Murray Butler; Labor and the League of Nations, by Ordway Tead; The European Commission of the Danube, by Edward Krehbiel. Address by President Wilson at the Metropolitan Opera House, New York, September 27, 1918. October, 1918.

132. The "Lusitania": Opinion of Court, United States District Court, Southern District of New York—In the the matter of the petition of the Cunard Steamship Company, limited, as owners of the Steamship "Lusitania," for limitation of its liability. November, 1918.

Special Bulletins:

The United States and Australia, by Percival R. Cole. March, 1910.*

Opening Address at the Lake Mohonk Conference on International Arbitration, by Nicholas Murray Butler. June, 1910.*

Mr. Carnegie's Letter to the Trustees of the Carnegie Endowment for the Advancement of Peace, and Resolutions adopted by the Trustees. January, 1911.*

Arbitration between Great Britain and the United States, by Cardinal Gibbons. May, 1911.

International Arbitration, by Sir Charles Fitzpatrick. August, 1911.*

The Dawn of World Peace, by William Howard Taft, President of the United States. November, 1911.*

Deutschland und Grossbritannien; eine Studie über Nationale Eigentümlichkeiten, by Lord Haldane. (In German).*

Address at Peace Dinner, December 30, by Andrew Carnegie. December, 1911.*

Great Britain and Germany; a Study in National Characteristics, by Lord Haldane. March, 1912.*

War Practically Preventable and Arguments for Universal Peace, by Rev. Michael Clune. June, 1912.*

Who Makes War? From the *London Times*. February, 1913.*

On Naval Armaments, by Rt. Hon. Winston Churchill. April, 1913.*

Profit and Patriotism, and Money-Making and War. Reprints. May, 1913.*

A New Year's Letter from Baron d'Estournelles de Constant. December, 1913.

The A B C of the Panama Canal Controversy. Reprinted from the Congressional Record, October 29, 1913. December, 1913.

Wanted—A Final Solution of the Japanese Problem, by Hamilton Holt. January, 1914.*

The South American Point of View, by Charles Hitchcock Sherrill. January, 1914.*

A Panama Primer. Reprinted from *The Independent*. March 30, 1914. April, 1914.*

The Causes Behind Mexico's Revolution, by Gilbert Reid. Reprint from the *New York Times*, April 27, 1914. June, 1914.*

The Japanese in California. June, 1914.*

The Changing Attitude toward War as Reflected in the American Press. September, 1914.

The Great War and Its Lessons, by Nicholas Murray Butler. October, 1914.*

Address of William H. Taft, May 17, 1914. October, 1914.

Contemporary War Poems. December, 1914.*

The War and Peace Problem, Material for the Study of International Polity, by John Mez. February, 1915.

Syllabus of Lectures on the War and Peace Problem for the Study of International Polity, by John Mez. February, 1915.

A Dozen Truths About Pacificism, by Alfred H. Fried, translated by John Mez. March, 1915.*

Educational Factors Toward Peace, by Leon Fraser. April, 1915.*

A Brief Outline of the Nature and Aims of Pacifism, by Alfred H. Fried. Translated by John Mez. April, 1915.*

Internationalism. A list of Current Periodicals selected and annotated by Frederick C. Hicks. May, 1915.*

Spirit of Militarism and Non-Military Preparation for Defense, by John Lovejoy Elliott and R. Tait McKenzie. June, 1915.*

Existing Alliances and a League of Peace, by John Bates Clark. July, 1915.*

Is Commerce War? by Henry Raymond Mussey. January, 1916.

Peace Literature of the War, by John Mez. January, 1916.

Is There a Substitute for Force in International Relations? by Suh Hu. Prize essay, International Polity Club Competition, awarded June, 1916.

Labor's War Aims: Memorandum on War Aims, adopted by the Inter-Allied Labor and Socialist Conference, February 22, 1918; The Allied Cause is the Cause of Socialist Internationalism: Joint Manifesto of the Social Democratic League of America and the Jewish Socialist League. June, 1918.

The Dawn in Germany? The Lichnowsky and other Disclosures, by James Brown Scott. November, 1918.

* Edition exhausted.

Copies of the above, so far as can be spared, will be sent to libraries and educational institutions for permanent preservation postpaid upon receipt of a request addressed to the Secretary of the American Association for International Conciliation.

A charge of five cents will be made for copies sent to individuals. Regular subscription rate twenty-five cents for one year, or one dollar for five years.

AMERICAN ASSOCIATION
FOR INTERNATIONAL CONCILIATION

COUNCIL OF DIRECTION OF THE
AMERICAN ASSOCIATION FOR INTERNATIONAL
CONCILIATION

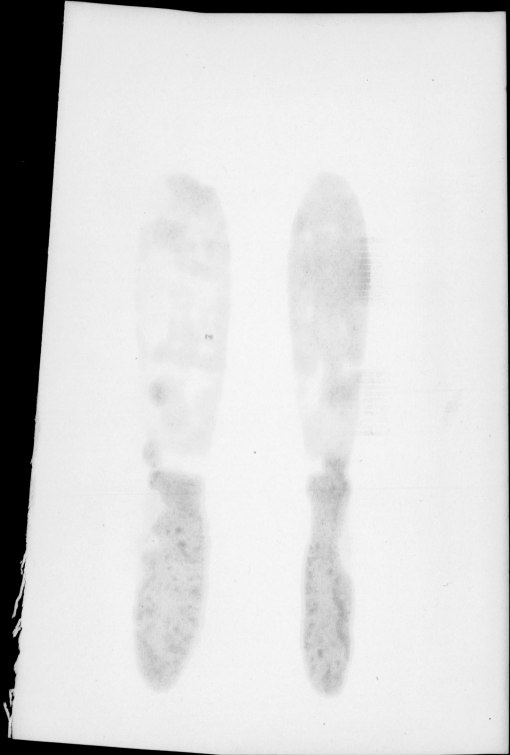